CISTERCIAN ABBEYS

HISTORY AND ARCHITECTURE

Copyright © 1998 for the English edition
Könemann Verlagsgesellschaft mbH
Bonner Str. 126, D-50968 Cologne

Translators of the English-language edition: Elizabeth Clegg, Caroline Higgitt, Marie-Noëlle Ryan
Editor of the English-language edition: Dr. John Crook
Typesetting: Goodfellow & Egan
Project coordination: Bettina Kaufmann and Stephan Küffner
Production manager: Detlev Schaper
Assistant: Nicola Leurs
Printing and binding: Imprimerie Jean Lamour, Maxéville
Printed in France

ISBN 3 - 89508 - 894 - 3

10 9 8 7 6 5 4 3 2

PHOTOGRAPHY BY HENRI GAUD
TEXT BY JEAN-FRANÇOIS LEROUX-DHUYS

CISTERCIAN ABBEYS

HISTORY AND ARCHITECTURE

KÖNEMANN

CONTENTS

INTRODUCTION

Nine centuries ago, several decades before the great cathedrals found their finest expression, the first Cistercian abbeys revealed the creative power of the medieval renaissance that was to fill Europe with masterpieces of stone and of faith. After the second half of the eleventh century, as the fears of the imminent end of the world in the year 1000 died down and the wounds of the epidemics and famines that had made that end seem such a real possibility began to heal, the Christian West came into its own. A new increase in population brought with it an economic expansion that exorcised the past. Feudalism was establishing itself on the ruins of the Carolingian era. Strengthened by the Gregorian reform that was to prove to be the most characteristic feature of the eleventh century, the Church demanded independence and purity, encouraging the development of the monastic Orders.

It was in this context that, like other religious reformers, the Benedictine Robert of Molesme, in his search for ever greater perfection after a number of previous experiments, founded the new monastery of Cîteaux in 1098. His successors Alberic and, in particular, Stephen Harding created the conditions necessary for the development of the Cistercian Order. It was a rigorous Order that demanded renunciation of the world and an asceticism that attracted the chivalrous nobility. For these men this was an adventure comparable to setting out on a Crusade, particularly if the ultimate aim, Bernard of Clairvaux's dream, was the extension of monastic virtues and the pre-eminence of the Church throughout the world. It was under Bernard's inspiration that, until the 1150s, the White Monks set up a network of communities over the entire face of Europe, created in the image of the heavenly Jerusalem. This initial stimulus lasted for a century. With its flowering of Cistercian abbeys, the twelfth century marked the high point of medieval monasticism.

Going beyond the self-sufficiency imposed by the founding Rule of St. Benedict, these abbeys became important centers having a significant impact on rural development. Their role in economic growth was to contribute to the development of towns in the thirteenth century. Thus the history of the Cistercians is entwined with the long progress of the joys and troubles of a merchant civilization in which the "Desert Fathers" were replaced by new Orders, Dominicans and Franciscans, whose growth coincided with that of the towns.

Nevertheless, the Cistercians were to retain this preoccupation with putting their own stamp on the landscape throughout the centuries, particularly in the eighteenth century, for they prove to be inveterate builders. This is why, despite the wars and revolutions that have destroyed the majority of the Cistercian abbeys, they still provide an exceptional heritage of outstanding sites and monuments.

Today, quite apart from any passing fashion for medieval monastic architecture, be it Benedictine with its capitals, tympana and historiated frescos, or Cistercian in its unadorned austerity of light and shade, there are hidden reasons that explain the attraction that so many people, tourists and historians alike, feel for this Cistercian world. For those of us who live among the stresses and strains of creeping urbanization, the abbeys seem to embody the values of an ideal rural life in a near-mythical way. The Cistercian monastery and the surrounding land which forms an integral part of it seems to give shape to the ideal of a self-sufficient – and almost ecological – style of farming, so different from the piecemeal approach of the modern world. The enclosed and isolated sites, almost always outside the town, are there to be discovered; a utopia that became a reality, for a few years at least; one which sought to bear witness to the perfection of human endeavor when linked to the sacred.

And like all utopias, whose function is to bring us back to fundamental questions, Cistercian history makes us meditate not only on the coherence between the taming of natural space and the social organization that underlies it, but also on the coherence between the ethics of life and the aesthetics of the works that are its product.

PART ONE

NINE CENTURIES AGO

ORIGINS AND FOUNDATION

The foundation of Molesme in 1075, preceding that of Cîteaux (1098) by 23 years, marked the beginning of the Cistercian adventure. It was one of a series of events that in just a few years, following the eleventh-century "half-time" period, drew a line under the political and moral chaos of the end of the early middle ages. Christianity was now to experience a period of expansion that would last for two centuries during which the Cistercians would play a major role.

The roots of this period of transformation in the West lie deep in history and may be traced first and foremost back to Rome, where everything began — both religious dogma and church architecture. But the long succession of generations that followed Constantine can hardly be ignored, for they added their own equally valid traditions to the initial model. The Cistercians could draw on a vast heritage from which to fashion those new styles of architecture that were to spring up in so many parts of Europe for centuries to come.

Previous pages
Double opening:
Fountains Abbey,
England.

Following page, on left:
Fontenay Abbey,
Burgundy, France.

Right:
Alcobaça Abbey,
Portugal. St. Benedict of
Nursia (c. 480–547),
father of western
monasticism. His Rule
was gradually accepted
by all monasteries.

CHAPTER I

THE ORIGINS OF CHRISTIANITY

THE ROMAN INHERITANCE

The unexpected alliance between the Roman Empire and the Church was the work of Constantine the Great: Christianity was to become the inspiration for a new and unrivaled Mediterranean civilization, which extended under Roman control from Spain to Palestine. Constantine realised that Christianity could bring new values that Roman institutions, falling into decline, were unable to provide on their own.

It was in this context that the late Roman emperors set themselves up as defenders of orthodoxy: Constantine called the Council of Nicæa (325) in order to define the divinity of Christ and the Trinity. Theodosius ordered that pagan temples should be closed, and subsequently destroyed—under pain of death.

From this date, and for centuries to come, a power struggle would take place between religious and political hierarchies, under cover of the defense of Christianity.

In the circumstances it was inevitable that the architectural *schema* of the first Christian churches was defined by Constantine, who financed the work. A kind of cultural revolution took place. For as long as people could remember, in traditional cults the temple had been reserved for the priests, while the people stood outside in the forecourt. The divinity was hidden. The Christians' innovation was their desire to come together in an assembly, the *ecclesia*, in order to celebrate, under the authority of the *episcopus*, the "miracle" of the Last Supper. The place where this happened became the meeting-place, as the Roman basilica or the covered portico of the agora in Athens had been. Here the crowd had found a hall permanently open to the activities of traders, with an apse reserved for judges in an extension at one end. Constantine adopted this architectural concept as the model for the Christian basilica. The bishop, who alone possessed the power to organize the sacraments, presided in the apse on a throne (*cathedra*) symbolizing his spiritual jurisdiction. The faithful assembled in the nave, and not only for religious ceremonies.

It was under Constantine, too, that a specifically Christian monasticism developed. From the first to the third centuries, the earliest eastern Christians had sometimes gathered together in groups of men and women, adopting a communal life of poverty and chastity, according to the teachings of the Gospels, but without cutting them-

---

CHRONOLOGY

1. Jesus
5 BC: birth of Jesus in Judea, a Roman protectorate
7 April AD 30: death of Jesus in Jerusalem

2. The Apostles
Period of oral teaching
• 30/44: persecution of Christian Jews by the Jewish community
• 36: Saul (St. Paul) is converted to Christianity
• 64/68: the Apostles agree to the spreading of the Gospel to non-Jews
Period of written teaching
• 65/100: composition of the 27 books of the New Testament
• 64/68: first Roman persecution under Nero (martyrdom of SS. Peter and Paul)

3. Mediterranean expansion
The entire Mediterranean including North Africa

The first bishoprics in Gaul after 250
Persecutions alternate with periods of religious peace

4. Alliance of the Church and Rome: Constantine the Great (306–337)
Christianity as a state religion (Edict of Milan, 313)
The Emperor as head of the Faith (Council of Nicæa, 325).
In the East
• Paul of Thebes and Anthony (†356), first hermits (anchorites)
• Pachomius founds (323) the first communal monastery (cenobites) at Tabennisi
• Basil (357): his *Monastic Constitutions*: obedience to the abbot, stability, and reform of morals
2. In the West
• Martin, hermit at Ligugé (361)
• Martin founds the community of Marmoutier (371)

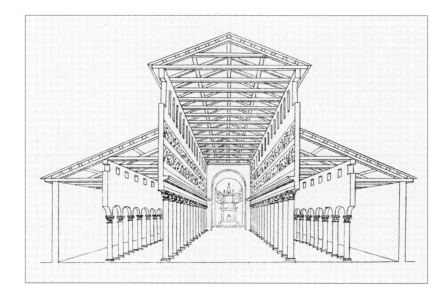

The first basilica of St Peter's in Rome, built by Constantine in 326, modeled on the Roman civic basilica and becoming the standard form for the Christian Church. (Reconstruction from Inventaire général, Architecture – Méthode et Vocabulaire, Paris, 1972)

selves off from the world. In these years when the Gospel was being spread openly, people were keenly aware of the obligation to profess their faith publicly, despite the threat of persecution.

As religious peace became established, the first monks appeared. When religious persecution came to an end, martyrdom was no longer the sole route to sainthood. Furthermore, official recognition of Christianity had brought about a relaxation in morality. New witnesses were needed and these were the monks, who offered their lives of self-mortification to God.

THE GERMANIC LEGACY

The civilization of the *Pax Romana*, that had assimilated Celtic culture and the new Christian religion, became the inheritance received by the West after the Roman and Byzantine empires went their separate ways (395). At the start of the fifth century the Barbarians arrived at the gates of the empire. The townsfolk of Gaul took refuge behind protecting walls. The religious hierarchy was concerned that the presence of the Church should made itself felt. This led to the creation of the "cathedral enclosure", an episcopal city in the heart of the secular town. It prefigured the enclosed space of the monasteries.

The invaders occupied Rome (476). The West was immediately plunged into new political turmoil as barbarian kingdoms set themselves up on the ruins of the empire. But the people remained strongly Romanized and, for the most part, Christian.

BENEDICT OF NURSIA

The spiritual journey of Benedict of Nursia was similar to that of all the "Founding Fathers". Like them, he was born into a well-off family, which provided him with a sound intellectual background. Like them, he was initially tempted to become a hermit in order to live his Faith the better. This was his attempt at living at Subiaco, but he did not achieve the balance he had hoped for. He then tried to bring together a few hermits who would dwell together as anchorites, organized in twelve houses of twelve monks, following the example of Moses and the twelve tribes, or Christ and the twelve apostles. This ended up with the whole community moving in 529 to a new monastic establishment, Montecassino, the drawing up of a Rule (534), the creation of a secondary establishment (Terracine) to house the excess number of disciples, the addition of a female convent thanks to the obedient Sister Scholastica (c. 480–543), and the writing, after Benedict's death in

the odor of sanctity in 547, of a Life for the use of his disciples, the *Dialogues* (592) of Gregory the Great.

There was nothing exceptional here. Yet the Rule, though long in competition with others, the Irish Rule in particular, was to become increasingly influential, would never be challenged, would always be invoked by successive monastic reformers. The Cistercian Order, like all the others, would be born under the banner of the Rule. The success of this text comes from the perfection of its form, its complete approach to everyday life as well as the spiritual life of the monks, the wisdom inherent in its advice on following a life of renunciation of the world.

The Rule confirms the merits of community life. Being a hermit may well be a path suited to those who are able to struggle on their own against the snares of flesh and thoughts. Rather, the Rule reaffirms the principle advanced by Basil of Cesarea from the fourth century: it is in community that "ordinary" monks, unheroically, can pray and obtain salvation together. The so-called "triple vow" of the Benedictines follows from this. Because he does not abandon his brothers in Christ, the monk makes a vow of *stability* within the monastery. Because the community elects its abbot, this implies that the *obedience* due to him should be the way of humility.

As for *moral conversion* (poverty, chastity, renunciation of the world), this allows the monk to devote himself to spiritual reading (*lectio divina*), to the Work of God (*Opus Dei*), so that it is not necessary to become a priest to be close to God. As well as these three vows, the Rule demands the *silence* appropriate to permanent communion with God, and the *work* which provides the best protection against the temptations of the devil.

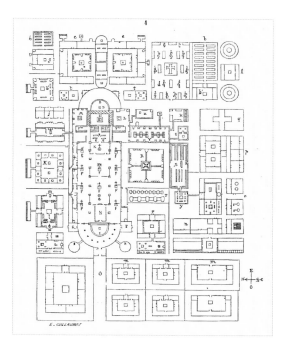

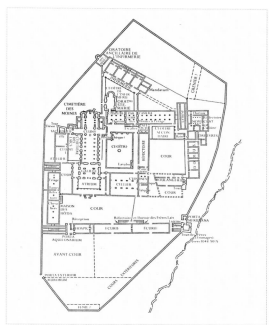

1 The Barbarians

The refined civilization of the Ostrogoths in Ravenna. Development of monasticism among the privileged classes. Benedict of Nursia founds the abbey of Monte Cassino (529). He draws up the Rule.

Columbanus founds Luxeuil (Central Europe receives the Gospel).

2. The Carolingians

Charlemagne takes control of the Empire and the Church. He is without equal on earth.

817: Benedict of Aniane brings together all monasteries under the one Benedictine Rule, emphasizing the exercise of the liturgy.

820: Saint-Riquier and the ideal of the "monastic town".

839: Saint-Gall and the ideal monastic plan.

910: foundation of the Benedictine Order of Cluny (that was to spread throughout Europe with 1,200 priories).

928: after the invasions, Jumièges is rebuilt and the monastic buildings are regrouped in a standard plan, the "conventual quadrangle".

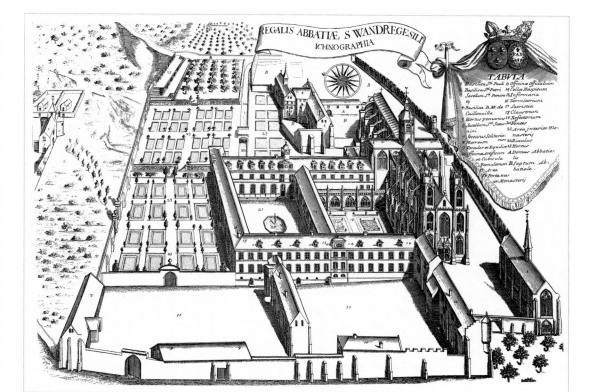

Above, from left to right:
• *Saint-Riquier Abbey, from the engraving by Paul Petau, 1913, Paris, BNF.*
• *Plan of Saint-Gall Abbey, c. 820, Saint-Gall, Stifts Bibliothek.*

• *Plan of the Abbey of Cluny II, c. 1050, reconstruction by Kenneth John Conant.*

Below:
Fontenelle, Abbey of Saint-Wandrille in the seventeenth century, Dom Michel Germain, Monasticon Gallicanum.

The Christian West,
second half of the
eleventh century.
1. Duchy of Upper
Lorraine (Nancy)
2. County of Burgundy
(Dole)
3. Duchy of Burgundy
(Dijon)
4. Royal domain of the
Île-de-France (Paris)
5. County of Champagne
(Troyes)

The spirit of conquest,
second half of the
eleventh century.

CHAPTER II

CHRISTIANITY IN THE LATE ELEVENTH CENTURY

THE POLITICAL SITUATION

The depression of the year 1000, whether a consequence or not of the terror predicted in the *Revelation of St. John the Divine* – "The Lord will return to judge the living and the dead" – favored a change in social attitudes, born of the suffering of famine and the violence of political change.

After 1050 things began to settle down. The energy of local princes defined a new political map of a West where the ambitions of kings could no longer be fulfilled.

The kings In Germany, Otto I proclaimed (962) the reestablishment of the Germanic Holy Roman Empire. But he could not have administered this Empire without the bishops, and this brought about conflicts with Rome once the pope sought to assert the administrative authority of the Church.

In France, the Capetian kings only had genuine authority over the royal domain of the Île-de-France, to which, of necessity, they devoted all their attention.

The local princes These dukes and counts were the heirs of the administrators of the *pagi* of the Carolingian empire, state functionaries whose position had become hereditary. Although in theory they were vassals both of the emperor and the king of France, they raised taxes and levied troops, behaving like independent sovereigns. The dukes of Burgundy and counts of Champagne in particular distinguished themselves, establishing the famous fairs which superseded Mediterranean trade.

SOCIAL REALITY

The fragmented political framework that had been established on the ruins of the Carolingian empire did not reflect the new social organization that governed the West on a day-to-day basis. The unity of Europe was preserved by a Christian faith that was unanimously accepted and practised within the structure of feudalism; from it derived the real power of a Church that had reformed itself in order to ensure its authority over kings, princes, and people.

Even though we may have some reservations about the social equilibrium too often attributed to this feudal society, it may still be characterized by referring to the famous theory of the "three orders", which evolved from the poem by Bishop Adalberon of Laon (1030). "The house of God, which people believe to be one, is divided into three: those who pray, those who go to war, and those who work. These three coexisting groups cannot be separated from each other; the services rendered by one are the condition of the activities of the two others; each in turn takes it on itself to support the whole."

The "bellatores" (warriors) Those who fight protect the whole community from the fear of any enemy who may invade the territory. In order to ensure peace, they are integrated into a hierarchy of "nobles" who pay homage to one another, the royal suzerain receiving homage from the local princes, while these in turn accept the vassalage of all the other petty lords who own an estate, the fief, deriving its legitimacy from the bloodline or lineage.

Jerpoint Abbey, Ireland.
"The Warrior"

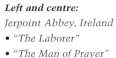

Left and centre:
Jerpoint Abbey, Ireland
• *"The Laborer"*
• *"The Man of Prayer"*

Right:
Vissy-Brod Abbey, Czech Republic. Pope Gregory VII.

The "laboratores" (workers) Those who work to protect the whole community from the fear of famine. These are the commoners, peasants, artisans, or rural serfs, who are tied by obligations of work and subsistence to a seigneurial estate. Crowded into hovels made of flimsy planks and lacking windows or furniture, these families are engaged in a perpetual struggle against famine. This precarious economic situation of a large segment of the population explains the success of the Cistercian institution of lay brothers.

The "oratores" (men of prayer) Those who pray protect the community from the fear of hell—no empty threat in an age where even the most intrepid knight in battle was terrified by the idea of dying outside the bosom of the Church. By praying within a liturgical framework, the priests and monks were performing a "public service" (*leitourgia*).

The Church was in full renewal, having known, in the year 1000, a degeneration similar to that being experienced by the political powers. Gregory VII, the monk Hildebrand, pope from 1073 to 1085, was the architect of the "new Roman Church" that was eager to separate itself from the comfortable but degrading authority of the political power. "In the fifth century, Pope Gelasius I had attempted to separate the two powers, spiritual and temporal; in

the ninth century, Charlemagne had assumed both powers himself; in 1075, Pope Gregory VII declared that all earthly power was subordinate to the spiritual power exercised by the Roman pontiff."[1] In his *Dictatus papæ*, of theocratic inspiration, Gregory VII stated that the election of the pope would henceforth be decided by the cardinals alone. He promulgated a number of disciplinary measures directed at the clergy: the celibacy of the priesthood, the forbidding of simony, the obligation for priests to confine their activities to pastoral duties. He claimed the right to nominate bishops, and in this lay the origins of the famous investiture controversy which forced the emperor, Henry IV, to come to him at Canossa seeking his pardon; it was a determining expression of papal ambition to hold universal power. The Church exercised this power by means of an administration of legates who controlled a geographic structure of archbishoprics and bishoprics whose assemblies (called synods or councils) ensured cohesion. But the Church's new power resulted less from this organization than from the introduction of religious practices that would appeal alike to the humble (the cult of relics) and the powerful (donations and pilgrimages).

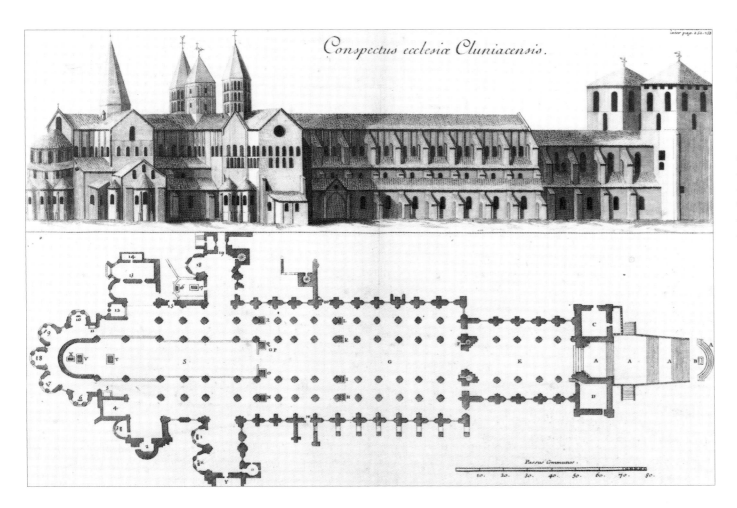

*View and plan of the abbey church of Cluny III. Engraving by P. F. Giffart. (*Annales ordinis S. Benedicti *by Mabillon, 1713)*

"Encouraged by a message from on high, Hugh built a basilica, like a tent for the glory of God, [...] of such splendor that if the inhabitants of heaven could content themselves with our terrestrial dwellings, one would say that here was the angels' courtyard." (Cluniac text. L'Esprit de Cluny, Zodiaque, 1963)

At the end of the eleventh century, the power of the Church became manifest: at Clermont, in 1095, the pope preached the Crusade that was to deliver Jerusalem from the hands of the Muslims, addressing his words to the princes and lords who were thus able to demonstrate their new vitality as a social group. No sovereign took part in this First Crusade, but the Church had accomplished its ambition to stand at the head of Christianity.

THE SITUATION OF MONASTICISM

For their part, the abbeys benefited greatly from the general clericalization of the West. They fascinated the feudal lords, for they represented the only islands of learning in a territory where nobles and serfs were often equally unlettered. The sum total of contemporary knowledge was represented in the libraries that had been rebuilt after the invasions. A famous abbey could enhance the prestige of a lord, who would contribute a portion of his wealth to it.

In addition, he was making an investment which would benefit his salvation.

"Who can count the vigils, hymns and psalms, prayers and daily offerings, the masses accompanied by floods of tears, performed by the monks? These disciples of Christ devote themselves utterly to these occupations, crucifying themselves in order to please God... Thus, noble Count, I advise you seriously to build such a fortress in your land, maintained by monks who will fight against Satan. There the hooded champions will prevail in a constant struggle with Behemoth, to the profit of your soul."[2] Recruits to the monasteries were almost exclusively aristocrats. The younger sons of noble families, such as Bernard of Clairvaux, could not all aspire to the positions of command reserved for members of the family. Instead, they became monks, taking a portion of the family inheritance with them.

The spirit of Cluny From its foundation in 910 the Cluniac Order revived, in reforming spirit, the

directives of Benedict of Aniane, initiating a spirituality that "took to extremes the splendor of ceremonial and the magnificence of the Temple of God".[3] In the face of such sanctity, donations poured in and the Cluniacs had more than enough to live on.

The monks' lives were entirely filled by psalmody. They chanted the psalms during the offices and in procession, they learned them in innumerable rehearsals, they read them again as food for their meditations in the cloister. And they copied them in the *scriptorium*, thus fulfilling the Rule's command to work (*laborare*), "avoiding at one and the same time manual labor which was deemed degrading and an intellectual labor for which too few monks would be suited".[4]

Emotional, even distorted, though this spirituality may have been, the very austere Peter Damian, counsellor of Pope Gregory VII, was overcome with admiration for it when he visited Cluny. It undoubtedly represented a certain propensity for emotionalism characteristic of the medieval mind.

The religious splendor also corresponded to a neo-Platonic view of the world adopted by the Church Fathers in their teachings: the world is an illusion, passions are chimeras, and man's existence is a short stay in a strange land. The true life is elsewhere and the monk aspires to finding it here and now in a grandiose liturgy celebrated for "the glory of God and the honor of men."[5]

And this grandiose liturgy was celebrated in the biggest church in the world! During the sixty years that Hugh of Semur was abbot (1049–1109), gifts and privileges never stopped pouring into Cluny. In 1088, work began on Cluny III, built on the foundations of the abbeys of Odo (Cluny I) and Mayeul (Cluny II) which were deemed too small for a community of more than 250 monks. But sights had been raised too high. At a time when major religious buildings were scarcely more than 300 feet (100m) long, a church 614 feet (187m) long was planned, with double transepts, six belfries or lantern towers, and a dozen apsidal chapels. This great building project, lasting for a century, was to weaken Cluny, particularly financially.

Its power was, in any case, being diluted as the 1,200 priories of the Order spread throughout Europe. Although controlled in theory by the mother house, these priories were becoming increasingly autonomous, often to the detriment of the observance of the Rule.

A return to the life of the hermit At the same time as the Church was becoming aware of the reforms necessary if it wished to recover its dignity and strength (the *Dictatus papæ* of Gregory VII in 1075), a number of reformers began to see the life of the hermit as a way of returning to the origins of Christianity. The Desert Fathers and their ideal of austerity had retained their seductive strength. Without abandoning the general principles of the Rule of St. Benedict of Nursia, some began to emphasize contemplation, others asceticism. They began to experiment with new ideas.

SOME MONASTIC REFORMS INSPIRED BY HERMIT MOVEMENTS IN THE ELEVENTH CENTURY

DATE	FOUNDER	INITIAL HERMITAGE	MONASTIC SITE	DESCENDANTS
1015	Romuald of Ravenna 951–1027	Arrezzo (Tuscany) 1012	Camaldoli (Tuscany) 1015	The Camaldolians Constitutions of 1085 1998 = 2 congregations in Italy
1039	John Gualbert 995–1073	Forest of Vallombrosa 1036	Vallombrosa (Tuscany) 1039	The Vallombrosians (Benedictine congregations since 1966)
1043	Peter Damian 1007–1072	Fabriano (Umbria) 1035	Fonte Avellana (Umbria) 1043	Merged with the Camaldolians
1044	Robert of Turlande 1001–1067	La Chaise Dieu (Auvergne) 1043	La Chaise Dieu 1044	Congregation of Casa Dei
1080	Stephen of Muret 1040-1124	Muret, near Ambazac 1076	Grandmont (Limousin) 1080	Order of Grandmont (until 1772)
1075	Robert of Molesme 1028–1111	Forest of Collau, near Tonnerre 1073	Molesme (Burgundy) 1075	Cîteaux (1098) and the Cistercians (1119)
1084	Bruno of Hartenfaust 1030–1101	Forest of Sèche Fontaine, near Molesme 1082	Grande Chartreuse (Dauphiné) 1084	The Carthusians "Customs" of 1136 1998 = 17 charterhouses
1101	Robert of Arbrissel 1045–1116	Forest of Craou (Normandy) 1095	Fontevrault (Anjou) 1101	Order of Fontevrault (until 1790)
1112	Vital of Mortain 1060–1122	Rochers de Mortain 1095	Savigny (Normandy) 1112	Congregation of Savigny Affiliated to Clairvaux in 1147
1142	Stephen of Obazine –1159	Forest of Aubazine (Limousin) 1140	Aubazine (Limousin) 1142	Congregation of Obazine Affiliated to Clairvaux in 1147

THE ARCHITECTURAL CONTEXT

At the turn of the twelfth century, builders had behind them a century of architectural renewal. Each decade had seen progress in the art of building.[6]

• The period 1000–1020
Stone replaces wood as the main material for civil, military, and religious buildings. Stone rubble, broken up with a hammer and set in plenty of mortar, creates a "mason's architecture" (Saint-Philibert-de-Tournus).

• The period 1020–1040
Incréasing numbers of stonemasons lead to an "architecture of bonded stone". The "Benedictine church plan" makes its first appearance, with its apse-and-ambulatory scheme, and smaller apses in the transept.

• The period 1040–1060
A key building: Notre-Dame-de-Jumièges, with its west-work, lantern tower over the crossing, three-storey elevation, built in dressed stone of standard dimensions.

• The period 1060–1080
The "façade harmonique" (twin-towered façade) symbolises the quest for truth in construction (churches of Saint-Étienne and La Trinité, in Caen).

• The period 1080–1100
The invention of the vault reduces the fear of fire in the roof timbers and gives a new impetus to the sung liturgy. First appearance of monumental decoration (tympana, voussoirs, and capitals).

Top, from left to right:
• *Tournus, Saint-Philibert.*
• *Dijon, Saint-Bénigne.*
• *Jumièges, Notre-Dame.*

Far left:
• *Caen, Abbey of La Trinité (Abbaye-aux-Dames).*
Left
• *Autun, Saint-Lazare.*

Vyssi-Brod Abbey, Czech Republic. Robert of Molesme. Religious statuary always shows the founding abbots carrying a model of their abbey church. Robert of Molesme is carrying two because he founded Molesme and then Citeaux.

CHAPTER III

FROM MOLESME TO CÎTEAUX

1075 ~ 1119

FOUNDATION AND GROWTH OF MOLESME (1075 - 1090)

Very little is known about the origins of Robert, the founder of Molesme. Born in about 1028, he was very young when he entered the Benedictine monastery of Montier-la-Celle, near Troyes, becaming prior in 1053. After more than twenty years of religious life, his fame had become so great that he was summoned to lead the abbey of Saint-Michel at Tonnerre. True to the spirit of the reformers of his time, Robert hoped to promote a renewal of the practice of monastic vocation. Unable to convince his community, he resigned his post in 1072. He accepted, as an expression of humility, to become prior of Saint-Ayoul at Provins, a simple daughter house of Montier-la-Celle. Disappointed once again by an over-traditional monasteric environment, he agreed to join the hermits in the forest of Collan, between Tonnerre and Chablis, who looked on him as their spiritual guide (1073).

After a few months of an exceedingly spartan life, Robert brought the hermits together in a new abbey at Molesme, a few miles south of the village of Les Riceys. For fifteen years the monastery followed the Benedictine Rule both in letter and spirit. Living a life of rigorous asceticism, the monks rediscovered the virtue of manual work. It was at this time (1082) that Bruno of Hartenfaust, a *scholasticus* from Cologne, retreated to the forest of Sèche-Fontaine, near Molesme. Robert encouraged him to follow his vocation as a hermit, and two years later Bruno founded the Grande-Chartreuse (1084).

MOLESME TODAY

Nothing remains of the abbey which Robert of Molesme founded in 1075. But a few great monastic buildings from the seventeenth and eighteenth centuries, erected by two enlightened commendatory abbots, still stand on the hill overlooking the little valley of La Laignes.

The abbey continued to flourish for more than two centuries after the death of its founder before a long period of troubles began. During the struggle between Charles the Bold and Louis IX the abbey was in the front line; it was taken, retaken, and pillaged by both princes in turn. In 1472 all the abbey's treasures were destroyed for ever: rich reliquaries, precious books, church ornaments. During the Wars of Religion tha abbey was sacked by Montgomery and the Huguenots. When peace returned, the first commendatory abbots appropriated the monastic income (80,000 *livres* from lands, woods, watercourses, and ironworks), rather than rebuilding the abbey ruins.[1]

A revival came with Abbots Armand de Bourbon and Charles de La Rochefoucault. The third abbey church, rebuilt in 1683, was the central element of a Classical ensemble of which a few parts survived the destruction of 1793, such as the monks' refectory, the work of Charles Aviler. This architect dreamed up various complex vaulting forms: fine technical experiments which have been properly conserved by the present owners.

As for the village created by the monks, still isolated in a particularly dense forest region, it has rediscovered wine-growing. The *vignerons* covet their neighbor's vineyard. A few miles downstream the monks of Molesme created the vineyard of Les Riceys, the only wine-producing estate in France which has achieved three *appellations contrôlées*, including the famous rosé which is only produced in good years. Here is an area in which the work of the monks still goes on.

1. E. NESLE, *Statistique monumentale, pittoresque et historique de la Côte d'Or*, Beaune, 1860.

But nothing is more likely to attract a crowd than hermits and a monastery in its enclosing walls. In 1083, the bishop of Langres, impressed by the spiritual life being led at Molesme, launched an appeal for charity on behalf of the abbey which met with all too generous a response—in the view of

the father abbot—from the feudal lords of Champagne and Burgundy. They showered the abbey with donations and Robert found himself no longer in a position to object to the fashion of the time whereby patrons "held court" in the institution that was the object of their protection.[4] Vocations and wealth flowed in together, but the spirit of Collan disappeared. Molesme became the mother abbey of a Benedictine congregation of 35 priories.[5] The abbey was to suffer a real identity crisis.

THE DIFFICULT ROAD TO CÎTEAUX (1090–1098)

The question of Molesme's future arose in 1090 when one of the original pioneers of Collan, Alberic, became prior. His desire for extreme rigor was supported by a newcomer to the abbey, Stephen Harding. A Benedictine monk from Sherborne (Dorset, England), he paused at Molesme on his return from a pilgrimage to Rome, and never resumed his journey. Robert proposed that the abbey should be reformed yet again, but the monks had abandoned their early ideals and were intent on returning to the traditional observance.

After a number of approaches to the neighboring hermits, Robert and 21 monks, including Alberic and Stephen Harding, decided to leave Molesme permanently and settle in the depths of the marshy forest of Cîteaux between Nuits-Saint-Georges and the Saône river. The monks occupied a "franc-alleu" (freehold)—that is to say, they paid no rent—ceded to them by one of Robert's cousins, the viscount of Beaune.[6]

Robert could not conceal his new retreat for long. He had abandoned his abbey, in theory a serious canonical sin. He traveled, therefore, to Lyon to obtain recognition for the new monastic site from the papal legate, in which he was successful. Robert glorified God at the "New Monastery" on 21 March 1098, St. Benedict's Day, chosen as the legal and symbolic date of its foundation.

At Molesme there was quite a furore. The community, abandoned by its abbot, felt it had lost its reputation. The monks appealed to the pope who, though not able to contradict his legate, decided to hold a synod at Port-d'Anselle, near Saint-Romain-des-Iles, south of Mâcon. In June 1099 this assembly of ecclesiastics annulled the vow of stability made by the monks of Cîteaux to Robert as abbot and recommended that it should be transferred to Alberic, his chosen successor. Robert returned to Molesme "in the interests of monastic peace".[7]

Before returning to his abbey of Molesme, Robert had spent two years at the head of the New Monastery. This was a decisive period, which determined the main lines that would be followed by the community, as much for the construction of future buildings as the organization of spiritual life. And yet none of the original documents of the Order refers to this time, as though suppressing any allusion to a period when the canonical existence of the abbey was not yet assured. What is more, these documents identify Alberic, rather than Robert, as the first abbot of Cîteaux. Robert underwent a *damnatio memoriæ* (erasing from memory) such as occurs now and then in religious history… This version of the history of the abbey continued until 1222, when Robert of Molesme was canonized. From that date he was venerated by the Order. The documents that branded his return to Molesme as a weakness, or even a betrayal, were expurgated at this time.[8]

THE ABBACY OF ALBERIC (AUGUST 1099 – JANUARY 1109): CÎTEAUX, CISTERCIAN ABBEY

Alberic,[9] prior of Molesme and then of the New Monastery, was promoted to abbot in August 1099. It was right and proper that he should be thus chosen by the monks. It seems to have been

admitted that he was the main inspiration in the departure from Molesme and Robert's mainstay in this spiritual adventure.

Alberic's objective was simple: to make the New Monastery an exemplary Benedictine abbey, with a strict observance of the Rule. Nothing more than this, as the writer of Chapter XV of the *Exordium parvum*, a summary of the Rule of St. Benedict, recalled a few decades later:

1. Statutes for the Cistercian monks who came from Molesme.

2. Since that time, this abbot and his brothers, not forgetting their promise, decreed unanimously that they would establish in this place the Rule of the blessed Benedict and would obey it, rejecting all things opposed to the Rule, namely: long-sleeved tunics and furs, fine linen shirts, caps and breeches, sheets and coverlets, bedspreads, as well as a variety of courses in the refectory, lard, and everything else that runs contrary to the purity of the Rule.

3. In this way, accepting the rigor of the Rule over the whole tenor of their lives, they conformed to it and followed its directions both for the ecclesiastical observances and for everything else.

4. Having thus "put off the old man", they rejoiced in having "put on the new".

5. And as they had found nothing in the Rule or in the life of St. Benedict that indicated that he, their teacher, had possessed churches or altars, offerings or burial dues, other men's tithes, ovens or mills, villages or peasants, and no sign either that women had entered his monastery or that the dead were buried there, save only his sister, they renounced all these things, saying:

6. "When blessed Father Benedict teaches that a monk should set himself apart from worldly activities, he gives a clear witness that these

---

Left:
Perhaps Abbot Robert resembled this anonymous monk from the tomb of Stephen, in the abbey founded by the latter at Obazine.

Facing page:
The forest of Cîteaux. "One learns more in the woods than in books. The trees and the rocks will teach you things you will not hear elsewhere." Bernard of Clairvaux. Letter 101 to Henri Murdach, Abbot of Vauclair.

things should find no place in the conduct or hearts of monks, who should strive to live out the meaning of their name by shunning such things as these."

13. And knowing, furthermore, that blessed Benedict had built his monasteries not in cities, towns or villages, but in places unfrequented and remote, these saintly men vowed to imitate him.

14. And as Benedict was also wont to set up the monasteries he had built with twelve monks and an abbot, they affirmed themselves ready to do the same.

The Rule was thus applied with the greatest severity, stripped of the additions made over the years. This seems to fit in with the character of Alberic. But it is noticeable that during this period not one candidate for the novitiate came seeking entry to the monastery, nor was any donation recorded. Indeed, the cartulary of Cîteaux shows that donations ceased the moment Robert was no longer there to receive them.[4] The petty nobility of the region must have been alarmed by the rigor of the New Monastery. The group of 21 monks that had arrived from Molesme soon numbered only a dozen survivors after the departure of Robert's closest supporters and the death of the older members, exhausted all too soon by the asceticism imposed on the community.

But an experiment of such a radical nature could not fail to interest both the duke of Burgundy and the religious hierarchy.

The bishop of Chalon, won over to the ideas of the Gregorian reform, obtained from the pope a deed that reassured Alberic, who was still fearful that the monks of Molesme, strengthened by their success in recovering their abbot Robert, might demand the return of other dissidents. Paschal II granted "Roman privilege" to the New Monastery. The abbey was thus placed under the direct protection of the Holy See, without for all that being removed from episcopal jurisdiction. The promulgation of this act most probably dates from 19 October 1100.[11]

Odo I, duke of Burgundy, made a donation of new land. The monks were able to leave the original site that had proved to be unsuitable, and move to the present site of the abbey, in the middle of a cultivated plain. This was probably in 1101, just before the duke's death in the Holy Land. The grateful monks agreed to bury him in the abbey church. This future ducal necropolis was then merely a small chapel with a single nave 49 feet (15m) long and 16 feet (5m) wide, still under construction (until 1106) and the only stone building in a monastery otherwise entirely constructed in wood.

STEPHEN HARDING AND THE CARTA CARITATIS (1109 – 23 DECEMBER 1119)

Two important events marked the beginning of the abbacy of Stephen Harding. The first, heavy with promise for the financial future of the Order, was the result of the new abbot's decision to encourage and accept donations.

Land and lay brothers The extreme rigor of the observance and the great poverty of the community under Alberic was leading the monastery into ruin; it was short of monks and lacked the capacity to feed those there were. With all the pragmatism of an abbot eager to attract vocations, Stephen, more effectively than Robert or Alberic, was successful in ensuring that "the abbey grew in wealth, without diminishing the spirit of religion".[6] The result was that Cîteaux obtained fifty major donations between 1109 and 1119. This was the starting point of an extensive domain for the abbey, but, more importantly, an opportunity to establish the principle of assistance from lay brothers and waged labor, as is recalled by the author of the famous Chapter XV of the *Exordium Parvum*:

9. Then, holding the world's wealth at naught, the new soldiers of Christ, poor as Christ was poor, debated among themselves by what exercise of brains or brawn they might provide for themselves and for the guests, rich and poor, whom the Rule orders should be received as Christ.

10. They decided therefore to receive, with the bishop's permission, bearded lay brothers, whom they would treat as themselves in life as in death— the status of monk excepted—and also hired men, for they did not see otherwise how they could observe fully, day and night, the precepts of the Rule.

11. Furthermore, in isolated places away from human habitation, they would accept land, vineyards, meadows, forests, and streams where they could build mills, but for their own use only and for fishing, as well as horses and different kinds of livestock useful to men's needs.

Facing page:
Stephen Harding, third abbot of Cîteaux. Twelfth-century illumination. Manuscript from Cîteaux, Commentaries on Jeremiah. (Dijon, B. M. Ms. 130, folio 104)

Left:
Poblet, Abbey of Notre-Dame, Spain. Bernard of Clairvaux.

12. And since they had set up farmsteads here and there for cultivation of the land, they decided that the aforesaid lay brothers, rather than the monks, should administer these farms, because monks, according to the Rule, should live within their cloister.

Bernard of Fontaine The second event that was to shape the spiritual and political future of the Cistercian world was the arrival as a novice, in 1113, of Bernard of Fontaine "accompanied by gentlemen of his family [four brothers and an uncle] and a few friends". Bernard had already brought this group together in Châtillon, as William of Saint-Thierry tells us.[12] For six months he tested them and assured himself of their faithfulness. It was a closely bonded group of men that entered Cîteaux. It was also the beginning of a real

enthusiasm on the part of the Burgundian nobility for the New Monastery.

Stephen Harding found that he had to manage the double problem of a sudden over-population of his site and the too strong presence of the Fontaine "clan" installed in the abbey.

Stephen Harding's profound sentiment that the New Monastery was the embodiment of the Rule of St. Benedict led him naturally to think of founding daughter abbeys that would spread good monastic practice. An expansion of this kind had certainly not been part of Robert of Molesme's original design, but there was no alternative to this. Thus, between 1113 and 1115 the four "first daughters" were successively created: La Ferté, Pontigny, Clairvaux (assigned to Bernard), and Morimond.

The founding texts Stephen Harding "feared then that all the efforts undertaken in order to return to a stricter and more perfect observation of the Rule might come to nothing. This was why he had the idea of writing a communal charter: the *Carta Caritatis* ('Charter of Divine Love'), so that charity and unanimity would bind together for always each foundation through the handing down of the customs established at Cîteaux."[8]

In order to have, in addition, an historical reference base, Stephen Harding began at the same time to produce a text, the *Exordium Cisterciensis Coenobii*, that would record the story of the foundation of Cîteaux and the intentions of its founder.

"Was this precaution sufficient to maintain the unanimity of the original Cistercians? This is a legitimate question, since today we possess three different versions of each of these two basic texts that traditionally have been thought to be undatable." Nor is it possible to authenticate all of them.

The *Carta Caritatis* was approved in September 1119 by the first official General Chapter, whose statute is contained in the *Carta*. On 23 December 1119, Pope Calixtus II, on his way to Saulieu, was given the text, together with that of the *Exordium Cisterciensis Ceonobii*, a short text of a more religious than historical character, that anticipates the *Exordium parvum*, written later. The pope confirmed its validity by the bull *Ad hoc in apostolici*. From that day onwards the monks no longer used the name of "New Monastery", for the Order of Cîteaux had been born.

The Consuetudines*: The "Cîteaux Constitution" The *Carta Caritatis* is, even today, a model of organization. Its innovation lies in the proposal for a system that preserves the independence of each participant in the whole within an interdependence that guarantees the respect of a centralized "general line". This Constitution eliminated the rigidity and inefficiencies of the essentially feudal pyramidal system that was usual in medieval religious Orders, and particularly that of the Cluniacs.

Each Cistercian abbey was therefore autonomous, electing its own abbot and without financial obligations to the mother house or the other monasteries. Corresponding to this horizontal arrangement was a vertical control that guaranteed

the unity of the Order. The abbot of Cîteaux visited each of the daughter abbeys every year—and particularly the four "first daughters"—in order to check that the Rule was being properly observed. The abbots of the daughter abbeys, in their turn, had to pay an annual visit to their priories, and even take control of them when there was no prior. Thus all the abbeys of the Order were arranged in dependent groups. The abbey of Cîteaux itself was visited by the abbots of the four "first daughters" that were considered to stand at the head of the affiliations and which, as such, held equal responsibility in the development of the Order.

It should be said that the local bishops could also intervene in abbey life at moments of serious difficulty. Unlike Cluny, the Cistercians had not sought to benefit from the privilege of exemption that would have removed them from the jurisdiction of the bishops and made them answerable only to Rome. This willingness to remain close to the local religious power, even though living far removed from inhabited places and excused from any apostolic task, was a notable characteristic of the Cistercian Constitution.

But a system of control was not enough. In order to develop the Order's internal legislation and preserve its special nature, as well as to record any possible general policies and to act as the public relations branch of the Church, a legislative body was needed. This was the General Chapter where all the abbots met once a year. The "parliamentary form" established by Stephen Harding is all the more remarkable in that it enabled decisions to be made without the arbitration of one senior member.[9] It was, however, agreed, for debates that were not unanimous, that the meeting should defer to the judgement of the abbot of Cîteaux, and not to the opinion of the majority. Even though so much in advance of its time, a monastery was not a democratic institution.

What was ahead of its time was the Order's supra-nationality. From the moment that it began to spread beyond the borders of France, the General Chapter considered that its interests and political decisions took precedence over those of states and principalities. Precursors of European unity, the Cistercians were to benefit in this respect from the widespread renown of Bernard of Clairvaux.

Cîteaux I, architecture and illuminated manuscripts Stephen Harding seems not to have been concerned—at least not before 1119—with developing an ambitious building program. Cîteaux was to keep its little chapel of 1106 and its wooden buildings for many years. On the other hand, one of these buildings housed an workshop for illuminated manuscripts that were of amazing quality. The *scriptorium* had been active since 1098. The letter from the papal legate stipulating Robert's return to Molesme also gave permission to the monks of the New Monastery to keep those books and liturgical objects that they had taken with them on leaving Molesme, "except for a breviary that they may keep only until St. John's Day so that they can copy it." Copying books was considered to be monks' work, and Cîteaux respected this from its foundation.

But Stephen Harding did better than copy and recopy them. In the same spirit of a return to the original sources of Christianity, he consulted rabbis and the different available translations of the Bible, in order to offer the Order the most authentic text possible. At the same time he initiated an important reform of the liturgy, and collected Gregorian hymns and melodies that made up the body of the religious texts to be sung during the offices.

Facing page:
Ex-libris from Cîteaux.
Twelfth-century
illumination.

Manuscript from Cîteaux. (Dijon, B. M. Ms. 151, folio 43)

LIBER SCE

MARIE I

INCIPIT

ET POST

ORBNMAR

INBROUDITH

PURITY AND POWER

When, after the fall of Rome, one domination succeeded another, not one of them had the power to erect a monumental ensemble of such coherence, breadth and extent.
Georges Duby, L'art cistercien

The Cistercian abbeys continue to impart a lesson written in the landscape, woods, and stones (…). No ideal or technical innovations has had such far-reaching consequences (…). The lessons of the Cistercians on the mastering of nature, of techniques and of building are of inestimable value.
Léon Pressouyre, Le rêve cistercien

SＣ̃ATVS BERNARDVS PRIMVS ABBAS ARCHICÆNOBĬ CLAREVALLIS.

Preceding page:
Abbey of Clairvaux,
Champagne. The
dormitory in the lay
brothers' range
(c. 1150).

Right:
Portrait of Bernard of
Clairvaux. Cathedral
Treasury, Troyes.

CHAPTER IV

BERNARD OF CLAIRVAUX

1120~1153

THE EXTRAORDINARY DEVELOPMENT OF THE CISTERCIANS IS GENERALLY MEASURED BY REFERENCE TO THE GREAT NUMBER OF FOUNDATIONS CREATED AFTER THE PROMULGATION OF THE *CARTA CARITATIS*. AT THE TIME OF THE APPROVAL OF THE BASIC TEXT BY POPE CALIXTUS II IN 1119, THE ORDER HAD ONLY TEN MONASTERIES. BY THE TIME BERNARD OF CLAIRVAUX DIED IN 1153, SOME THIRTY YEARS LATER, IT EMBRACED 351 ABBEYS, OF WHICH HALF WERE OUTSIDE FRANCE AND 169 ATTACHED TO CLAIRVAUX ALONE.

A MAN OF GOD IN A CHRISTIAN WORLD

In fact, the major importance of the Cistercians should not be measured only in terms of such quantitative criteria. Their power was political in the broadest sense of the word, and was realized principally through Bernard of Clairvaux, whose authority and influence were felt beyond his abbey and its daughter houses, and even beyond the Order itself, eclipsing the abbot of Cîteaux on the public stage.

For thirty years Bernard of Clairvaux exercised a religious and political power that was almost unequaled. He stands in history as the outstanding participant in a period when a man of God—fortified by the principles of the Gregorian reform still fresh in people's minds—could become involved, and be used by popes, kings, and princes, in the defense of a Christian West controlled for a time by a single Church.

The political and social framework of the early twelfth century, where kingdoms were of shaky status and local powers were in the midst of restructuring, before the first manifestations of monarchist centralization and the demands of the towns, goes some way to explain the extent of power left in the hands of the Church.

But this does not explain how and why Bernard of Clairvaux was able to seize the initiative to such an extent, becoming rapidly the most famous man of his age and the major influence in a period in desperate need of capable and trustworthy leaders.

To start with, the abbot of Clairvaux was endowed with an irresistible personal charisma. Even if we ignore the legends and miracles attributed to him by a hagiography that has obscured his real merits, he must be credited with a rare talent for organizing and leading others. The first sign of his persuasiveness, when he convinced all his brothers and his closest relatives to enter Cîteaux with him, remains a significant example of an exceptional personality.

Bernard of Clairvaux's inspiration was to place his actions under the banner of purity invoked by the monastic reform movement as a whole, and particularly by the Order of Cîteaux. In earlier centuries, prelates had not been known for their moral purity and disinterestedness, and the Church had lost all credibility and power.

In his writings *On The Steps of Humility and Pride*, Bernard of Clairvaux reveals the psychological mechanism of his "interior tension": a desire for the renunciation of the world through humility and a will to act on the world through charity.[1] It is clear in this respect that the year 1118, that he spent outside the abbey walls, "in a hut like those shelters assigned to lepers at crossroads,"[2] refusing

Sedlec Abbey, Czech Republic. Bernard of Clairvaux, the "mellifluous doctor", preaching.

The Cistercian cult of
Mary.

Right:
Zlata Koruna Abbey,
Czech Republic.

Facing page:
Zdar Abbey, Czech
Republic

all nourishment, in an exaltation of humility and asceticism, was a trial that he imposed on himself to test his faith and his will to triumph over man's inevitable end. This kind of achievement became an essential part of an aura attributed at the time to the exploits of God's chosen, the fame of which was to spread all over the Christian world.

Defense of the poor Bernard of Clairvaux's purity of action was first exercised in favor of the common people still struggling to find a crust to eat. In 1124, while he was writing his famous *Apologia ad Guillelmum*, hundreds of peasants were fed each day at the gatehouse of his abbey. The abbot's words took on a revolutionary tone:

"The church shines with splendor on all sides, but the poor are hungry… The walls of the church are covered with gold, but the children of the church go naked… Ah Lord! if the folly of it all does not shame us, surely the expense might stick in our throats?… You will seal my lips saying that it is not for a monk to judge, please God that you seal my eyes also so that I may not see. But if I held my peace, the poor, the naked, and the starving would rise up and cry out…"

The cult of the Virgin Mary Bernard of Clairvaux was well aware that he lived in a time that was marked by the emergence of a new sensibility based on the discovery of profane love, and, in particular, that of women. A number of theologians and prelates of the official Church saw this as nothing but the sin that leads to Hell—as depicted in the Last Judgements on the tympana that were beginning to appear on church portals.

Bernard took a page out of the troubadours' book. He placed love at the heart of his mystical theology, and sublimated it into devotion to the Virgin, queen of Heaven. The Cistercians kept women out of their monasteries, but all the abbeys were placed under the protection of Our Lady, and

CHRONOLOGY

1124: the *Apologia ad Guillelmum*, against Cluny

1126: The letter to Suger, to "convert" him.

1128: Council of Troyes (drawing up the statutes of the Templars)

1140: Council of Sens: condemnation of Abelard

1143: Letters to the bishops, against Arnold of Brescia.

1147: Enthusiasm of Bernard for the writings of Hildegard of Bingen. Poitiers, sermons on the Trinity against Gilbert de la Porée. The Clairvaux pope Eugenius III consecrates Fontenay

1153: *Treaty of Consideration*, for the Pope

the *Salve Regina* (the antiphon of Le Puy) became, under the influence of Bernard of Clairvaux, the last devotion of each day in all Cistercian communities. Warming to his fantastic talent for writing, Bernard of Clairvaux, the "honey-tongued Doctor", developed endless elaborations on the theme of the love of God and of his Church in the extraordinary series of 86 sermons on the Song of Solomon.

A MONK OUTSIDE HIS MONASTERY

For Bernard of Clairvaux, filled with the principles at the basis of Christianity, political action and religious action were one. If the place of the Church in the world depended on it, he was quite prepared to become involved, even to the detriment of the monastic vows that obliged him to keep within the walls of his cloister.

But it was from these Christian principles that he drew his capacity for invention. His power was not attached to any hereditary title, nor was it the prize of any election. It was not conquered by force, nor was it a privilege bought with money. It existed only through the aura linked to the purity of his life as a monk. He knew it. He made use of it and added to it. He allowed legend to create an image of him performing miracles and marvels, for the greater glory of God. A small half-starved monk, swamped in the famous, undyed, wool robe of the Cistercians, unable to keep down the little food that he agreed to take, without any other escort than a secretary who wrote under his dictation during the long hours of traveling, how could he fail to stand out in the assemblies of prelates and lords dressed in purple and armor?

The schism of Anacletus The defense of the "true" papacy between 1130 and 1137 mobilized Bernard of Clairvaux, and made the abbot into one of the foremost political men of his day. Two popes had been elected at the same time. Kings and

princes gave the abbot of Clairvaux the task of settling the situation. The abbot recognized the legitimacy of Innocent II over Anacletus II, on the basis that he was the most worthy, not because the election had been more or less legitimate. He ended up by winning his case after several years of negotiations. The schism had managed to avoid the intervention of armed forces that might have given too much power to the victor to the detriment of the Church. It was a monk who was able to give the pope that power that "alone can be called universal".[1]

The Second Crusade (1146–1151) With the Crusade, Bernard of Clairvaux took on a political role of even greater importance. Always concerned

to be involved when the established order, that he believed was decreed by God, was breached, he put himself forward for the task of preacher of a new "holy war". But "the ultimate failure that brought about its end was already written in the manner in which it was embarked upon […] The mistakes of the crusaders were not the only reason for defeat. The ignorance of the preacher of those temporal matters that presented themselves, his obstinate determination to ignore the realities that rose up before him, convinced that reality should bow down before the demands of the sovereign rules that were the expression of a truth against which nothing could resist, this disdain for circumstances [all ran the risk] of leading to disastrous results—which is what happened."[2]

THE DEATH OF BERNARD

Afflicted by illness, isolated at the center of the Order in which his influence was diminishing, deeply affected by the deaths of his friends (Suger and Thibaut of Champagne in 1151, and Eugene III in July 1153), Bernard of Clairvaux returned to his abbey to find serenity at last. The saint became again a man who knew doubt and asked himself if he had not been the "chimera of his century"…

He died on 20 August 1153 and the great men of the entire world rushed to Clairvaux for his burial in the abbey church, before the altar of Our Lady—in a popular and spontaneous canonization that the monks hoped would soon be made official. With this in mind, the *Vita sancti Bernardi* was begun during his lifetime. Was it this over-hastiness, or the excessive hagiography in the text that led the papacy to ask for it to be rewritten, with additional documentation? It was necessary to wait for the canonization of Thomas à Becket in 1173, considered by Rome as having priority, before Bernard was finally glorified in 1174.

Meanwhile, without waiting, the monks of Clairvaux demolished the square east end of the abbey church, replacing it with an apse and ambulatory scheme with nine radiating chapels. The community, in a state of great exaltation, wished to create a shrine of light around the man whom they considered as the founder of the Order. At the same time they replaced the original Romanesque roof with a rib vault. The ceremony of St. Bernard's canonization took place, therefore, in a brand new Gothic church.

Above:
Fontenay Abbey, Burgundy. Virgin of Fontenay. Thirteenth-century Burgundian School.

Right:
Portalegre Abbey, Portugal. The Death of St. Bernard. Azulejos from the Lisbon workshops, early eighteenth century.

CHAPTER V

MONASTIC ARCHITECTURE ACCORDING TO BERNARD OF CLAIRVAUX

IN TRUTH, CISTERCIAN ARCHITECTURE OWES EVERYTHING TO HIM. *ST.* BERNARD WAS INDEED THE PATRON OF THIS VAST BUILDING *SITE* AND, AS THEY SAY, THE MASTER BUILDER. FOR THIS ART WAS INSEPARABLE FROM THE ETHICAL *SYSTEM* OF WHICH BERNARD WAS THE INCARNATION, ONE THAT HE WISHED AT ALL COSTS TO IMPOSE ON THE UNIVERSE, AND IN THE FIRST INSTANCE ON THE MONKS OF HIS ORDER.

GEORGES DUBY, *L'ART CISTERCIEN*, PARIS, 1976[1]

EARLY CISTERCIAN ARCHITECTURE

The amazing expansion of the Cistercian Order expressed itself physically in the appearance of hundreds of building sites. But the first abbeys were not those of brick and stone that have come down to us through the centuries. When an abbot and his first twelve monks, generally accompanied by a few lay brothers, arrived at the site of their future monastery, they lived at first in huts built of logs, in a symbolic return to the hermitage. This allowed for an easy change of site, should the first one prove to be less than perfect. If it appeared to be suitable for the monastic life, a chapel was immediately built, together with the first communal buildings. These early dwellings were hastily built, timber-framed constructions, using mud or unfired bricks, not intended to be permanent. It was then possible to take in novices and live a truly communal life according to the principles of the Rule.

The lack of documentation or archeological evidence means that little is known about the architecture of these first buildings constructed by the "pioneering" generation of Cistercians. The modest and temporary structures, probably erected as needed, must have constituted a kind of village without a master plan but surrounded by a protecting wall of wood or by hedges.

FOUNDATION DATES OF ABBEYS, AND DATES FOR THE START AND END OF WORK ON THE ABBEY CHURCHES

1. The first ten abbeys of the Order

ABBEY	FOUNDATION	MOTHER HOUSE	WORK BEGUN	WORK FINISHED
CÎTEAUX	1098		1140	1150
LA FERTÉ	1113	Cîteaux	1140/1160	1210/1220
PONTIGNY	1114	Cîteaux	1140	1170
CLAIRVAUX	1115	Cîteaux	1135	1145
MORIMOND	1115	Cîteaux	1150	1160
PREUILLY	1118	Cîteaux	1170	1200
TROIS-FONTAINES	1118	Clairvaux	1160	1190
FONTENAY	1119	Clairvaux	1139	1147
BONNEVAUX	1119	Cîteaux	1140	1240
BOURRAS	1119	Pontigny		

2. Examples of some northern French and Belgian abbeys founded before 1150

ABBEY	FOUNDATION	MOTHER HOUSE	WORK BEGUN	WORK FINISHED
VAUCELLES	1131	Clairvaux	1191	1235
TER-DUINEN	1138	Clairvaux	1214	1262
CLAIRMARAIS	1140	Clairvaux	1225	1257
CERCAMP	1141	Pontigny	1221	1262
VILLERS II	1146	Clairvaux	1210/1240	1250/1272
LOOS	1146	Clairvaux	1223/1251	1279/1289
AULNE	1147	Clairvaux	1200	1250
CAMBRON	1148	Morimond	1164/1196	1214/1240

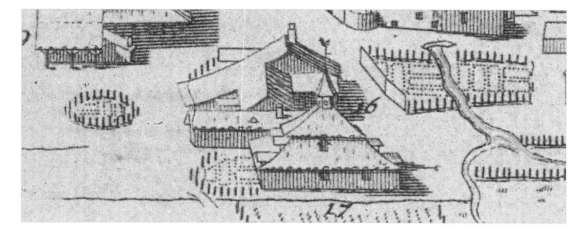

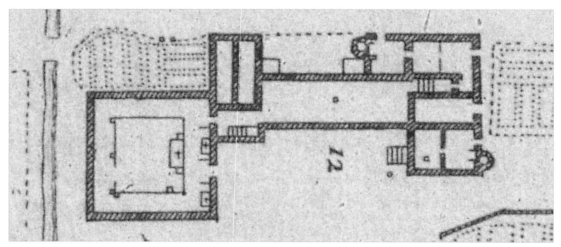

Excavations of some of the early churches, begun before 1140, have uncovered modest basilicas, lacking a transept or apse, with a nave flanked by rectangular piers supporting the roof beams. Examples are found at Rein in the Steiermark region of present-day Austria (1129), Taglieto in Liguria (1120), and Tintern Major in Wales (1131).

At Clairvaux, the *monasterium vetus* (Clairvaux I) still figured prominently in the plan and famous perspective drawings by Milley in 1708. It was little more than a kind of barn to which was attached a chapel, 56 feet square on plan (17m x 17m), with a rectangular ambulatory marking off a central space that was probably constructed in stone. The building was covered by a pagoda-like roof cut through by a central gutter, with several gables, and surmounted by a belfry mounted on a small lantern tower. This fine piece of medieval carpentry must have replaced the original construction of a century or two earlier, of which we know nothing.

Such provisional arrangements were to last for a generation. When the Order was in its beginnings it took at least twenty years for the abbeys to emerge from the phase of "taming the land, clearing it, and turning it to agricultural use" and to accumulate sufficient capital, mainly through donations, for it to be possible to envisage building an abbey that could be called permanent. Thus the building work could last for several decades, and could even be halted for long periods if the donors became less generous. Certain abbeys continued as building sites for more than a century (see Box).

THE ORIGINS OF CISTERCIAN ARCHITECTURE

The Order's first great building campaign was opened by Bernard of Clairvaux when, in 1135, he laid the foundation stone of the great abbey church and the medieval monastery known as Clairvaux II. Even Cîteaux had to wait until 1140, more than forty years after its foundation, before work started on its abbey church.

This date of 1135 is significant. Stephen Harding had stepped down as abbot of Cîteaux in 1133, dying the following year when the General Chapter discussed, for the first time since the *Apologia*, the question of architecture and decora-

Above:

Abbey of Clairvaux, Champagne. The Monasterium Vetus *(1115-1134) as it looked in 1708. (Engraving by Dom Milley. B. M. Troyes)*

Facing page:

The cloister of Thoronet Abbey in Provence. The few entirely Romanesque Cistercian abbeys are the traditional embodiment of the asceticism and simplicity of the Order's architecture.

On the other hand, the oratories were already the object of particular attention. At Cîteaux, the stone chapel of the original monastery was consecrated, according to an inscription on the façade, as early as 1106. Still there in the eighteenth century, it was described by visitors as "quite small, vaulted, and very pretty,"[2] with an aisleless nave 79 feet long (24m). It is unlikely that the vault was the original roof.

tion. Could it be that Stephen tried to delay, for as long as he had the strength, the erection of the great buildings of the Order, for fear that they might not be in keeping with the spirit of poverty of the founding fathers? He may have been afraid that the Order might repeat the Cluniac experience and succumb to that spirit of competition and achievement inherent in periods of architectural expansion. But Bernard of Clairvaux, confident of his spiritual hold over the Order, was prepared to fight for a Cistercian architecture where simplicity was the watchword. It is possible, nevertheless, that Stephen Harding had a presentiment that the very act of building for the long term inevitably brought with it the risk of falling for the fascination of huge building campaigns, involving major financial outlays, that might divert too much away from the spirit of future communities.

Bernard of Clairvaux may also have had such a presentiment when Godefroi de La Roche Vaneau, prior of the abbey, at a loss as to where to lodge so many monks and lay brothers even when daughter foundations were multiplying, begged Bernard to build Clairvaux II.

A deliberate architectural program Since the Order was forced to build, a framework of rules and recommendations had to be provided that would allow the abbots of the daughter houses to have buildings adapted to the Cistercian monastic life. Thus was born, under strong pressure from Bernard, who was convinced that there were traps to be avoided, the program that would be imposed on the architects of the new Cistercian abbeys. Naturally, nothing was written down, for architectural knowledge was at that time a specialized area, transmitted orally within closed guilds.

Like any building program, that of the abbeys involved a functional *schema* defining the general organization of the abbey, that for convenience can be called the "typical plan", together with architectural recommendations concerned particularly with the "formal part", the decoration, and everything which contributed to the spirit of a project.

An architectural program respected As one approaches the sites where many of the Cistercian abbeys are hidden away, this unity is clearly visible: the same functional *schema* and formal aspects were adopted at Fontenay in Burgundy, at Poblet in Catalonia, at Maulbronn in Germany, and at Fountains in England. They provide a clear illustration that their architecture is derived from a process that respected the essential supremacy of a single program. For the Cistercians, builders of some 750 abbeys, and innumerable barns, storehouses, mills, forges, and town houses, this program was imposed systematically, and it is unmistakably inscribed in the landscape, the buildings, and the ruins that still remain more than eight centuries after the building monks started their work. Knowing the persuasiveness needed by any master builder to ensure that his program is not altered in any way during the course of construction in order to facilitate progress as ever new and unexpected obstacles crop up for the architect and the builders, we can appreciate the extent to which Cistercian architecture bears the imprint of a strong control over the work.

The program and the Rule For Bernard of Clairvaux and the Cistercians, the priority was to build a monastery that would provide the monks with an environment suited to a strongly communal life. Thus the program had to translate the Rule of St. Benedict into spatial terms. The fundamental doctrine of Cîteaux is recalled in the article devoted to the building of abbeys in the *Capitula* (IX. 6/7): "In order that an indissoluble unity may be maintained for ever between the abbeys, it has been established in the first place that everyone should understand in the same way the Rule of the blessed Benedict, nor should they depart from it by one iota." Thus the Rule generated the program that in turn generated the plan.

The Rule, always very concrete, says almost everything about the organization of a monastic complex. But, in addition, it says even more about the spirit that ought to result from this plan. For the Cistercians and Bernard of Clairvaux, the asceticism and poverty practised on a daily basis by the monks represented the spirit of Cîteaux that architecture should translate (for all architecture reveals a culture or an ethic), favoring in return the development of a monastic life even closer to perfection (all architecture is sanctioned in this way by usage). It was a quite different reading of the Rule that had led Benedict of Aniane and the Cluniacs to build their sumptuous churches laden with works of art.

Asceticism and poverty in architecture In architecture, poverty often means something temporary and the Cistercians, unlike the monks of the Order of Grandmont, wanted none of this. Their buildings were intended to last, to withstand time. Asceticism is not the same as poverty. "We should be clear about the notion of poverty. It was more a question of simplicity. For Cistercian thinking, it was not a question of concessions on the quality of building materials, the perfection of the planning, or the choice of the most tried and tested types of construction."[3]

The spirit of Cîteaux was rather to eliminate all ostentation and the superfluous, to choose always the simplest solution, to strip bare as far as possible any kind of artificial language of construction that was no more than a concession to architectural fashion.

On the matter of art, the *Capitula* (XXXVI) are succinct: "It is completely forbidden to have sculptures. As for paintings, they are permitted only on crosses, and the latter must be of wood."

The Cistercian program and the exaltation of St. Bernard As a good master builder, Bernard of Clairvaux was tireless in the circulation of his directives. His letters, copied and recopied, were read in every abbey of the Order. His most famous letter, the one that brought about the conflict between Cîteaux and Cluny, speaks, amongst other things, of architecture and the decorative arts. This letter, the *Apologia ad Guillelmum* (1123–1125), is one of the texts that best illustrates Bernard's great talent as a writer.[4] In deploring the "excessive height of the oratories, their extravagant length, their inordinate width, their costly furnishings", he is stigmatizing Cluny, even if he admits that it is "all done for the glory of God". He condemns, and the reader understands that it is necessary to

Above:
Chauvigny, Collegiate Church of Saint-Pierre, Poitou. Capital of dragon (death), devouring a Christian. Second half of twelfth-century.

Facing page:
Alcobaça Abbey, Portugal. Room of the Kings. Panel no. 7 representing the surveyors marking out the land given to the abbey by the king. Early eighteenth-century azulejos.

do the opposite of what he denounces: nothing should distract the eye and the spirit from the idea of God. And yet, it would be a mistake to see the ideas of the abbot of Clairvaux as merely Manichean, rejecting all forms of art. Here was a man who polished his prose, just like any other writer concerned with literary effect. The *Apologia* should be read as the words of a preacher where the debt to the poor takes precedence over aesthetic preoccupations, anachronistic in the early twelfth century. Referring to St. Paul, Bernard distinguishes between "spiritual" and "fleshly" men and implies that the architecture of the cloister and that of the parish church can be different:

"St. Bernard denounced the oriental bestiary and the pagan bestiary, as councils had done before him [...]. All these representations were very unChristian [...]. If the cathedrals of the second half of the twelfth century became "bibles in stone", if the illuminating episodes of the Gospel replaced themes from the Apocalypse and obscure stories from the Old Testament, if the mermaids and griffins were replaced by the figures of Christ, the Virgin, and the saints, it was due to the radiant authority of St. Bernard."

Responsibility for the work The system of government of the Cistercian Order (extensive decentralization and strong control) was decisive for the respect for the Cistercian aesthetic. Bernard of Clairvaux set the example by involving himself closely in the building work being carried on at the abbeys that he visited. The Life of the saint depicts him as a mystic always deep in prayer—capable of walking all day by Lake Geneva without ever noticing the water! In fact, we know that he was capable of being extremely practical: he understood, for example, how to have the site of the first abbey established at Villers modified in such a way as to adapt it better to the water supply.

Respect for the program meant, for the most part, that each abbot who built a new abbey faithfully reproduced the plan. In turn he transmitted the architectural message that he had followed to the daughter house. Every year all the abbots gathered together at Cîteaux, where they were able to get back to basics in the General Chapter. Architecture was at the top of the agenda.

The cellarer, the *custos operum* As the abbeys were being built, it was the cellarer monks who took charge of the day-to-day overseeing of the work, just as they did for everything else concerning the economic life of the community. Some were so successful at this job that their names have been preserved; one was Gerard, the cellarer of Clairvaux and Bernard's brother. When he died, the father abbot wept and praised him with the words:

"When it came to buildings, fields, gardens or watercourses, arts or agricultural work, was there anything that Gerard did not know? He could direct the masons, the smiths, the farmers, the shoemakers, and the weavers without difficulty."[5]

Among these masons whose work he oversaw, some were responsible for the building while others executed the work (stone-cutters and hired hands), united in the same guild though divided according to responsibility for the work.

The architects of the Cistercian abbeys Viollet-le-Duc comments in his *Dictionnaire*[6] that, in the chaos of the early Middle Ages, the huge monasteries that preserved knowledge, thanks to their libraries and schools, had available to them a body of master builders whose job it was to design the buildings and oversee their construction. This function as architects—to use the modern term—emerged from the monasteries at the time the

cathedrals were being built, the latter being over-seen by master builders trained in the workshops of independent architects or in the workshops that were formed on the site itself.

Did the Cistercians have architects among their monks and lay brothers, or did they call upon the services of independent master builders? This question has long been debated. The hagiographic myth that the monks did all their own building is still current, and there are medieval carvings that show monks and lay brothers engaged in building. The illuminations painted in monastic manuscripts contribute to this legend. But this is to ignore the fact that architecture and stone cutting are not jobs for amateurs, even if the Rule stated

Above:
Stove at Salem Abbey, Germany. The stone-cutter's workshop.

Right:
Illumination of carpenter monks. Citeaux manuscript, Morales in Job by St. Gregory. Beginning of twelfth century. (B. M. Dijon, Ms. 170, folio 59).

1

2

3

4

that monks should practise all trades. Neither monks nor lay brothers could have spent the several years needed to learn the trade as apprentices before taking the risk of constructing such important buildings as abbey churches. Furthermore, it would not have been possible for the monks to work efficiently, continuously or profitably on the site, when their day was broken up by the various offices. And it was the *opus Dei* that had priority.

According to Marcel Aubert, for Clairvaux II and then for other daughter houses Bernard of Clairvaux used the services of the architect monks Achard and Geoffrey of Ainai.[7] This hypothesis is not entirely convincing. It is more probable that these two monks were outstanding organizers, whose job it was to deal with the financial and human problems that must certainly arisen on the larger sites. Alain Erlande-Brandenburg has pointed out that the respective duties of the master of the works and the architect have always been performed by professionals. This would have been nothing but good sense, given the technical expertise required for the conception and direction of an important building project. It was, furthermore, at this time that the organization of the building sites with an *operarius*—a figure often confused with the architect—came about.[8] Gerard, Achard, and Geoffrey of Ainai were described as *operarii*. Marcel Aubert himself cites several texts which indicate the presence of lay master builders and wage-earning workers on the abbey sites. The

masons' marks still to be seen on the stones of the pillars and vaults of the abbeys add further weight to this view.

ANALYSIS OF THE BERNARDINE PROGRAM

By the time Bernard of Clairvaux died, the Order had created 351 abbeys the length and breadth of Europe and about a hundred of these had already embarked on building work. This figure is further evidence against the theory that the master builders and stonemasons came from within the monastic communities themselves. How could so many have been trained at once?

The influence of the principles laid down by Bernard of Clairvaux at the time his abbey was under construction was evidently considerable. Thanks to the publication of Anselme Dimier's enormous *Recueil de plans d'églises cisterciennes*,[9] it can be seen that the 69 daughter houses of Clairvaux founded before 1153 follow all the programmatic principles adopted by the famous abbot. The same architectural design is also found, however, at Cîteaux and in the majority of daughter houses dependent on other abbeys. The Rule that supplied the norm had become part of the landscape.

Masons' marks

Right:
1. *and 2. Clairvaux*
Abbey, Champagne.
3. *Poblet Abbey, Spain*
4. *Veruela Abbey, Spain.*

Facing page:
Sénanque Abbey,
Provence.

1

2

3

4

Illumination of monks cutting down a tree. Cîteaux manuscript. Morales in Job by St. Gregory. Beginning of twelfth century. (B. M. Dijon, Ms. 173, folio 41).

1. The Rule and the site

The monastery should, if possible, be arranged that all necessary things, such as water, mill, garden, and various crafts may be within the enclosure …

> *Rule*, Chapter 66

Let no monastery be built within towns, castles, or villas (farms).

> *Capitula*, IX.2

The wilderness   For Robert of Molesme and his disciples, the application of the Rule was bathed in a nostalgia for the Desert Fathers that Benedict himself had known and envied (C.I.5).

For the medieval West, the "desert" meant the forest. The Cistercians made this their "Egyptian wilderness". Here they could find the "solitary wastes" dear to contemplatives, but also the wood that provided the necessary masterial for the various crafts. The forest-wilderness had preserved its mythical character as the temple of pagan cults and the refuge of runaway serfs, charcoal-burners, hunters of wild honey, and other woodland folk who wandered in the forest like nomads in the desert. They were regarded with suspicion by those of fixed abode, and they endowed the forest with a marginality that had always attracted hermits and was still appealing to the cenobites.[10]

Between Vosges and Morvan, the Ardennes and the Langres plateau, the medieval forest had preserved the thick density of the ancient Gaulish forest of Septentrion that so impressed the Romans that Gaul was known as "hairy". Clairvaux, Morimond, and Pontigny were little more than significant clearings in the heart of this forested land, impregnated with legendary terrors that could only be vanquished through prayer.

The White Monks were to be found in all the forests of Europe, along with many other monastic communities that cleared the land to cultivate it or to obtain wood for building, firewood, or tools. In the face of this general situation, the Cistercians reacted and managed their forests with an eye to the future, thanks to their policy of coppicing. Well marked with high stones bearing the arms of the abbey and broken up by carefully maintained clearings, the Cistercian forest became a model of wise management that was revived in part by Colbert with his forestry reforms.

The water of the valleys   The self-sufficient life of the monastery made it vital for the Cistercians to choose forest sites that were well supplied with water. They knew that sufficient water was a precondition for effective cultivation. For this reason they never founded an abbey on a hill, as happened at Vézelay, where the pilgrims' path was guided upwards by their eyes.

The newly promoted Cistercian abbots, sent out across Europe to establish new houses, began by making a careful survey of the valleys in the region whither they had been called by a local bishop or lord. Contrary to common practice, they often turned down prestigious sites that had been ear-marked for their use, preferring forest clearings bordered by rivers that could be turned to good use. The water would be used to turn mill-wheels, activate the forge bellows, for ablutions to wash away the sweat of toil, to flush out the latrines, and to fill the fishponds where the monks farmed the carp that made up a large part of their diet and that of the poor people who came to the abbey gate. A simple spring for drinking water was also necessary, but was not on its own enough to justify selection as a monastic site.

The documents reveal evidence that the search for a suitable site could be long:

"There was at the abbey of Balerne an abbot named Burcard who was surveying the region of Buillon in search of a site suitable for the Cistercian life. Two monks came and said that they knew of such a place suitable for the religious life and provided with water."[31]

The importance of a good site was such that the majority of abbeys started out on a temporary site while waiting to build the definitive church in a place best suited to the abbey's need for water. Such was the case of Clairvaux I (1115–34), whose buildings were converted into outhouses twenty years after its foundation, as well as the first sites of Villers-en-Brabant, Acey in the Franche-Comté, or Le Thoronet in Provence. If the site chosen turned out to be badly irrigated, the monks might have to dig major channels requiring often complex and always significant labor, given the techniques

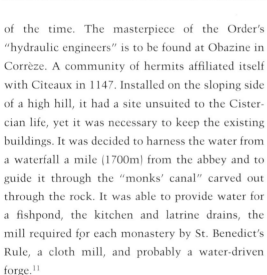

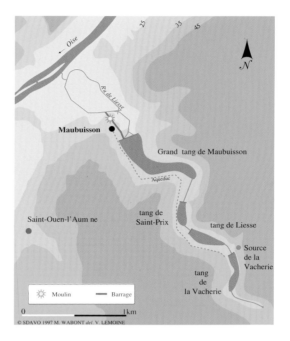

of the time. The masterpiece of the Order's "hydraulic engineers" is to be found at Obazine in Corrèze. A community of hermits affiliated itself with Cîteaux in 1147. Installed on the sloping side of a high hill, it had a site unsuited to the Cistercian life, yet it was necessary to keep the existing buildings. It was decided to harness the water from a waterfall a mile (1700m) from the abbey and to guide it through the "monks' canal" carved out through the rock. It was able to provide water for a fishpond, the kitchen and latrine drains, the mill required for each monastery by St. Benedict's Rule, a cloth mill, and probably a water-driven forge.[11]

The proximity of the rivers, systematically sought out, was translated into a variety of solutions when monastic buildings were established.[12] The White Monks often guarded against floods by building on terraces overlooking the river, as in the cases of Pontigny, Huerta, and Zwettl. To bring the water to the abbey it was therefore necessary to create a race with a head of water upstream of the site. In the case of abbeys in the valley bottom, a dam was built to channel the excess flow of water (Fontenay) or alternatively to have sufficient water permanently available by means of a pond (Fontmorigny). An exit channel directed the flow of water towards the low point of the monastery. More unusual is the monastery of Sittichenbach, where two deep tunnels cut through the rock

collected the water which percolated through it in order to feed a pond and activate a mill.

A special relationship existed between the Cistercians and water. As with so many things in the Middle Ages, it had a symbolic value. It was both the water of baptism that washes away original sin and the water of Genesis at the beginning of the world. Thus it is not surprising that water features in the place names given to the Cistercian abbeys.[13] Fontenay, Trois-Fontaines, Fontfroide (*Fons frigida*), Aiguebelle (*Aquabella*), Belaigue (*Bella aqua*), Auberive, Haute-Fontaine, Aubepierre, Bonnefontaine, Bonaigue (*Bona Aqua*), and even Sénanque (*Sana aqua* or perhaps *Sine aqua*)... And the water runs through the valleys of Clairvaux (Claravallis), Vauluisant, Vauclair, Le Val, Bonnecombe, Valsauve, Valsainte, Bellevaux,Bellecombes, Bellevaux, Bonnefontaine, Bonneval, Bonnevaux, Valbonne, and Valbenoîte.

Access to the abbey When a river runs through a forest, one is never far from a path. Thus it was that the Cistercian abbeys were never very distant from the road network of the time. Deep in the forest, they may have seemed cut off from the world, but often the distance from the road was no more than a few hundred yards.

Cîteaux, thought of as lost in the marshes, was only a hour's walk (about three miles [5km]) from the ducal road that cut through the Vouge by way

From left to right:
• *The monks' canal at Obazine, Limousin (diverted from the Coyroux) in the mountain above the abbey.*
• *Alcobaça Abbey, Portugal. The*

seventeenth-century basin with running water in the "modern kitchen".
• *Maubuisson Abbey, Île-de-France. Map of the watercourses constructed above the abbey.*

of the present-day village of Saint-Bernard. It was reached by following the river.

But the "first daughter" houses were even closer to the roads. The road from La Ferté led to Saint-Ambreuil in little over two miles (3km). The gate of Mormond gave directly on to the road, albeit a small one, between Damblain and Fresnoy. The same was true for Pontigny, situated by the bridge over the Serein, the river marking the frontier between the counties of Auxerre and Champagne. This choice of site was not without political calculation.

The site of Clairvaux is, in this regard, even more astonishing. Bernard did not choose it only because it represented a good opportunity for a donation by his cousin Josbert the Red, viscount of La Ferté. His family owned plenty of other pieces of land equally suitable for use as a Cistercian abbey! It was true that the land of Clairvaux, placed in a steep valley at right-angles to the Aube, between two thickly wooded hillsides, was rich in alluvial soil from the river, while the east-west orientation

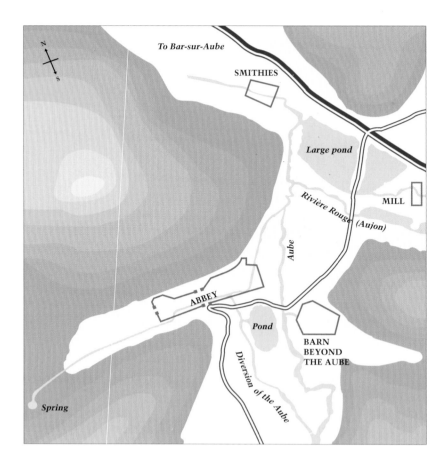

Site of Clairvaux Abbey, Champagne. An isolated valley in the forest, well oriented east-west; a river, ponds and an unpolluted spring; proximity to the main road to the Champagne fairs. After J. M. Musso, ACMH.

meant that it received plenty of sun. But the real reason for the choice of site for Clairvaux was its position in relation to the roads. The ancient Agrippan Way from Lyon to Reims, the main link between Italy and England, passed less than a mile from the abbey. The counts of Champagne protected this road, once again the major axis of European trade, since it served the Champagne fairs. Ten miles (16km) away, in Bar-sur-Aube, one of the towns where the fairs were held, the city gates were opened every year to travelers from every Christian land in the West. Clairvaux had a town house in Bar-sur-Aube; there Bernard of Clairvaux found himself at the heart of Europe.

2. The Rule and the cloister

The tools of good works are these. In the first place, to love the Lord God with all one's heart, all one's soul, and all one's strength. [...] Now the workshop, wherein we shall diligently execute all these tasks, is the monastic enclosure ...

Rule, Chapter 4.

The Rule also says:

At the gate of the monastery let there be placed a wise old man, who understands how to give and receive a message, and whose years will keep him from leaving his post. [...] The monastery should, if possible, be arranged so that ... the monks may not be compelled to wander outside it, for that will in no way benefit their souls.

Rule, Chapter 66.

A brother who by his own fault leaves the monastery should, if he wish to return, first promise full amendment for having gone away; and then be received back in the lowest place...

Rule, Chapter 29.

The *Capitula* are emphatic:

Let nothing be constructed beyond the monastery gates

IX.5

The monk is not allowed to live outside the monastery walls. The monks whose habitation, according to the Rule, must be the cloister, may go to the granges each time that he is sent, but never to stay there for a long time.

XVI.1/2

WATER AT CLAIRVAUX

A branch of the river, passing through the numerous workshops of the abbey, is blessed by all for the services it renders... The river first leaps forward impetuously to the mill, where it busies itself here and there, grinding the grain under the weight of the millstones and shaking the fine sieve that separates the flour from the chaff. And now it rushes on to the next building where it fills the boiler and offers itself up to the fire that heats it to prepare the monks' beer if the wine harvest has been poor. But the river does not give up here. It is the turn of the fullers working next to the mill to call on it. Having concerned itself with preparing nourishment for the monks it now thinks of their clothing. It never refuses to do what is asked of it. It raises and lowers in turn the heavy pounders, hammers, or to put it another way, the wooden feet, thus sparing the brothers much heavy labor... How many horses would become exhausted, how many men would tire their arms in these labors that are performed for us by our gracious river to whom we owe our clothes and our food? When it emerges from turning so many wheels so rapidly, it is foaming as if whipped. Next it enters the tannery, where it prepares the leather needed for the brothers' footwear. It is both hard-working and energetic. Then, dividing up into a multitude of smaller channels, it sets off to different parts of the monastery, seeking diligently where it can be of service, whether to cook or soak, crush or water, wash or grind, never refusing its cooperation. At last, to complete its work, it carries away the waste and leaves everything clean.

Descriptio monasterii claravallensis, Patrologia latina, vol. 185, cols. 570A–571B

Poblet Abbey, Spain. The Guests' Chapel. St. Benedict said: "All guests who arrive shall be welcomed like Christ himself, for He will say one day: I was your guest and you welcomed me (Rule C. 53.1)." All abbeys had a guest-house, but set apart from the "conventual quadrangle" so as to avoid disturbance to the life of the community.

It is clear that the Cistercian abbey was an enclosed space and the walls were never merely symbolic. All the monastery buildings, including the workshops and gardens, had to be situated within the enclosure, away from the eyes of strangers. At the time of Bernard of Clairvaux, many enclosing walls were still made of wood. Later all were built in stone or brick, reinforced with defensive watchtowers to protect the monastery from the armed marauders who roamed the countryside.

It was at this symbolic place where the inside met the outside world that princes came to bring their donations and the poor to seek food. The twelfth-century gatehouses that still exist are simple buildings, square on plan, pierced by a pair of vaulted passages, one for wheeled vehicles and the other for those on foot. It was impossible to escape the eyes of the porter as there was only one gate.

Next to the gatehouse was the "strangers'" chapel, this term referring to those who were not members of the monastic community or that of the lay brothers. For the Sunday mass and feast days, this chapel was used by visitors to the monastery,

who stayed in the men's or women's guest-house. It was used also by those of both sexes who were part of the *familia*, that is to say the servants and the people of the immediate neighborhood. Normally, however, such people were expected to attend mass in their parish church, even if it was a considerable distance away.

While the monastery was supposed to be a prefiguration of the Heavenly Jerusalem, the monks did not retain the symbolic twelve gates (St. John, chapter 21). Enclosure was strict, but it was not the "bodily constraint" of a prison. The wall also represented protection, refuge, and a promise of serenity linked to assured security, the determined limit of a chosen territory, and therefore sacred. A retreat from the world has always involved such ambiguity.

3. The Rule and monastic layout

A new abbot should not be sent into a new place without at least twelve monks [...] and without having first put up the following buildings: the oratory, the refectory, the dormitory, the guest-

house, and the gatehouse, so that they may, as soon as they arrive at the place, serve God and live according to the Rule.

   Capitula, IX,4

The tradition of the cloister   There is no contemporary indication as to the ground plan of the abbeys, and yet they were all built according to a similar general *schema*. If we are surprised, it is to forget the programmatic power of tradition that complemented explicit directives. A constant is that the Rule and commentaries on it did not deal with what was obvious in the highly ritualized world of the Middle Ages. Bernard of Clairvaux never stated what tradition made explicit.

When the Cistercians began to construct their abbeys, after 1135, the Benedictines had already had more than a century of architectural experience. The founding fathers of Cîteaux understood the principles, for they had been Benedictines. For Bernard of Clairvaux, who had visited all the great abbeys of his time, there was no reason to leave out any of the traditional elements of the Benedictine

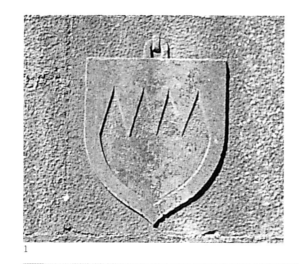

1

2

3

4

5

Coats of arms

1. Hore Abbey, Ireland

2. Kilcooly Abbey, Ireland

3. Fontenay Abbey, France

4. Ter Doest Abbey, Belgium

5. Melrose Abbey, Scotland

6. Heiligenkreuz Abbey, Austria

7. Tarouca Abbey, Portugal

6

7

WALLS

If I were a gardener, the wall would interest me more than the garden, or rather the garden would need to consist only of the wall [...] I would return again and again to this wall, telling myself that behind it there is nothing, or almost nothing: a tumult, the din of which is scarcely perceptible, or— why not?—lands full of marvels, but which do not awaken my curiosity in the slightest [...] If I were a gardener, I would touch this wall as a sick man, dying a good death, reaches out to the angel.

Pierre Sansot, *L'Espace et son double*

I am very fond of enclosed spaces, clearly defined, abolishing all that surrounds them, creating a universe that can be taken in in a glance and that can easily be listed. I find enclosure comforting.

Jean Dubuffet, *Bâtons rompus*

To enclose, that is man's great dream. To find the completeness of childhood repose, this is a desire that reawakens after a peaceful dream ... When you analyze the Jonah story (in the belly of the whale), you see it as appearing as a measure of well-being. The Jonah complex marks all our images of refuge with a primitive sign of soft, warm, safe well-being. It is an absolute of intimacy, an absolute of the contented unconsciousness.

Gaston Bachelard,
La terre et les rêveries du repos

THE RECRUITMENT OF CISTERCIAN MONKS

The White Monks applied the social norms of their time: anyone wishing to enter their monasteries as a choir monk had to give evidence of his nobility. It was a requirement that novices be able to read Latin. This condition was not always applied, should political circumstances require it to be ignored: a powerful lord, Gobert d'Apremont, for example, wished to become a Cistercian at Villers-en-Brabant. It would not have been easy to refuse him entry under the pretext that he was illiterate. In the event, he learned a few psalms, though he did not understand their meaning. In the choir he was sometimes overcome by boredom, and would chew on a peppercorn to wake himself up! By contrast, the Cistercians admired some of their community who were not of noble origin because they were good *litterati*.

abbey, starting with the cloister. This had been inspired by the Carolingian farm, influenced in its turn by the central atrium of the villas of the colonizers in the Gallo–Roman era. Thus the Cistercians also experienced life in the cloister, an enclosed space consisting of buildings enclosed within walls, that was the basis of monastic architectural composition in the twelfth century, even if the abbey church, placed symbolically on the highest piece of ground, and hence away from the river, represented its backbone.

But the Cistercian abbey was not merely a cloister attached to a church. What most characterized it was the unvarying arrangement of the different functions in the buildings forming the monastic enclave. While this arrangement was undoubtedly established according to functional criteria, there were also sociological aspects to it.

Two monasteries in one abbey There were two monasteries in the abbey, that of the choir monks,

men of noble family, and that of the lay brothers (*conversi*) who were vitally necessary to the economic self-sufficiency of the whole.[14]

Besides the church and the cloister, reserved essentially for the monks, the abbey had two clearly distinguished buildings, one for each community, without communicating access. To the east lay the choir monks' range giving on to the transept of the church so that they could go directly to the services; on the opposite side to the west was the lay brothers' range, open to the gate-house and the secular world.

The Bernardine plan of the conventual quadrangle
Influenced by tradition, justified by the Rule, decreed by a directive hierarchy and set up by users who preached obedience as a virtue, the functional and social organization of Cistercian abbeys, defined by Bernard of Clairvaux at the time when he was building his own abbey, was to be reproduced from abbey to abbey for centuries to come. The only variations resulted from the need to adapt to a particular site or local building techniques.

Even Cîteaux, from 1140, reproduced the plan of Clairvaux. In the meantime, Bernard had launched the building of Fontenay (whose church was built between 1139 and 1147), the daughter house dearest to his heart. He visited the site several times. Fontenay can be considered the prototype of the Cistercian abbey, because Clairvaux rapidly became oversized, a veritable monastic city with a perpetual building site, with its 800 monks and lay brothers, its servants, guests, and poor people.

Thus, what we know of Clairvaux and what we can still see at Fontenay, together with the many analyses of Cistercian buildings subsequently built in Europe, make it possible to posit the existence of a functional program for the buildings of the conventual quadrangle and their spatial organization (see the typical plan).

- **The abbey church** The Cistercian church derived its Latin cross plan from that of the traditional basilica. It was oriented, i.e. turned *ad orientem*, like the early church buildings. The symbolism of this arrangement was derived from the tradition of religions that worshipped the god of the new day, like the early Christians who did it to distinguish themselves from the Jews with their requirement to look towards the Temple. The east end of a Cistercian church was provided with windows or *oculi* that allowed in the sun to light up the sanctuary.[15]

The sanctuary The sanctuary (1) had in its center the high altar. The simplicity of the Cistercian Order extended to the ritual of the mass and thus

the space was not large. Nevertheless, the eyes of those present would have converged on the celebrant, and they needed to have a good view of him. For this reason, the sanctuary was raised above the floor of the church by at least two steps, with the altar itself raised on a further step. The high altar of twelfth-century churches was a simple stone construction, on which was placed a slab incised with the five consecration crosses. The wooden processional cross, placed up against the east end,

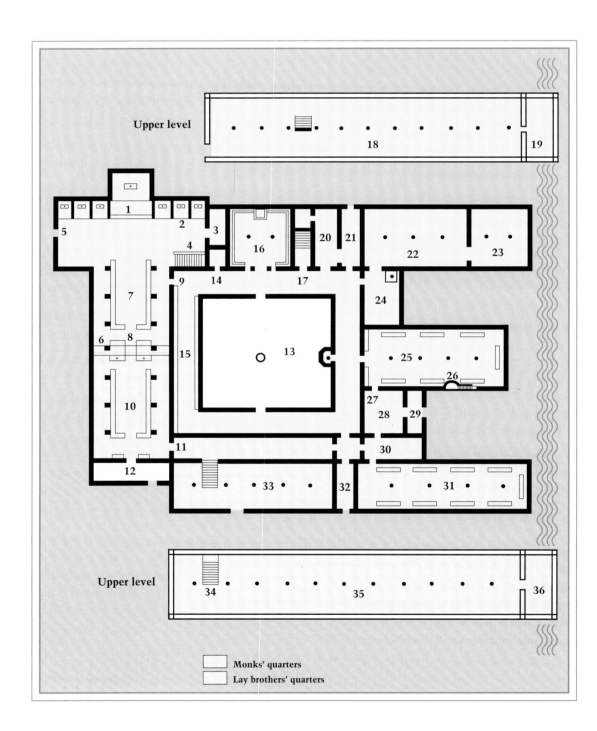

Upper level

18   19

Upper level

34   35   36

▢ Monks' quarters
▢ Lay brothers' quarters

THE CISTERCIAN ABBEY ACCORDING TO BERNARD OF CLAIRVAUX:

Functional program of the buildings of the conventual quadrangle and their arrangement (typical plan)

1. Sanctuary and main altar.
2. Transept chapels and secondary altars.
3. Sacristy.
4. Night stairs.
5. "Porte des morts".
6. Screen.
7. Monks' choir.
8. Bench for the sick and infirm.
9. Door to cloister (for the monks).
10. Lay brothers' choir.
11. Lay brothers' door to passage.
12. Narthex.
13. Well in cloister garth.
14. *Armarium* (Book closet).
15. Walk of the *collatio*.
16. Chapter House.
17. Day stairs leading to:
18. Monks' dormitory and
19. Latrines (rere-dorter).
20. Monks' Parlor or auditorium.
21. Monks' passage.
22. Monks' day-room (*scriptorium*).
23. Novices' day-room.
24. Warming house.
25. Monks' refectory.
26. Reader's pulpit.
27. Hatch.
28. Kitchen.
29. Stores.
30. Lay brothers' parlor or auditorium.
31. Lay brothers' refectory.
32. Lay brothers' passage.
33. Storeroom.
34. Lay brothers' stair leading to:
35. Lay brothers' dormitory.
36. Latrines (rere-dorter).

was of plain construction and bore the image of Christ. This was the only decoration authorized by the *Capitula* of 1119 (C.XXVI). The quality of the altar cloths and the liturgical objects was similarly prescribed:

"The altar cloths and the vestments of the ministers should not be of silk, with the exception of the stole and the maniple. The chasuble should be of a plain color. All ornaments, sacred vessels, and liturgical objects should be free of gold, silver, or precious stones, except for the chalice and the fistula, that may be of silver gilt." (C.XXV)

At the back of the sanctuary was a square east end. This was a particularly notable feature of Cistercian architecture, and one inspired by Bernard. Nevertheless, some historians have attached too much importance to the significance of the square east end, which is better explained as the sort of solution that any mason might offer his master builder, who was working to a limited budget and who would approve of any simplification of architectural forms. Furthermore, the Cistercians were not the first to use the square east end. Although the rounded apse had been the preferred form of east end for Christian places of worship since the time of Constantine, from the eleventh century many churches in the Burgundian countryside were constructed, for reasons of economy, with a square *chevet* of this sort.

Built into the south wall on the same side as the pulpit, an arched credence niche contained the cruet and a small basin usually with two holes, one to carry away to the outside the water used for the purification of the sacred vessels, and "the other for the water from the ablutions performed after the consecration of the Host; this flowed into the foundations, in holy ground."[18]

In the same wall was a cupboard for the vessels and books used in the mass, closed with a wooden door. Another cupboard was provided for the unconsecrated Host, and sometimes even for the abbey's relics.

The transept Functioning as a large vestibule, here could be found the chapels [2] used by ordained monks for their private masses. There were generally two, sometimes three, chapels in either transept, placed against the straight wall to the east and separated one from the other so that the celebrants were not disturbed. Many monks were not priests and were not required to celebrate mass every day, which is why the number of private altars was so small. To provide more such altars the abbey church of Clairvaux II had chapels on both sides of each transept.

The three-doored transept The door of the sacristy (3), always in the south gable wall, opened into a small room, dimly lit and sometimes without any windows. This was the *vestiarium*

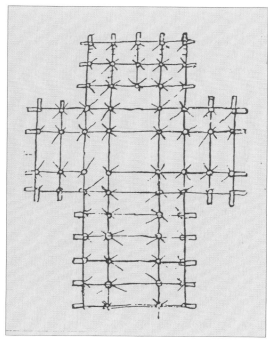

Far left:

Silvacane Abbey, Provence. The nave of the abbey church with a pointed barrel vault has reinforcing arches rising from half columns that end, following the Cistercian usage, on corbels ten feet (3m) from the ground.

Left:

Plan of a church constructed from square modules, from Villard de Honnecourt's Album.

VILLARD DE HONNECOURT

With his early thirteenth-century drawing of the basic plan of a "church of the Order of Cîteaux" as it was in the twelfth century, Villard de Honnecourt shows us that the square, Bernardine east end was probably the formal outcome of a treatment by medieval masons of the basilical plan. The Cistercian church fitted into a series of square modules following a relationship between the length of the nave and the width of the transept (6/4 according to Villard de Honnecourt). Whether or not this relationship is significant, the important thing was the obvious identification between this architectural layout and the symbolic plan of the City described in the *Revelation of St. John the Divine* (1:14), that of the cosmos in esoteric tradition, but also that of the "square man" described by Hildegarde of Bingen, the abbess of Rupertsberg, who sought the authority of Bernard of Clairvaux to validate her visions.[16]

The vast rectangular ambulatories constructed around the original square-ended sanctuaries that we find at numerous late twelfth- and early thirteenth-century Cistercian houses (Cîteaux II, Morimond II, Ebrach, Byland…), while remaining faithful to the Bernardine plan and the spirit of that drawn by Villard de Honnecourt, was a response to the new need for extra chapels.[17]

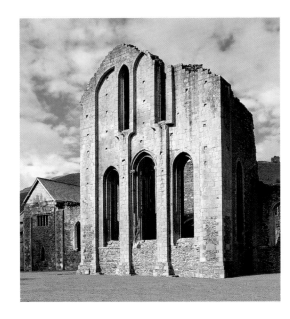

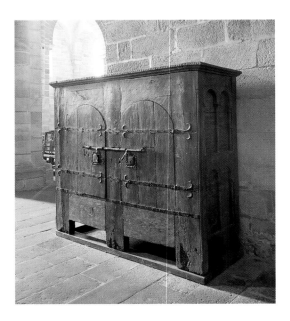

Above, from left to right:
• *Valle Crucis Abbey, Wales. The square east end of the sanctuary of the church.*
• *Obazine Abbey, Limousin. The twelfth-century liturgical cupboard in the sacristy.*

Below:
• *Silvanès Abbey, Rouergue. The night stairs.*

where the priestly napkins and vestments were kept in cupboards, niches carved into the walls, or hand-carved wooden chests.

The door to the monks' dormitory (4) was at the top of the night stairs. It was used for the night offices by the monks, who were thus able to enter the church directly from their dormitory. Like all stairways of this period, it was straight and wide, so that the monks could process down it in double file. It was always placed against the west wall of the transept, on the side of the monks' dormitory.

The "porte des morts" (5) facing the two other doors, opened on to the monks' cemetery, a small piece of ground enclosed by a low wall. When a monk died the whole community hurried to his bedside. He was laid cruciform on a mat covered with ashes. After reciting the office for the dead, the monks buried him, without a coffin, dressed in his tunic and cowl, the hood lowered over his face. The tomb, oriented east-west like the church, was marked by a wooden cross placed at the head. No burials were allowed, in theory, within the church, and no lay person, even a benefactor, was granted burial in the monks' cemetery.

The nave The Cistercian nave was flanked by side aisles. This might seem surprising, since the reformed liturgy had reduced the importance of processions and forbade the attendance at services of people from outside. There was no need for space for movement along the sides of the church. Some smaller abbey churches, however, had a single nave only: L'Étoile, Grosbot, Boschaud, Le Pin… Generally, though, the Order built churches that could accommodate rapidly expanding communities, with a central nave wide enough to take extra rows of stalls, and this led to the need for supporting side aisles.

Reflecting the arrangement of the abbey where the two communities of monks lived separately,

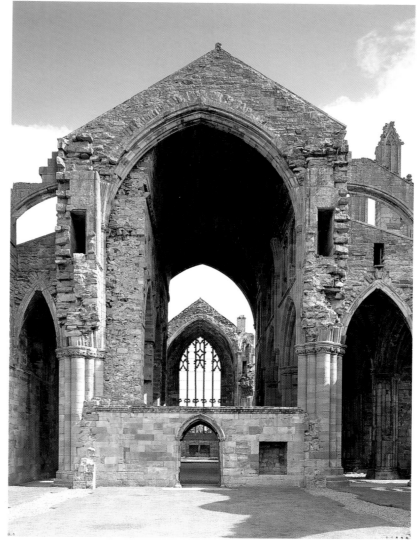

Far left:
*Flaran Abbey,
Aquitaine. The Porte des
Morts ("Door of the
dead").*

Left:
*Melrose Abbey,
Scotland. The nave of
the church and the "high
screen" separating the
monks' choir (under the
still existing vault) and
the lay brothers' choir.*

the nave was cut into two by a "high screen" (6) that marked two distinct choirs.

The monks' choir   The monks' choir (7) consisted of stalls resting against the piers of the first few bays and extending into part of the transept. They returned round the end of the choir so as to allow the abbot's and prior's stalls to face the sanctuary. Each stall, with its hinged seat with a "misericord", was allocated to a particular monk according to his seniority in the monastery. Thus he retained the same neighbors for the whole of his religious life. It was in this stall that the greater part of the days and hours of the choir monk was spent.

The daily timetable (*horarium*)   *As soon as the signal for the Divine Office has been heard, let them stop what they are doing and assemble with the greatest speed, yet soberly, so that no occasion be given for levity. Let nothing, therefore, be put before the Work of God.*

   Rule, chapter 43.

   At midnight I will rise to give thanks unto thee [...] Seven times a day do I praise thee: because of thy righteous judgements.

   Psalm 119, verses 62 and 164

St. Benedict had arranged the days and hours of the monastery in line with this text. Everything was laid down with the Rule's usual precision and humanity.

In the winter time, that is from the first day of November to Easter, the monks will rise at the eighth hour of the night, so that they can rest for a little more than half the night and get up refreshed. [...] From Easter to the aforesaid first of November, let the hour of rising be so arranged that there be a very short interval after matins, in which the brethren may go out for the necessities of nature, to be followed at once by lauds, which should be said at dawn...

   Rule, chapter 8.

And the Rule continues, from chapter 9 to 20, laying down:
– How many psalms are to be said at the night office
– How the night office is to be said in summer
– How the night office is to be said on Sundays
– How the office of lauds is to be said
– How lauds shall be said on ordinary days
– How the night office is to be performed on saints' days
– At what seasons Alleluia is to be said
– How the work of God is to be performed in the day-time
– How many psalms are to be said at these hours
– In what order the psalms are to be said
– The manner of saying the divine office
– Of reverence in prayer

Time and bells   The marking of time was of paramount importance to the monks. The controller of the time was the sacristan. During the day, he would use a sundial. At night, and on overcast days, he had to make use of other methods for measuring time. One possibility was not available to him: the mechanical clock. This was not invented until the 1300s, and it is first mentioned by Dante who refers to its religious role: "A clock calls the bride of Christ to matins...."[19]

The clepsydra was used in monasteries with great skill. This ancient water-powered device had been invented two thousand years earlier by the Egyptians and the Chinese, and had been more commonly used in antiquity than in the Middle Ages. There are no completely preserved clepsydras today, but the workings of the one at the abbey of Villers-la-Ville are well understood.[20]

The sacristan knew how to vary the length of the hours according to the seasons and determine the variable times of the offices. He had a warning system worked by a release mechanism that alerted him to the time when he should go and wake up the community for the night office.

In a Cistercian monastery, the sacristan had three bells with which he regulated the day. The great church bell announced mass, meals, and the offices attended by the lay brothers. As the latter might be in the fields, permission was granted that a bell might be raised up into a bell-tower. Its weight was limited, however, to 500 pounds, making it possible for the sacristan to pull it unaided, and the bell-tower was not to be constructed in stone, which would have smacked of ostentation! A bell-tower was only allowed if made of wood. Later, many abbeys built stone bell-towers, but always placed on the transept crossing.

The monks also obeyed a second bell, known as the "horologium", hanging in a small arcade in the end wall of the transept next to their dormitory. This bell announced the beginning of the day and then those offices that were attended by the choir monks only.

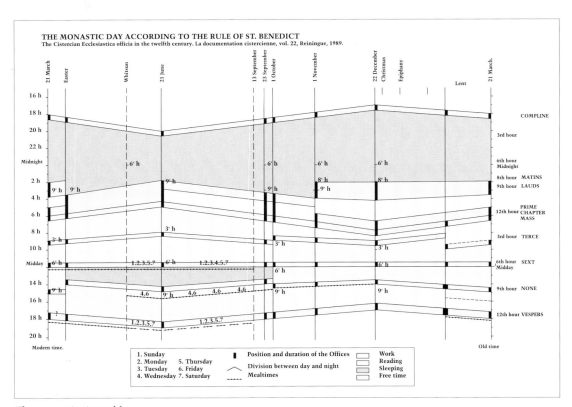

THE MONASTIC DAY ACCORDING TO THE RULE OF ST. BENEDICT
The Cistercian Ecclesiastica officia in the twelfth century. La documentation cistercienne, vol. 22, Reiningue, 1989.

The monastic timetable (horarium) *according to the twelfth-century* Cistercian Ecclesiastica officia.

Finally, after the sacristan had rung the bell for mealtime, the prior of the monastery would take over, ringing the third abbey bell, which hung in a turret above the refectory with a rope hanging down beside his chair, for the *Benedicite* and the graces.

The monks' retrochoir The monks' choir included, between the stalls and the high screen, a retrochoir (8) where the old, infirm, or sick monks would sit, along with those weakened by blood-letting.

All these monks, whether healthy or not, reached the cloister through the one door that, by day, provided a communication between the church and the rest of the abbey, and which passed into the chapter house walk (9).

The choir and the lay brothers' passage The lay brothers' choir was in the western bays of the nave. From here they could hear the offices but not see the high altar. Secondary altars were placed against the high screen so that mass could be given by the abbey lay brothers on Sundays to those who came to the abbey on that day from their granges.

The lay brothers returned to their quarters by a door (11) that opened into the lay brothers' passage. This long corridor without windows but, unusually, open to the sky, ran along the west walk of the cloister. Was it that the lay brothers were insufficiently respectful of the rule of silence, or were they thought too dirty to be allowed to pass through the cloister? In an architectural ensemble where every element had been carefully thought about and

where economies were endlessly sought after, this elaborate arrangement speaks volumes about the social segregation that lay at the heart of the abbey. Yet the institution fascinated outsiders, and great lords and educated clerics like Milon of Montbard, Bernard of Clairvaux's uncle, Alain of Lille, a famous "*scholasticus*", or Salomon of Austria, prince and heir to the kingdom, managed to get round the taboo and the regulations in order to become lay brothers, presenting themselves as mere commoners in a spirit of true humility. At the end of the twelfth century, the General Chapter forbade nobles from becoming lay brothers.

The church door The nave was often prolonged beyond the west façade by a simple porch (12) that sheltered a small side door. Since important guests with the right to follow the offices in a side aisle rarely came to the abbey, the monks of the first abbeys voluntarily withdrew the use of the west door for receiving or ceremonies. The façade was pierced only by narrow windows or small oculi, generally grouped in threes to symbolize the Trinity. To opt for such simplicity must have seemed all the more provocative in that, at the same period, the Romanesque churches of the Benedictines and bishops were exploiting the theatricality of the façade (e.g. at Notre-Dame-la-Grande in Poitiers) and the iconographic possibilities of tympana, trumeaux, and voussoirs on the great portals of churches like those at Moissac, Souillac, Beaulieu-sur-Dordogne, Autun, Conques, and Vézelay.

• The cloister On one side, the church, always lying east-west, occupied the high ground of the monastic site. On the other, the service buildings had to be built alongside the river. The cloister was placed in the center, against the nave of the church, and more to the south or to the north depending on the configuration of the site. Marcel Aubert has carefully analyzed all the ground plans, concluding that: "The proportion of abbeys where the cloister lies to the south of the church, being consequently exposed to the sun, seems rather greater than the reverse."[21] In fact, it appears that in northern Europe, wherever possible, the cloister was built in a position to receive the sun (as at Clairvaux, Fontenay, and Cîteaux), while in regions where it is hotter in the summer, the shade of the nave was used to keep the cloister cool (as at Fontfroide, Sénanque, and Le Thoronet).

Without exception, the cloisters had a square, or almost square, plan (each side being between 80 and 100 feet (25–32m), surrounded by a continuous covered walk of regular arcading opening on to a garth through a central portico. In the middle,

Above:
Byland Abbey, England

Left:
• *Zlata Koruna Abbey, Czech Republic. Sundial.*
• *Casamari Abbey, Italy. The small calling bell in the cloister (in addition to the three bells of the monastic day).*

TEMPORA TEMPORI RECTIVS VTET

The cloister at Noirlac Abbey, Berry.

where the four segments of grass that formed a square intersected, there was a well, or a basin, to collect rainwater. Some commentators have interpreted this as "the *omphalos*, the navel of the

world and center of the cosmos. Through it passes the axis of the world, this spiritual ladder, the feet of which plunge down into the kingdom of the shadowy nether world."[42] This is to see the cloister, a place for meditation, as another Zen garden… More prosaically, the monks washed their clothes here with water drawn from the well and dried them on the grass. Here too they received their regular haircut, with the crown tonsure.

The eastern cloister walk This was the most frequented of the cloister walks both because it led to the church, where the monks went seven times during the day, and because here were to be found all the rooms in which their daily life took place.

The monks came and went, but always without noise or words. The Rule recommended to the monks "the love of silence", as practised formerly by the hermits and founding fathers of monasticism. Benedict did not prescribe absolute silence, allowing speaking in cases of necessity. He saw no mystical significance in silence, but rather a moral importance. Firstly, in order to cultivate humility, only the master speaks and teaches. Then, in order to practise charity, for by speaking too much one falls into sin. Benedict quotes the prophet's terrifying words: "Life and death are in the power of the tongue." (C.VI.5)

When the Cistercians needed to communicate without breaking the silence, or even just to discuss a piece of work to be carried out, they used a sign language that had been used at Cluny since the beginning of the tenth century. The codification of a vocabulary of 296 signs, carried out around 1005 by the Cluniac monk Ulric, allowed this new language to spread to the monasteries of the congregation of Hirsau, who became ardent propagators of the system. "But it was at Cîteaux that it was used most strictly."[23] For the exchanges of day-to-day life, the monks' sign language was not like that of deaf-mutes who, through a succession of letters or syllables, are able to carry on a full conversation including abstract notions. The monks simply used coded or mimed gestures to indicate an "optical onomatopoeia".

The *armarium* (almery, or book closet) At the door into the church, the monks could find, in a

niche in the wall of the eastern walk, those books needed for their meditation (*lectio divina*). This *armarium* (14), sometimes enlarged to the detriment of the sacristy behind, also contained works belonging to the precentor of the community.

The *Capitula* of 1119 say:

C.XI: "A new abbot should not be sent to a new place […] without the following books: a psalter, a hymnal, a collection of prayers, an antiphoner, a gradual, a Rule, and a missal."

C.X: The same texts should be had everywhere: the missal, the text of the Gospels and the Epistles, the collection of prayers, the gradual, the antiphon, the hymnal, the psalter, the lectionary, the Rule, and the calendar."

These texts were the indispensable elements of the liturgical life of the community.

The precentor looked after all these hand-written books, produced in the abbey *scriptorium* and existing in only a few exemplars. His responsibility over the *armarium* was linked to the major role played by the psalms in the liturgy of the hours. The monks sang for several hours every day, as did Stephen Harding, who is supposed to have sung as he walked from Scotland to Rome and then from Rome to Molesme in order to work out a good way of chanting the psalms. This sung recitation, *recto tono*, with its few very short melodic inflections, required great musical ability. The modal scales of Gregorian chant, first introduced during the reign of Pope Gregory in around A.D. 600, and then reformed by the Carolingians before a Cistercian reform by Stephen Harding then by Bernard of Clairvaux himself, are of great complexity.[24] The monk's life was lived to the rhythm of this lyrical incantation that must have filled even his hours of silence.

The omnipresence of chant in the liturgical life could not fail to have an influence on the architecture and led the master builders to favor solutions that allowed the best acoustic and least echo. The decision to vault the abbey churches was certainly influenced by the Cistercians' profound wish to worship God with the purest of chant.

The chapter house "As often as any important business has to be done in the monastery, let the abbot call together the whole community and himself explain the matter. And, having heard the advice of the brethren, let him take counsel with himself and then do what he shall judge most expedient. [...] Let the brethren give their advice with all deference and humility [...] but in everything [...] let all follow the Rule as master. [...] The abbot himself, however, should do all things in the fear of God and observance of the Rule ..."

Rule, chapter 3.

There was always important business to conduct, even in a monastery cut off from the world, for every community harbors tensions that need to be dealt with quickly lest they become the source of rumor or conflicts that could be harmful to spiritual life. Therefore, the abbot called the community together every morning in the chapter house (16) which was so named because the abbot started each meeting with a reading and commen- tary on a chapter (*capitulum*) of the Rule. This was a good introduction to the *culpæ* where each monk accused himself publicly of any failure to observe the Rule. "In a group of men whose life was regu- lated in the smallest detail, where each one, in principle, demanded the maximum of himself, blamed himself for the slightest thing, allowed nothing to slip through and was reluctant to forgive himself, the occasions for sin were endless."[26] At

---

THE CISTERCIANS' SACRED TEXTS

For the liturgy of the mass:
- the missal containing the texts of the prayers and descriptions of the liturgical rituals applicable to the mass for every day of the year (ordinary, saints' days, church festivals);
- the text of the four Gospels and the 21 Epistles (thirteen by St. Paul) that make up the New Testament;
- the gradual (or antiphoner of the mass) containing the chants of the mass;
- the lectionary containing the Bible readings chosen for the mass and the celebration of the sacraments;
- the collection of prayers of imploration to God.

For the liturgy of the "hours"
- the hymnal that introduces the hymns and chants for the profession of faith in the liturgy;
- the psalter that gathers together the 150 texts of the Book of Psalms of the Bible, the basis of monastic prayer since the beginning of monasticism on account of their prophetic dimension; they were recited in their entirety over a period of one week of the monastic office—the antiphoner of the office containing the chants of the liturgy of the hours.

ACOUSTIC JARS

The search for the best possible acoustics in buildings and other places used for theatrical productions or music goes back more than 25 centuries to the ancient Greeks. First approached empirically and then increasingly scientifically from the time of Pythagoras (sixth century BC), the Cistercians too were aware of the need for good acoustics. Their master builders, as accomplished professionals, inserted—as recommended by Vitruvius—amphora- shaped pottery vases into the vaults of the abbey churches and chapels during their construction, at a depth of between four inches and one foot (100–300mm) behind the surface. Embedded in the infilling, only the lip of the jar remained showing on the upper surface of the vault. There does not seem to have been any rule governing their positioning, which was sometimes in lines and sometimes randomly scattered, nor the number used, which varied from a few up to as many as a hundred in one building. Recent studies, however, carried out in those sites still possessing such an arrangement and where the jars have not been blocked up with rubble, reveal that they can have a reinforcing effect on choral singing, depending on where they are positioned, by extending and amplifying the sound at the same time as reducing the echo.[25]

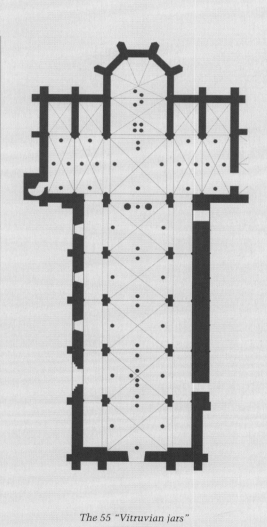

The 55 "Vitruvian jars"
in the church of Loc-Dieu
(taken from Camille de Montalivet, 1997).

Fontfroide Abbey, Languedoc. The chapter house, later twelfth century.

the time of Bernard of Clairvaux, this self-accusation was completed with the "proclamation": any fault against the Rule could be denounced by another brother (*delatio*) and be duly punished (by fasting, exclusion from the offices, or corporal punishment). More serious faults emerged in private confession and the guilty monk could be punished by imprisonment (in the monastery), or even by expulsion.

It was in the chapter house that the monks, on the death or at the deposition or retirement of the abbot, gathered to elect his successor. This "democratic" procedure, in reality very circumscribed given the presence and influence of the father abbot, was one of the innovations of the Cistercian Order and one reason for its success. Even when elected the abbot continued to be the Roman *pater familias*, vigilant and caring. "The abbot must know that the Father of the family will hold it as the shepherd's fault if there is any neglect of his flock." (*Rule*, chapter 2)

The architecture of the chapter house reflected the dignity of its function. An openwork doorway and two open bays in the eastern walk of the cloister provided access and light. They also allowed the lay brothers standing in the cloister to hear the general sermons given by the abbot on feast days. They had no voting rights, and were only allowed to cross the threshold of the chapter house twice: first, on the day when they asked to be received into the noviciate, and secondly when they made their profession.

Three windows in the exterior wall let in the morning light when the community of monks met together after prime. The room was square, each wall having a double row of benches. The simple, dignified throne of the abbot was placed opposite the door. In the center, between the columns supporting the vault, was a lectern.

The day stair and the monks' dormitory The monks used this stair (17) to go to their dormitory (18) in the evening, or in the middle of the day in the hot season when a mid-day siesta was required. They also used it to reach the latrines (19) that were generally to be found against the gable wall of the dormitory, above a channel diverted off the river, that made it possible to keep this potentially insalubrious place clean.

"How the monks are to sleep.
Let them sleep each one in a separate bed. […] If it be possible, let them all sleep in one place. […] Let them sleep clothed and girt with girdles or cords…"
Rule, chapter 22.

In the dormitory the monks slept in their tunics and leggings but without their heavy leather boots, their cowls—made of the natural-colored wool, undyed as a sign of simplicity, that earned them their name of the "White Monks")—or the black scapular which was originally a work apron

worn over the tunic. The latter garments were placed on a long, wooden bar that ran the length of the dormitory and served in place of a locker.

The dormitory had no more than a low partition between the mattresses, with no curtain dividing them off from the central passageway. A legend of the Virgin Mary tells how, as she passed by blessing the monks as they slept, she had to turn away from those who slept with too little on. Having a mattress to oneself was something of a novelty. In the twelfth century it was the common lot of all families, from the poor in their hovels to lords in the single large room of their keep, to sleep in a single, communal bed. Even in the hospitals, three or four shared a bed. But as living habits changed, the monks began to feel the oppressiveness of this obligatory communalism: "The dormitory was one of the high points of monastic mortification […] and it is easy to understand why the monks fought so hard for the right to abandon communal dormitories."[27] The General Chapter of the Order did its best to delay the inevitable move towards individual cells, but from the beginning of the thirteenth century curtains were installed in the dormitories.

Cistercian hygiene Little is known about the degree of hygiene existing in the first Cistercian abbeys, but we may suppose that it was not very good. A description by Césaire d'Heisterbach relates that one nobleman wishing to become a novice with the Cistercians was reluctant to step over the monastery entrance on account of the dirtiness of the monks. Given the arrangements in Cistercian monasteries for the removal of used and dirty water, it seems that the buildings were properly washed and cleaned—but this cleanliness seems not to have extended to the monks themselves. While Cistercian architecture is characterized by the exceptional rigor with which it separated out the different uses for the buildings, avoiding the need for multi-purpose buildings, there was no room designated for bathing. The rules that lay down with an almost excessively minute detail every action of a monk's daily life, including how to lie on his mattress, how to pull down the hood of his cowl over his face when going to the latrines, how to shave and cut his hair, how to let blood, say nothing about the monk's washing

Royaumont Abbey, Île-de-France. The thirteenth-century building housing the latrines, constructed over a cleansing water channel.

arrangements. The monks washed their hands, and perhaps their faces, in the *lavatorium*, a basin in the cloister, before going into the refectory. The only obligatory ablutions took place once a week on Saturday evenings, with the ceremony of *mandatum* when, as a mark of humility and charity, the monks washed each other's feet. Benedict of Nursia was known to "grant" baths in special circumstances. But Bernard of Clairvaux did not allow for such activities in his architectural program, since at that time bath-houses had a reputation for being places of immorality and perdition. Nakedness so terrified the founding fathers of Cîteaux that the monks were not allowed to remove their leggings at night, and at the *mandatum* they had to keep their bare feet hidden under their robes so that they should not be visible. No doubt the monks considered that personal dirtiness was an extra trial to be endured, following the example of Benedict of Aniane, who so neglected his bodily comfort as to be covered in lice that infested his rough skin.

The parlor "It is proper that the abbot should have charge of appointments to offices within his monastery. [...] However, if he should deem that it is expedient, he may, with the advice of his brothers fearing God, choose a monk and establish him as prior. This prior will carry out humbly that which his abbot asks of him."

Rule, chapter 65.

The prior looked after the administration of the community from his "office" in a narrow space in the choir monks' range beside the day stair, which allowed him to store his "dossiers" in the space beneath the stairs. Sometimes this arrangement was organized as a strongroom, with a wooden door and large locks, to protect the abbey's "treasure", consisting of the charters of its foundation and possessions along with the details of property brought by the monks when they entered the monastery. The prior sat on a stone bench to receive monks concerned with the organization of the daily offices, novices needing instruction, copyists, and all those who worked, to tell them what they should be doing. Here talking was allowed, hence the name "parlor" (20). Since the prior listened, it was also the "*auditorium*".

At Clairvaux, in Bernard's time, the prior was soon allowed a huge room in keeping with the importance of the abbey. The abbot therefore installed his secretary Nicholas in the old parlor. A large proportion of the finest Bernardine texts must therefore have been dictated in this uncomfortable, understair cupboard in stark contrast with the glowing prose, filled with the symbolic images and cadenced words of the letters and sermons of "the honey-tongued Doctor".

The passage to the infirmary, and the gardens and orchards

"Idleness is the enemy of the soul. The brethren, therefore, must be occupied at stated hours in manual labor…"

Rule, chapter 48.

Whether they went to work in the *scriptorium* to copy the sacred texts, or to the garden, or more rarely, the fields, the monks used the passage (21).

Right:

Poblet Abbey, Spain. The cloister lavatorium. The hexagonal aedicule was built around 1200. The two superimposed basins are of marble.

Below:

Furness Abbey, England. Façade of the twelfth-century monks' dormitory.

In the spirit of Benedict of Nursia, the main reason for this manual labor was not to earn a living but to avoid idleness. Experience had shown that abbeys supplied by peasants and donations, even to the benefit of the *opus Dei* and interminable offices, abandoned the spirit of the early monks. The Cistercians advocated self-sufficiency, as recommended in the Rule. The work connected with this type of enterprise was shared between the monks and the lay brothers.

"If the conditions of the place, or their poverty, makes it necessary for them to do their own harvesting, let the monks not be discontented, for it is then that they are truly monks, when they live by the labor of their own hands, like our Fathers and the Apostles."

Rule, chapter 48.

"The monks of our Order should gain their living from the work of their hands, from the cultivation of the land, and the rearing of flocks. For this reason, it is permitted for us to possess, for our personal use, ponds, forests, vines, pastures, lands distant from secular habitation, and animals [...]. In order to exploit, upkeep and maintain all this in good state, we can have, near the monastery, or far off, granges that will be overseen and administered by the lay brothers."

Capitula, XV

Since the monks, while not spending the entire day in their stalls, as at Cluny, had even so to devote some six hours to the *opus Dei* and *lectio divina*, and this at intervals too close together to make it feasible to work at any distance from the church, and since in any case it was not desirable for the monk to go out of the walls ("the monk may go to the granges each time he is sent, but never to stay for long" (*Capitula*, XVI)); since, furthermore, it was more useful to occupy them with work for which they were suited rather than laboring in the field, Cistercian abbeys reserved to monks the care of the sick, tending the monastery garden, and copying manuscripts.

"The care of the sick must come before all other things. They shall be served as Christ should be served [..]. The abbot will take the greatest care that they are not neglected in any way. Those brothers who are ill will be allowed a separate cell and an attendant, God-fearing, diligent, and caring. The use of baths will be offered to the sick whenever it is expedient. [...] Very weak patients will also be allowed to eat meat so that they may recover their strength."

Rule, chapter 36.

All the abbeys had large infirmaries, for there were many sick monks. The combination of poor hygiene, excessive blood-letting, an unbalanced diet, and often extreme asceticism was unlikely to encourage good general health.

The passage led directly to the infirmary, always placed to the east of the monastery so that the prevailing westerly winds would blow the noxious vapors away from the cloister. In the course of time, in the larger abbeys, the infirmary became organized as an annex of the monastery, around its own "little cloister".

Gardens and orchards "The monastery shall be built in such a way that [...] the garden is enclosed within it. In the garden [... the monk] shall always have his head down and eyes downcast ..."

Rule, chapters 66 and 7.

In every monastery there were, as well as an orchard, several cultivated and regularly maintained gardens. The cloister, on the other hand, as a place for gathering, was simply grassed. There was the vegetable garden, where "the vigorous vegetable plants push up their green sprouts", as the author of the plan of Saint-Gall puts it, listing the eighteen varieties recommended to the monks for their vegetarian diet: onions, leeks, cabbage, nigellus for flavoring, parsley, chervil, shallots, lettuce, garlic, radishes, beans, and peas... Missing were potatoes, tomatoes, and haricot beans, for these did not reach Europe until the discovery of America.

Near the infirmary was another, smaller, garden. This was the *herbularius*, the famous monastic herb (or "simples") garden that still has much to offer today's proponents of natural medicine. Here plants were grown that could be used as medicine, "simply", without any preparation. The number of species grown was large and included surprising plants like the rose (that calmed the nerves) and the lily (used against snake bites). The poppy could be found there, for a sponge soaked in an infusion of poppy juice relieved the pain of wounds. A beautiful medicinal garden has been reconstructed and can be visited today in the ruins of Vauclair abbey. Father Courtois and his team of archeologists have reconstructed a checkerboard garden on the basis of excavations carried out at Orvel and at the actual site at Vauclair. Four hundred different kinds of plants are grown there.[28]

The monks' day-room and the warming room (calefactory) "As for Abbot Robert's chapel and the other things that he had brought with him when he left Molesme for the new monastery, we have decided that all remains the property of the brothers of the new monastery, except for a lectionary that they may keep until the feast of St. John the Baptist, so that they may copy it."

Exordium parvum, decree of Hugh, papal legate, VII.8

From this we see that there must have been a *scriptorium* at Cîteaux from the first foundation of the abbey. Without sacred texts there could be no liturgy based on reading. When one considers the enormous demand for books generated by the newly created abbeys, it can easily be understood how the chief work of the monks was copying on to parchment and vellum (the latter for sacred texts). When, long after their foundation, the abbeys became important centers, this activity took place in buildings provided exclusively for this work, just as a cloister was set aside for the novices. But for a long time and in all abbeys, copying took place in the monks' day-room (22) and its annex, the calefactory or warming room (24).

Left:
Stove at Salem, Germany. Monks in the abbey garden and orchard.

Facing page:
Furness Abbey, England. The infirmary.

Parchment was used until the end of the Roman Empire. All ancient literature was thus handed down in unique exemplars by an entirely craft-based system of reproduction that required a huge number of copyists, some laymen, but mostly clerics, who copied, commented, annotated, and decorated with illuminations all the written knowledge that had come down to them. It is an extraordinary story. "Completely ignored by populations who spoke no Latin, a few literate monks attempted—for they were after all the heirs to Latin culture—to preserve the old texts. Over the course of many centuries they copied not only Christian texts but also pagan ones, illuminating them so that perhaps the light of knowledge would also fall on those—the vast majority—who could not read."[29]

THE MONKS' PHARMACOPOEIA

A tisane of dill is excellent for the stomach. An infusion of angelica is diuretic and purgative. Asperule in an infusion is soothing. Tisane of bergamot relaxes. Bettonica cures breathing problems. An infusion of cornflowers relieves irritated eyes. A tisane of borage is excellent for sore throats. A tisane of camomile helps the stomach. Be wary of the very poisonous foxglove. Tisane of hyssop is excellent for respiratory problems. An infusion of lavender soothes headaches. Marjoram in a tisane is sovereign against rheumatic pains. Mint improves the taste of other plants in a tisane. Chewing the leaves of rosemary sweetens the breath. An infusion of savory helps digestion. Sage is indispensable for the stomach. A concentrated infusion of marigold treats burns and small scratches. Against fever, a tisane of elder can be used. An infusion of thyme is wonderful for a cough.

The libraries of Cîteaux and Clairvaux, obviously much more complete that those of the smaller abbeys still struggling to clear their land and put up their first buildings, represented a source of books going well beyond religious texts alone. In the mid-thirteenth century Cîteaux possessed some hundred *codices* (a codex, unlike the roll that had long been used, allowed sheets of parchment written on both sides to be bound together). Clairvaux listed 300, and went on to produce, following the plan laid down by Bernard, a total collection of 1,800 works (1,400 of which are still in the Troyes library). Christian authors make up the bulk of this total, but there are also texts by Cicero, Virgil, Terence, Pliny, and all those Latin authors that Bernard had studied at Châtillon.

The Great Bible of Clairvaux, in six volumes, finished in 1151, remains the masterpiece of Bernard of Clairvaux's time. The parchment, very white and fine, is ornamented with blue and red initials with geometric interlace. The abbot forbade the use of gold or the representation of the human figure, recommending a strict monochrome style.

This monochrome style, that was used in the Cistercian *scriptoria* for several decades, was in complete contrast with the illuminations made at Cîteaux before 1140, when the influence of Bernard of Clairvaux had not yet prevailed over Stephen Harding's marked taste for exuberance and color. In the early years, before the writing of the *Apologia ad Guillelmum* in 1124, the first Cîteaux style contained examples of "humor, the grotesque, the marvelous and the humdrum, all rendered with a sharp sense for detail combined with a superb freedom of line."[30] Stephen Harding's *Bible* of 1109, the *Moralia in Job* of 1111, and St. Augustine's *Commentaries on the Psalms* are good examples. Subsequently Stephen Harding, influenced but not entirely convinced by Bernard's austerity, instituted a second Cîteaux style, serious and idealized, borrowed from Byzantine art. The St Jerome *Commentaries on the Bible* are typical of this style.

This artistic activity implies that the abbeys had available animal skins—generally from sheep—in sufficient numbers and that the lay brothers, under the supervision of the precentor, had

mastered the craft of producing parchment. This meant cutting up the animals, washing the skins in river water, steeping them in a bath of lime to remove the hairs, stretching them on a frame, bleaching them with chalk and pumicing them. These processes are described and illustrated in Diderot and d'Alembert's *Encyclopédie*. The same operations were still being used in the eighteenth century for leather and bookbinding.

Significant numbers of good quality sheep would have been required to keep the abbey's copyists supplied with skins. At Clairvaux in 1121 a specialized grange was established. The flock had more than a thousand sheep. The Cistercians acquired a taste for sheep rearing and soon became leaders in the wool market both on the Continent and in England.

The copyist's task was a tedious one, involving the production of five or six quarto folios a day. It was tiring work for the eyes and the *scriptorium* monks had to have good eyesight, there being as yet no lenses or spectacles. A copyist could reproduce forty books in the course of his life and to

Facing page:
Sénanque Abbey, Provence. The warming room, with the only fireplace in the abbey. The base of the single column (restored in the nineteenth century) is decorated with four turtles representing the four cardinal points.

Below:
Fontenay Abbey, Burgundy. The monks' day-room, with numerous large windows enabling the copyists to work with daylight.

Stylistic evolution of Cistercian illumination.

Left to right:
• *First style ("fantastic"), Stephen Harding (B. M. Dijon, Ms. 173, folio 103v)*
• *Second style ("Byzantine"), Cîteaux. (B. M. Dijon, Ms. 135, folio 107v)*
• *Third style (monochrome), Clairvaux (B. M. Troyes, Ms. 128, folio 1).*

copy a bible could take several years. As orders increased, a degree of specialization crept in, the production of a book being shared out between copyists, correctors, illuminators, and binders.

The pigments were prepared in the warming room, using earths or minerals (malachite), flower stamens (saffron), or plant roots (madder). Each color had its own binder and adhesive. A kind of alchemy led to a continual improvement in the manufacture of the inks, while the preparation of brushes, bone styluses, goose quills, pen knives (to scratch out mistakes), compasses, and rulers became a job for skilled experts.

Would the warming room have existed if it had not been for the work of manuscript copying in the Cistercian abbeys? In the winter, the copyists were allowed to come and warm up their hands before the wood fire. In Burgundy and Champagne, where the first Cistercian daughter abbeys were established, and where the winters were long and harsh, this permission was essential. The monks were also allowed to come into the warming room to grease the leather of their shoes, while for bloodletting the warming room became a kind of annex of the infirmary.

Villers-la-Ville Abbey, Belgium. The monks' refectory is designed like a church, since the communal meal is a form of mass.

The novices' day-room The novices were integrated into the monastery, living the same routine as the monks. They learned the art of copying at the same time as that of praising God. For this reason the novices' day-room (23) was attached to the monks' day-room. "The tradition of the Order has always had it that the first novices' day-rooms were placed at the end of the east wing: the abbot inspectors of the seventeenth and eighteenth centuries show this clearly in their descriptions of the state of the more or less ruined rooms of an old abbey."[31] Probation lasted for a year under the spiritual direction of a master of novices, "an older monk, skilled in the winning of souls" *Rule*, chapter 58.

The refectory "For the daily meal, we esteem that two cooked dishes on the table are sufficient, so that he who is not able to eat one of them can take of the other. Let two dishes suffice for all the brothers then, and if there is more fruit or green vegetables, they can be added. A pound loaf of bread, carefully weighed, will be enough for each day, whether there is a single meal (in Lent) or two

[…]; all shall abstain absolutely from the flesh of four-footed animals."
Rule, chapter 39.

"If a brother shall be found guilty of a lesser fault, let him be excluded from sharing the common table."
Rule, chapter 24.

The monks ate together in a refectory (25) that had to be placed near the kitchens, which in turn had to be near the river or other arrangement to supply water for cooking and cleaning. This meant that the refectory was on the other side of the cloister from the church, and wasreached by the walk that opened on to the *lavatorium* which projected into the covered walkway.

As the Cistercians had always built with an eye to future expansion, the refectories were important rooms which, with rare exceptions, extended at right-angles to the cloister gallery so as not to take up all the room between the monks' range and that of the lay brothers. Long tables ran along either side of the long room. The monks, sitting on benches on

one side of the table only, ate in silence, the food being brought by the "monk of the week". He fetched the dishes from the hatch (27), an opening in the wall into the kitchen, sometimes called the "providence".

There was usually a pulpit (26) in a niche in the west wall of the refectory, reached by a small stair built for the purpose in the thickness of the wall. Each week the abbot chose a reader to declaim extracts from the Bible in Latin, between the *Benedicite* and the *Deo Gratias* that marked the beginning and end of the meal (*Rule*, chapter 38).

Ritualized in this way, the meal was more like a religious office. The monks walked in procession into the refectory, having first washed their hands together in the large basin in the cloister. This explains why refectories, as much as churches and chapter houses, were the object of careful and almost spectacular architecture.

The vegetarian diet prescribed by the Rule was, like the regulations for the dormitory, one of the subjects of debate that regularly cropped up in the Order's meetings through the centuries. Meat was considered to be a stimulant by the Desert Fathers,

THE COWL AND MODESTY

The proper dress for attendance in the choir was the long and ample cowl. Since, however, the original tunics were only knee-length—like the clothes of the peasants—and since the Rule had failed to anticipate the need for undergarments, the cowl was also worn in the refectory where the monks sat facing one another...

and their example was followed. This ban on meat was not supported by any Biblical reference, however, unless it was prompted by nostalgia for the Earthly Paradise where Adam and Eve were vegetarians in a just world where animals lived at peace with men (Isaiah XI.6-9). The new world that emerged after the Flood accepted that man could sow fear over the world and in heaven: "Every moving thing that liveth shall be meat for you; even as the green herb have I given you all things." (Genesis, IX.3.)

The cloister fountain   "The abbot will pour water over the hands of his guests. After this ablution the

verse will be said: "We wait for thy loving-kindness, O God: in the midst of thy temple." (Psalm 48, verse 8.)

Rule, chapter 53.

Fresh water came, whenever possible, not from the river and the channels constructed by the monks, but from a spring protected from any pollution, drawn off above the abbey and channeled to the cloister fountain, opposite the entrance door to the refectory.

This precious water, symbol of that purity for which the Cistercians strove, justified the luxury of a well designed fountain and not merely the

Right:
Alcobaça Abbey, Portugal. The reader's pulpit and the stair leading to it built into the thickness of the west wall.

Far right:
Above:
Abbey of Tintern Major, Wales. The serving hatch in the monks' refectory.

Below:
Fountains Abbey, England. The monks' refectory standing over the river.

installation of a simple tank. It was enclosed within a pavilion, often of octagonal plan. The water rose up a central column, feeding a high basin from which it flowed through a number of small holes fitted with pipes or taps into a lower basin, and thence to the monastery drains. The pavilion provided an excuse for the architects to show off—the only ostentation they were allowed to display in the abbey. No pavilions survive from the first abbeys, but Viollet-le-Duc has left a drawing of the splendid lavabo at Fontenay.[32]

The lay brothers' quarters "In order to exploit [the abbey properties], keep them up and maintain them in good condition we may have near the monastery, or further off, granges that will be overseen and administered by the lay brothers.

These lay brothers are taken on by us as our fellows and our helpers, in the same way that we welcome monks; for us they are brothers and they share equally in our spiritual and our material goods, just as the monks do."
Capitula, XV and XX

The lay brothers or *conversi* were religious men subject to strict Cistercian discipline, whose job it was to deal with the material business of the abbey. They were to be found, therefore, at the very heart of the monastery, busy with domestic chores, in the workshops within the walls, and in the granges beyond the abbey.

The status of the lay brothers Although the system of lay brothers was not a Cistercian innova-

tion, no Order had previously used such a large number of them, and to such good effect, over a period of at least two centuries. At the time of Benedict of Nursia, the monks themselves took part in the manual and agricultural tasks. After Benedict of Aniane, religious duties took up all the monks' time and the monasteries, whole-heartedly embracing the feudal system, were supplied with food by their peasants. In order to free themselves from the social and political constraints that resulted from this situation, the eleventh-century reformers, Jean Gualbert at Vallombrosa and the first Carthusians and Grandmontines, made servants an integral part of their communities.

The *usus conversorum* that laid down the rules for the daily life of the lay brothers were composed by Stephen Harding and regularly amended by the

Valmagne Abbey, Languedoc. The sound of the water falling from one basin to the one below seems to enhance the silence of the cloister.

General Chapters. The lay brothers were recruited from among the local peasants, who were still living in extreme poverty in the twelfth century despite the beginnings of a significant modernization in agricultural methods. With the Cistercians they could find food and security, things they could not count on from their lords. In addition, their religious faith and the good reputation of the Order favored recruitment.

After a year-long novitiate in which to learn by heart the basic prayers and elements of monastic discipline, the lay brothers took the same vows as the monks. But they had to remain illiterate, forbidden to read, excluded from the administration of the monastery, and prevented from becoming monks. "They were peasants, and they remained such. They prayed a little more than formerly, but in their own way, very simply. They would offer instead the sweat of their brow [...] The choir monks and the lay brothers existed on different levels. Between them existed the love that binds brothers, but the barrier between them could not be penetrated: it was not possible to move from one group to the other, and each lived in their own quarters."[33] In the mid-twelfth century there were 300 monks and 500 lay brothers at Clairvaux; 100 monks and 130 lay brothers at Vaucelles; 100 monks and 300 lay brothers at Pontigny; 140 monks and 500 lay brothers at Rievaulx…

The kitchen The kitchen (28) was one of the few places where monks and lay brothers came together, for here the meals were prepared for the two groups, which received, theoretically at least, the same food (*usus conversorum*, chapter 14). The monk-cook of the week was helped by the lay brother in charge not only of the upkeep of this room but also of the bakehouse situated in the abbey outhouses.

Cistercian kitchens combined the two kinds of fireplaces known in the Middle Ages, the wall fireplace still used today, and the central hearth with its great hood, a heating system that today is little more than an occasional novelty. On either side of the kitchen were storerooms (29).

The lay brothers' parlor "As cellarer of the monastery, a member of the community should be chosen who is experienced, sober and mature in character, who is neither a great eater, nor haughty, excitable, unfair, narrow-minded, or a spend-thrift. He should fear God and be like a father to the whole community."

Rule, chapter 31.

The cellarer was in charge of the entire material life of the abbey, and it was his duty to look after the lay brothers, together with the hired workers taken on by the abbey when needed, for example as seasonal farmhands or during building work. Like the prior for the monks, the cellarer had his parlor (30), where he saw the lay brothers; it was fitted with stone benches and a cupboard for the "dossiers". He allocated the work to be done, and it was he who usually held the weekly chapter of the lay brothers, generally standing in for the abbot.

On Sundays and major religious holidays, the lay brothers came in from their granges to hear mass in the abbey church. Their journey there and back had to be made in the space of one day, which meant building granges no more than seven or eight miles (12km) from the abbey; though this rule was not always observed, which explains why chapels were found in the more distant granges.

The cellarer also went to inspect the workshops and granges. Gerard, the cellarer at Clairvaux, is praised in the *Exordium magnum* because he "ate with the lay brothers, was content to eat their food, drank water as they did, and was not prepared to be served with special foods or larger portions than usual."[55]

Stove at Salem, Germany. Lay brothers praying while working in the fields.

The lay brothers' quarters The lay brothers' quarters always included, on the ground floor, a refectory (31) and a partly underground storeroom (33), separated by the passage (32) that led out towards the exterior. On the floor above was the dormitory (35), a vast, single roofed space and always the largest room in the abbey. While the majority of lay brothers slept and lived in the granges, it was necessary to be able to accommodate and feed them when they came to the monastery.

With the demise of the lay brothers in the thirteenth and fourteenth centuries, their quarters were turned over to other uses. As the building was close to the gatehouse, it could be altered to become a guest-house, an abbot's lodgings, a library or even a simple grange.

After the French Revolution, the lay brothers' range was generally spared from the general destruction, while the other buildings were demolished for building stone. The industrialists and farmers who had become landowners thus had at their disposal vast areas for production or storage. The abbey of Clairvaux was taken over by the prison administration and transformed into a prison in 1808. The lay brothers' range was used for more than a century as a store for heavy machinery.

Social segregation, architectural unity Although so uncompromising on the subject of their buildings and how they should be lived in, going so far as to erect stone screens to separate themselves from the lay brothers in church, the Cistercians did not let this segregation affect the quality of the building. Every part of the abbey received the same care and concern for solidity . There was no difference between the monks' dormitory and that of the lay brothers. The forge at Fontenay is an even better example: a work place was no less sacred than a liturgical one, no spaces were left unaccounted for, every building was totally integrated. Cistercian architecture formed a whole.

4. The Rule and the abbey lands

In order to exploit, keep up, and maintain in a good state [the abbey properties] we may have near the monastery, or further off, granges that will be overseen and administered by the lay brothers.
Capitula, XV

The Cistercians had rejected the seigneurial system with their rejection of the world. This meant that they lost the rents, tithes, and other feudal rights authorized by their status as monks. Their search for uncultivated land led them far away from the farming centers, but made it easy for them to establish large estates. This sometimes involved evicting the peasants living on their land in the name of the monks' need for solitude. They had condemned themselves to self-sufficiency. In the spirit of the founders of the Order, self-sufficiency was a pledge of virtue, of asceticism through work. But was it carried out by the monks on their own?

The extraordinary success of the Cistercian economy remains the most perfect historical example of a self-managed enterprise that was both agricultural and industrial. An exceptional entrepreneurial spirit was not necessarily a monastic virtue, but it was a quality possessed in good measure by the Cistercian abbots and cellarers. By

From left to right:
• *Arouca Abbey, Portugal. The kitchen with its central hearth, as at Alcobaça, but also at Longpoint.*
• *The chapel of the wine grange (called the cellar) at Clairvaux, Colombé-le-Sec, Champagne.*

Because of its distance from the abbey, the lay brothers stayed at the grange on ordinary Sundays.
• *Stove at Salem, Germany. Lay brothers in the kitchen.*

Fountains Abbey, England. The undercroft of the lay brothers' range.

using labor motivated by faith—though this was not sufficient to prevent a number of revolts in the thirteenth century—it was possible for several decades to obtain constant and high quality work. It was cheap labor, although not free as is often said, for the lay brothers had to be lodged, fed, and clothed, but the cost was certainly less that that of even the most exploited workers of the period. The system of granges was also remarkable in that it provided a model for expansion by the successive addition of decentralized units of production.

The Cistercian economy modeled its physical space according to its principles of organization. Even today, the countryside and the farm buildings bear witness to its originality and perfection. Since the work of Robert Fossier,[35] who pioneered the understanding of this specific dimension of the White Monks, and the conference on "Cistercian Space", held at Fontfroide in 1993,[36] it is no longer possible to think of a Cistercian abbey as merely a monastic enclave of church and cloister. It is instead a complex ensemble that molded a territory starting from a focus of religious life, incorporating workshops on the spot and agricultural or industrial granges further off.

The outhouses A large part of the economic life of the abbey took place within the enclosed space between the encircling walls and the conventual quadrangle.

Fontenay has preserved several of the buildings put up when the abbey was first established. Still visible are the bakehouse with its bread oven, the dovecote, the mill and, especially, the forge, completed before the end of the twelfth century.

The dovecote (*columbarium*) In the feudal period, the construction of a dovecote, like that of a bake-

Above:
Bouchet Abbey, near Valence. The monastic cellar is still used today to store wine.

Right:
Fontenay Abbey, Burgundy. The beautiful twelfth-century forge.

house, was a privilege reserved for the local lord. Fontenay had "pigeon rights", and could sell the birds or eat their meat or eggs (fowl not being quadrupeds, the monks were allowed them). The *columbarium*, being of stone, was different from the smaller, wooden dovecote that only those few farmers owning over 36 acres of land were allowed to build. All abbeys had a *columbarium* with several hundred nesting holes, reached by a stair that rotated round a central post, a masterpiece of the carpenter's art. The *columbarium* at Fontenay is a cylindrical tower with a conical roof, surrounded by a thick, masonry wall. Around the structure at mid-height runs a stringcourse acting as a dripstone, designed to stop rodents entering the little window reserved for the pigeons.[37]

The forge It was rare for iron-working installations to be placed within the area of the outhouses because of the nuisance they caused (noise and smoke), and the large amounts of raw material that needed to be brought to them (ore and wood). At Fontenay there was only one forge, but this was so important and so beautiful that it has been the object of an intensive investigation by Paul Benoît

and his team. Following in the footsteps of pioneers of the history of technology such as Bertrand Gille,[38] Benoît has demonstrated the major importance of the monastic metal industry and, in particular, that of the Cistercians. At Fontenay, the site of the forge was clearly determined by the presence of a large waterfall, over eight feet (2.5m) high, with the regular rate of flow essential to operate a tilt hammer. The mine of Munières was a third of a mile (500m) away, and production developed rapidly between a furnace in the Grand Jailly forest and a forge on the river. 180 feet (55m) long, the building consists of four vaulted rooms, arranged in a line, each of two bays separated by four columns. The first probably dates from the 1130s and must have been built across the waterfall at the time the network for the water supply was set up. The three others seem to have been built a few years later, to house a tilt hammer and the hearths used to heat up raw metal and ingots before forging.[39]

The workshops With the triumphant economic expansion of the Cistercians after 1150, the outhouses became ever larger and more ornate, taking up a considerably larger space than the

monastic buildings proper. Here could be found: the masons' lodge with stone-cutters and sculptors; the workshops of other craftsmen involved in building, including carpenters, joiners, and locksmiths; and other crafts, including weavers, shoemakers, curriers, and parchment makers. The *usus conversorum* reminded lay brothers that these workshops should be places of silence, just like the monastic enclave of which the workshops represented a spiritual extension.

The granges The grange was the basic unit of production for Cistercian abbeys. Today the French word means a barn, a large covered building used to contain the harvest of some agricultural product. For the Cistercians it meant a production site of any kind. There are records of cereal granges, wine granges (or storehouses), and metalworking granges.

When the cultivable land was near the abbey, a grange was built within the monastery, as at Clairvaux. But the real importance of the granges was that they made it possible to exploit distant properties. At each grange there was a "master of the grange" or *grangiarius*, a lay brother selected for his experience and his devotion, and answerable only

Left:
Fontenay Abbey, Burgundy. Water cascading from the forge.

Facing page:
Villers-la-Ville Abbey, Belgium. The brewery (interior and exterior). The tradition of monastic brewing goes back to the Middle Ages, since the domestic water supply was often polluted.

Right:
Fontenay Abbey,
Belgium. Waterfall of the
smithy.

Facing page:
Abbey of Villers-la-Ville,
Belgium. The brewery
(views of the interior and
exterior). The tradition
of brewing by monks
goes back to the Middle
Ages, due to the often
polluted quality of the
local water supply.

to the cellarer whose instructions he carried out. In this way, the abbeys were able to organize production and expansion starting from a basis of a single piece of land of 500 to 750 acres (200–300ha), often with a specialized function because of their geological or climatic particularities. This method of organization, even more than the adoption of new techniques, explains the success of the Cistercian economy. "It filled the place of the feudal manor, but much more effectively. The feudal system divided up the vast seigneurial domains into isolated and virtually independent units, where the peasants, held back by their servile condition and the rights of the lords, had been left to their old ways without any plan for development or communal organization, with the lord being interested only in collecting his rents [...] A complicated and ineffective system of rights and mutual obliga-

tions based on ancient customs had triumphed over economic considerations."[40] In the granges, the number of lay brothers was dependent on the number of jobs to be done, the monks only joining them for harvests, sometimes with extra paid hands.

The success of the grange system became clear in the 1130s, when the feudal lords discovered that the Cistercians were successfully exploiting those lands that they had been given because they were apparently worthless: native forest, moors, and marshes in particular. Making this land fit for cultivation, by drainage or irrigation, was the Order's great achievement in the mid-twelfth century. Three particular examples spring to mind. From 1138, the abbey of Chiaravalle, near Milan, began to irrigate the dry lands of its domain by means of a canal drawing water from the Po. In

Right:
Fraville, first of the Clairvaux granges and perhaps the first grange to be managed by Cistercians. Cluny ceded the benefice to it in 1122.

Below, top to bottom:
• *Ter Doest grange, built around 1275 at Lissewege in Belgium*
• *Vaulerent, thirteenth-century grange belonging to Chaalis (Île-de-France).*

• *Late twelfth-century cellar of the wine grange of Colombé-le-Sec, where Clairvaux grew Arbanne grapes on some 250 acres (100ha) of land. Wine treated by the champagne method is still produced in this grange.*

1144, Count Rothenburg gave some marshy land to the Cistercians of Walkenried. In a few years they had so successfully drained the marshes that they became known as the famous "golden fields" of the Thuringian valley. From 1139, the abbey of Dunes began to turn nearly forty square miles (10,000ha) of sandy desert on the Flemish coast into fertile soil. Two centuries later it had 25 granges in this area. The Cistercians did less deforesting than they are generally credited with, but, on the other hand, they made a large amount of land useful for cultivation. For them, the forest represented capital that should not be squandered and the White Monks knew how to manage it well, so as to have at all times a good supply of firewood, mature trees for building, and branches from which to make hurdles for sheep-pens.

Every grange, in addition to the work buildings, had a dormitory and refectory, a lodge for the *grangiarius* and, naturally, a chapel. But the General Chapter had forbidden the celebration of mass in these chapels, wishing the lay brothers to return to soak up the atmosphere of the abbey once a week, for the Sunday mass and feast days. The more distant granges became like miniature abbeys, with an enclosing wall, orchards, gardens, and bread oven. The main building concentrated under the one roof the majority of the grange's functions. There was, however, also a gatehouse and a small guest-house, since hospitality was always provided for travelers who got caught out. "On this account, a lamp burned all night in a small niche provided above or next to the door of these rural buildings, like a beacon to guide [the traveler] and encourage him on his journey."[41]

This tradition was continued through the centuries. It was in the guest-house of the grange of Outre-Aube that Joan of Arc found refuge on the way to Chinon with the small, and still anonymous, troop supplied by the lord of Baudricourt. The Clairvaux monks had refused hospitality to this woman dressed in soldier's clothes, but the lay brothers of their nearby grange took her in. This grange of Outre-Aube is today a hamlet, where a number of the original buildings and walls can still be made out.

THE GRANGE OF OUTRE-AUBE

A. Gate towards the forest and Saint-Malachie fountain

B. Rue de la Fontaine Saint-Malachie (flows into the Aube 220 yards (200m) further on)

C. Grange with five aisles (burned down in 1986), and grange of seven aisles with foundations visible on an aerial photograph taken by raking light.

D. The house of the grange-master and the lay brothers, still standing, but altered

E. Agricultural buildings, one still standing but altered

F. Gatehouse and guest-house, existing but altered

G. Enclosing wall

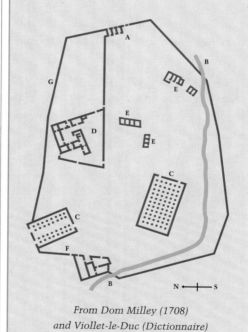

From Dom Milley (1708)
and Viollet-le-Duc (Dictionnaire)

MAP OF THE GRANGES AND STOREHOUSES BELONGING TO CLAIRVAUX [42]

The first of all, Fraville (in the commune of Arconville, three miles [5km] from Clairvaux), was granted, in 1122, an exemption from paying tithes. This generous decision, granted to the poor abbey of Clairvaux by the very rich Cluniac abbot Pons de Mergueil, anticipated the general exemption from the tax that was granted to the Cistercians in 1132 by Pope Innocent II. In 1156, another pope attempted to take back this exorbitant privilege, for the bishops and other congregations were losing income in proportion to the donations being attracted by Cistercian expansion. They had to wait until the Lateran Council of 1215 for this situation to change: the (very considerable) wealth acquired before this date continued to be exempt from tax, while new wealth would have to be governed by the common law.

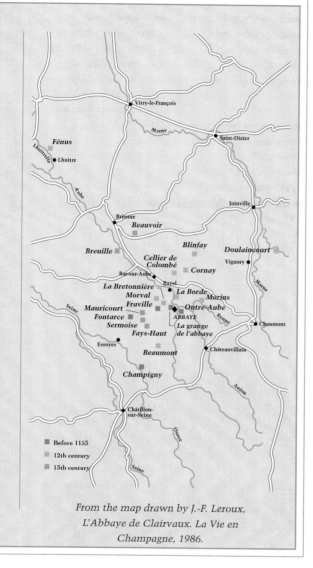

From the map drawn by J.-F. Leroux,
L'Abbaye de Clairvaux. La Vie en
Champagne, 1986.

CHAPTER VI

ROMANESQUE ARCHITECTURE IN THE EARLY CISTERCIAN PERIOD

The challenge for the Cistercians was how to translate the great functional program established as dogma by Bernard of Clairvaux into architectural reality. As at any period, the master builders had at their disposal the formal context of the existing architectural heritage and the building techniques then current. But these needed to be interpreted in the spirit of Cîteaux and of the *Apologia ad Guillelmum*. Bernard of Clairvaux, and the father abbots who considered themselves to be his disciples, were careful to choose master builders who felt that they were mediators of the Rule, caring little for mere show or formal solutions that could not be justified by this uncompromising program. Nevertheless, the importance of the architect was important: the adaptation of the new monastery to the constraints of the site, decisions about the elevations and roofing – the very essence of architecture – and the selection of materials and control over how they were used. This last task was an important one, in a community for which perfection of execution had a spiritual value.

In 1135, when Bernard of Clairvaux agreed to allow work to start on his great abbey (Clairvaux II), Romanesque architecture had reached its apogee. Stonemasons had been perfecting their techniques for over a century, while the *façade harmonique*, echoing the structure behind it, had been known for fifty years. From the beginning of the twelfth century vaulting was becoming the norm, but while the barrel vault, even the pointed tunnel vault had been well mastered, groin vaulting was still at the experimental stage. In 1125, five years before the dedication of the abbey church of Cluny III – the largest church in Chris-

tendom – begun by Abbot Hugh in 1077, a recently constructed vault collapsed. It was a telling reminder to the innovators that the limitations of weight still existed!

Clairvaux was the first of the Cistercian abbeys to develop Bernard's functional plan along the lines of the Romanesque canons of the day, but the remains of the first buildings of the mother house are not sufficiently extensive to allow us to judge their quality. The abbey church and cloister of Fontenay (1137–47), on the other hand, were built at the same time as the great abbey church of Clairvaux II (1135–45) and provide much evidence for the architectural vocabulary used by the Cistercians during the first decade of their history as builders.

THE CHURCH OF FONTENAY

The church at Fontenay, of simple plan with a transept, consists of a nave of eight bays, with pointed tunnel vaulting reinforced by transverse arches. It was flanked by aisles with transverse barrel vaults, a rather old-fashioned solution that did not eliminate exterior buttresses, but allowed for side lighting in the nave. Like all small churches in eleventh-century Burgundy, the church of Fontenay did not have upper storeys over the aisles. There was no gallery and no clerestory.

The capitals were undecorated and the bases lacked multiple roll-moldings. There was no display here, but rather a deliberate simplicity. The sanctuary was also had a barrel vault, but it was lower than the nave, allowing the diaphragm wall of the east end of the nave above the crossing at the

transept to be pierced with five windows lighting the monks' choir. What the architecture lacked in ornament was made up for by a white light that, during daylight hours, sculpted the shape of the masses and modified the colors of the building stone.

THE CLOISTER AT FONTENAY

Built during the same decade as the church, the cloister unites the traditional strength of Romanesque buildings with an elegance that draws its rhythm from the arcading. Vaulted in a continuous barrel vault (1), articulated by blind arcading (2), the cloister walks open on to the central garth through semi-circular arches (3) arranged in pairs under a relieving arch (4) resting on solid piers (5); the paired sub-arches are supported by short, twinned columns (6) resting on a low plinth wall (7). The waterleaf capitals are scarcely more elaborate than those of the church (see photograph on p. 86).

TECHNICAL PROGRESS IN THE 1140S: BIRTH OF GOTHIC ARCHITECTURE

As the building of the first Cistercians abbeys got under way and the churches of Clairvaux and Fontenay were dedicated, a number of bishops and Benedictine abbots were beginning to think about rebuilding or enlarging their eleventh-century buildings in a more contemporary style. Their architects were faced with a double conundrum: how to build "entirely of stone" churches or monastic buildings that would be higher, bigger,

CISTERCIAN LIGHT

*The panes of the windows shall be white,
without a cross and without colors.*
Capitula

The light was white thanks to a colorless glass that the architects of the Cistercian churches cut into simple, stylized shapes, and inserted in lead cames. There were no figures or historiated motifs in colored glass, as were beginning to develop elsewhere at this period of the mid-twelfth century. The brightness of the white light was augmented by reflection from the whitewashed stone walls (to which the Cistercians, with a surprisingly fanciful touch, liked to add ochre lines simulating masonry joints!).

The General Chapter fought successfully throughout the twelfth century against the introduction of color, but gradually the Cistercian abbeys succumbed to the temptation. The thirteenth-century stained glass makers ended up by seducing them just as they had seduced the canons in charge of the cathedral works.

In recent times the white glass of Cistercian churches has been the object of several studies, and of some debate. The glass made by Pierre Soulages in 1994 for the windows of the Benedictine church of Conques looks back to the sheets of alabaster that can still be seen in Cistercian churches in Aragon and Navarre. Georges Duby has written: "Perhaps there is only one kind of Cistercian painting, that of Soulages."[4] The black lines that run down his windows have a strength and a rigor that could support a metaphorical meaning, complying at the same time with the decorative neutrality recommended by Bernard of Clairvaux. Paradoxically, while praising the work of Soulages, the result of painstaking research, Georges Duby also points out the unsuitability of Conques for this particular experiment by reminding us that the monks of this pilgrimage church were not Cistercians, and that consequently they had already got into the custom of "transposing on to the windows the multicolored figurative designs of manuscript illumination,"[5] using them to teach the Bible in the same way as they used the capitals and historiated tympana of their great churches.

While Soulages was busy at Conques, Jean Ricardon was working at Acey, where the monks decided in 1992 to put new glass in the windows of their twelfth-century church. They gave their stained glass maker a double task: "Not to fall into pastiche through soulless imitation of the olden days, and not to deny the Cistercian spirit of this place, while still using the techniques of a modern age."[6] Large single sheets of glass were used, treated with a mixture of glass-painting techniques in grisaille (gray, black, blue, and white), vitrified enamels, and sand-blasting. The procedure was exemplary in its aims, but resulted in a work of art that was rather too dominant for that particular site. It was Jean-Pierre Raynaud, with the windows he created for Noirlac in 1977, who most successfully recreated the sense of Cistercian light. "Cistercian art reaches its greatest complexity in the simplest of ways, arriving at the irrational through reason, attaining gentleness through power [...] Surely Jean-Pierre Raynaud can have had no other aim in mind when he sought perfect joy in the rejection of all artifice and the choice of stripped-down simplicity? [...] Self-effacement in the presence of the naked work. At Noirlac, the harmony is stunning."[7]

and lighter, without adding greatly to the building costs. The answer was provided by a technical revolution. "It was in the course of the 1140s that Gothic architecture was defined, through three monuments: Saint-Denis, Sens, and Angers."[8] Although bitterly disputed by experts, the choice of these buildings brings together a set of technical innovations: the non load-bearing wall entirely of ashlar; the rib vault that distributes the weight on to the piers; the iron tie-bars that stabilize the lateral pull; the three-storey elevation (main arcade, gallery or triforium, and clerestory) allowing maximum light; the flying buttress that took the place of the simple buttress that was often insufficient to stabilize the weight.

These techniques did not all emerge simultaneously, nor were they used in all parts of a single building at once. Some techniques have proved difficult to date: it was long believed that the first rib vault had been constructed at Durham in 1093, when it now appears that it was a repeat of an experiment carried out at Saint-Étienne, Caen, in around 1120;[9] similarly, it was believed that the vaulting rib was no more than a reinforcement for the groin vault, which may sometimes have been the case, but is clearly incorrect when one looks at the ruins of old churches where the Gothic "skeleton" remains even though the vault has collapsed. It would appear that Gothic architecture is the result in part of a state of mind that was receptive to new experiments and theories, such as the acceptance of decompartmentalization and the transparency of volumes. Erwin Panofsky has

written a definitive text on this subject: *Gothic Architecture and Scholasticism*.[10] In his introduction he speculates on the role that might have been played in the very evolution of architecture by a master builder as determined as Suger, abbot of Saint-Denis and then regent to the kingdom—the only man ever feared by Bernard of Clairvaux.

THE LAY BROTHERS' RANGE AT CLAIRVAUX

In the timetable for the building of Clairvaux II, the church must have taken priority, along with the cloister and the choir monks' quarters. When the church was dedicated in 1145, the lay brothers' range may not have been started, but the logic of construction and stylistic analysis allow us to date it from around 1150. Probably the last building that Bernard of Clairvaux saw before his death, it was obviously the subject of particular care from all the hired workers and lay brothers who built it.

The Romanesque abbey church and cloister no longer exist, but the lay brothers' range is still there, the only remaining evidence of Bernard's abbey. At right-angles to the abbey, it forms the western wing of the monastic layout. Over 250 feet (80m) long, it has two storeys, each divided into three aisles of fourteen bays. Partly below ground level, the lower storey was used for the two different functions of refectory and storeroom, divided at the eighth bay by the passage. The upper floor was the dormitory. A steep, gabled roof topped the whole. The internal bay structure is reflected

externally by buttresses supporting semi-circular relieving arches, as in the storeroom at Dijon or the infirmary at Ourscamp.

The unknown architect who carried out the construction of this building was aware of the technical innovations of early Gothic art, and he used semi-circular arches, ribbed in the Gothic style, to support the storeroom vault.

Marcel Aubert has drawn attention to the storeroom's conoid corbels to date to the mid-twelfth century this typically Cistercian technique whereby the vaulting ribs are supported by corbels set in the walls. In this way it was possible to create more floor space, both in the storerooms and in the dormitories, refectories, and even in the church in order to fit in more stalls.

On the upper floor the lay brothers' dormitory gives an impression of immense spaciousness, for the three aisles extend without interruption over some 250 feet (76m), giving a floor space of nearly 1,800 square feet (1,500m²) under a single roof. Restoration work has revealed a pale stone for the arches and whitewashed facings for the web of the groin vaults. It is fortunate that with this lay brothers' building at Clairvaux one of the most beautiful groin-vaulted rooms in the history of Cistercian architecture has been preserved, together with a storeroom that provides evidence of the Cistercians' ability to taken advantage of every technical innovation that was available to builders.

Previous pages:
Fontenay Abbey, Burgundy. Nave of the church and cloister.

Facing page:
Stained glass Obazine, Limousin. Noirlac, Berry. Sénanque, Provence. Acey, Franche-Comté.

Right:
Four types of vault, from Glossaire, *Zodiaque*.

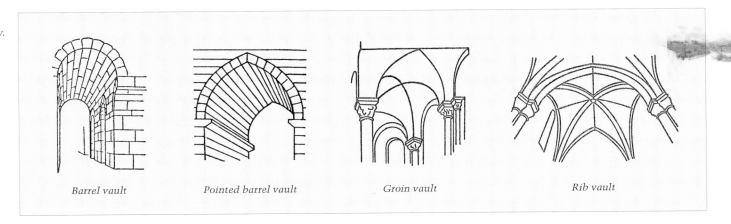

Barrel vault　　　　Pointed barrel vault　　　　Groin vault　　　　Rib vault

Cistercian corbels

1. Flaran, Aquitaine.
2. Valmagne, Langedoc.
3. Casamari, Italy.
4. Santes Creus, Spain.
5. Clairvaux, Champagne.
6. Kaisheim, Germany.
7. Poblet, Spain.
8. Chiaravalle della
Colomba, Italy.
9. Veruela, Spain.

Facing page:
Abbey of Clairvaux II.
The undercroft of the lay
brothers' range, c. 1150
(see illustration of the
dormitory, p. 30).

THE POWER AND THE GLORY

THE CISTERCIANS FROM 1153 TO 1265

With the passing of the generation of the founding fathers, the Cistercian Order continued to expand. For a century, the principles of organization established by Stephen Harding, together with the contributions made by Bernard of Clairvaux, remained the reference points for the White Monks. As long as this unanimity lasted—until 1265 when the disagreements between Cîteaux and Clairvaux became inevitable and open—the Cistercians continued to spread throughout Europe. Their presence on the political and religious stage became more important. Their economic power was becoming as significant as their influence on the evolution of architecture.

CHAPTER VII

CISTERCIAN EUROPE

THE VERY PRINCIPLE OF HOW THE ORDER SHOULD DEVELOP WAS INEVITABLY THE SUBJECT OF MUCH HEART SEARCHING AT THE GENERAL CHAPTER. IT SEEMS CLEAR THAT UNTIL HE RETIRED IN 1133 STEPHEN HARDING CONTROLLED THE PACE AT WHICH NEW ABBEYS WERE CREATED.₁ THEREAFTER GROWTH WAS ENTHUSIASTICALLY ENCOURAGED BY BERNARD OF CLAIRVAUX. AN ATTEMPT AT REINING BACK WAS MADE IMMEDIATELY AFTER HIS DEATH IN 1153, BUT EXPANSION SOON STARTED UP AGAIN, CONTINUING UNTIL THE END OF THE THIRTEENTH CENTURY.

Patterns of growth *The first period of expansion* Under Stephen Harding the Order had adhered scrupulously at grass-roots level to the principles of the *Carta Caritatis*. The new abbeys forming part of the system of mother and daughter houses grew in response to the increase in recruitment, establishing good working relations with the bishops and local lords. The four first daughter houses (La Ferté, Pontigny, Morimond, and Clairvaux), founded between 1113 and 1115, were encouraged to spread further, but the abbot of Cîteaux continued to control the setting up of new foundations. In fifteen years, between 1115 and 1130, he accepted only about thirty new abbeys, i.e. about two a year.

After 1130, however, the movement began to snowball, forty new daughter houses being created in three years by Clairvaux and Morimond. This rate of over ten new foundations a year continued for two decades. The momentum given by Bernard of Clairvaux and Gautier of Morimond (formerly the prior of Clairvaux) was maintained by Raynard, a monk from Clairvaux elected to the highest position in the Order. The figures speak for themselves: the Order numbered 322 abbeys in 1150, and contacts already established at this date brought the total up to 351 by 1153, when Bernard died.

The second wave of expansion and doubling of the number of foundations In 1152, Bernard of Clairvaux, sick, and depressed by the failure of the

Crusade, did not attend the General Chapter. A new abbot presided, Gossuin, from an abbey directly dependent on Cîteaux, the ever wise mother house, rather than on one of the four original daughter houses that were traditionally more enterprising. The Chapter condemned the recent affiliation of whole congregations of Benedictines, even "reformed" ones like the Order of Savigny which attached itself to Clairvaux with 29 of its abbeys in 1147. The General Chapter decided to limit the number of new foundations. Requests continued nevertheless to flood in from all over

Europe, from the pope and the bishops, from kings and princes. Expansion was not halted, even if it bore within itself the germ of all those risks inherent in large institutions, particularly the temptation for those abbeys far away from Burgundy and the influence of their mother house to become autonomous.

Every year the "Cîteaux storks" and their attendants took to the roads of Europe, traveling from abbey to abbey, converging on the General Chapter that opened on 14 September, Holy Cross Day. For some abbots from distant abbeys the

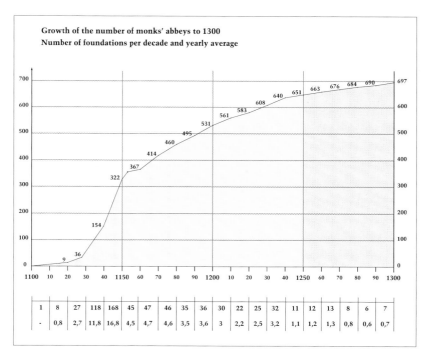

Growth of the number of monks' abbeys to 1300
Number of foundations per decade and yearly average

	1	8	27	118	168	45	47	46	35	36	30	22	25	32	11	12	13	8	6	7
	-	0,8	2,7	11,8	16,8	4,5	4,7	4,6	3,5	3,6	3	2,2	2,5	3,2	1,1	1,2	1,3	0,8	0,6	0,7

Facing page:
Alcobaça Abbey,
Portugal. The façade,
sixteenth to eighteenth
century.

NUMBER OF ABBEYS PER FILIATION

FILIATION	1150	1153	1200	1250
Cîteaux	59		59	70
Morimond	83		138	165
La Ferté Pontigny	29		56	76
Clairvaux	151	169	270	339
TOTAL	322	351	523	651
Clairvaux's share	47%	48%	51%	52%

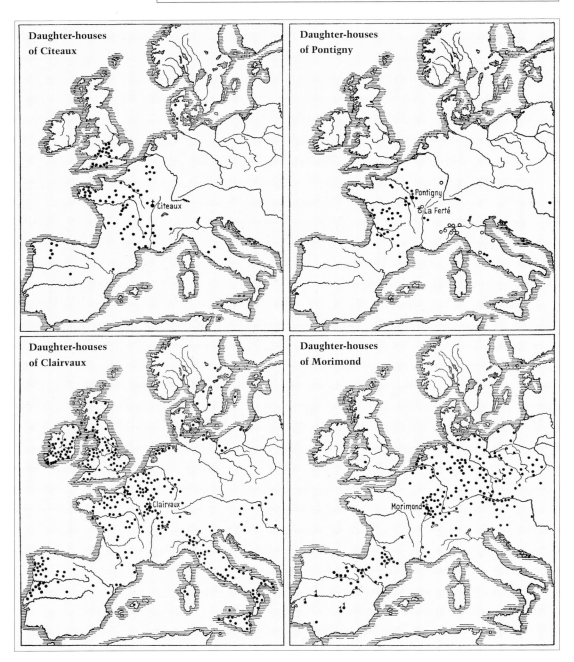

Daughter-houses of Cîteaux

Daughter-houses of Pontigny

Daughter-houses of Clairvaux

Daughter-houses of Morimond

journey could take several weeks. They were excused from coming to Cîteaux every year. In fact, the General Chapter never received more than a third of the abbots; furthermore, there were only 300 seats in the chapter house!

At the end of the thirteenth century, at its peak, the Order consisted of some 700 abbeys. Later foundations were few in number—some forty up to 1500, and then another fifteen or so up to the French Revolution—and not enough to replace the number of abbeys destroyed or dissolved, victims of the events of history. In total, the Order founded 754 monasteries, of which only 400 were still active by the time of the Revolution.

THE CISTERCIANS IN EUROPE

The Order was represented in every country of Christian Europe, and even in the Middle East, whither the Cistercians had followed their "brothers", the Knights Templar.

In France and outside France Naturally France was the main center of the Cistercian Order, with particularly large numbers of abbeys in the two provinces of Burgundy and Champagne, the birthplace of Cîteaux and its four original daughter houses.

However, although more than half the Order's foundations (183 out of 351) were French at the time of Bernard of Clairvaux's death in 1153, subsequently only a third (244 out of 754) of the total number of abbeys were on French soil. From 1180, the Order considered that its mission to "colonize" on the frontiers of the Christian world should take priority. New foundations were established, in cooperation with the Premonstratensians, in Poland, Bohemia, and on the Iberian Peninsula of the *Reconquista*.

Outside France the Cistercian presence had grown, with 510 abbeys proudly carrying the standard of Cîteaux. Four countries in particular were significant: England (65 abbeys), Italy (98), Spain (57), and the Holy Roman Empire (71). Morimond was influential in the Empire thanks to its four very active and prolific daughter houses: (Kamp, which produced more than fifty daughter houses, Altenberg, Lucelle, and Ebrach). From these bridgeheads, eastern Europe was conquered in due course.

Morimond and Clairvaux In fact, expansionist activity was only truly supported by Clairvaux and Morimond. The directly dependent daughter houses of Cîteaux were few in number, and the mother house was too busy with its administrative duties and the organization of the annual Chapter. Pontigny and La Ferté, for their part, did not have sufficiently large numbers of new recruits to allow a significant expansion.

Clairvaux, on the other hand, had assumed a dominant position. The large numbers of recruits made it possible to send monks all over Europe. With 339 foundations, it represented, in 1250, 52% of all Cistercian abbeys. Its relative size had, indeed, increased over a century (in 1150, its 151 foundations represented 47% of the Order's abbeys). Outside France, the Clairvaux abbeys benefited from the effective work of those personally devoted to Bernard of Clairvaux, whom they had met and admired on the occasion of his many journeys through Europe. At the time of their incorporation into the Clairvaux house (1147), the Benedictines of Savigny brought with them thirteen English abbeys. The friendship of Malachy, the bishop of Armagh who spent his last years at Clairvaux, resulted in a flowering of Irish abbeys, beginning with the "house" of Mellifont (1142) which, in less than fifty years, gave rise to a network of 24 abbeys. In Italy, the abbey of Casamari (1140) alone produced fifteen more founda-

tions, particularly through its daughter house of Sambucina di Calabria (1160). Poblet in Catalonia (1151) and Alcobaça in Portugal (1148) were also to play an important role in the development of Clairvaux beyond the Pyrenees.

Above:
Illumination of soldier
defeating a dragon.
Cîteaux manuscript.
(B. M. Dijon, Ms. 173,
folio 20)

Facing page:
Royaumont Abbey,
founded by Cîteaux and
St. Louis in 1228.

CHAPTER VIII

POLITICAL AND RELIGIOUS GLORY

As the thirteenth century dawned, Christianity had as yet no inklings of the great change that was to rock its very foundations with the arrival of an urban and trading population ready to ally itself with the universities and support a strong central power. This new triple alliance was to destroy the old provincial alliance of the monk, the lord, and the peasant. There were those, like Arnaud of Brescia, who had predicted these events, but they were regarded as eccentrics. Neither the Church nor the Cistercians paid any heed.

After the death of Bernard of Clairvaux, the White Monks occupied center stage in public life. They were present at every Crusade and advised the king. The Order was duly rewarded. The Fourth Lateran Council singled it out as a model to be imitated. Most satisfying of all was the moment when the Benedictine abbots were invited to adopt structures copied from those of Cîteaux, including regular visits from superiors and a General Chapter. They were advised to invite two Cistercian abbots to help them, "for the Cistercians have

long had the custom of bringing such chapters together!"

A PASSION FOR CRUSADING

The interest manifested by Bernard of Clairvaux throughout his life in military matters had given rise to a similar interest among members of the Order, partly, no doubt, on account of the large numbers of recruits from the feudal nobility. For many decades the Cistercians followed his example and volunteered for all those campaigns where the "defense of Christianity" could more or less justify their presence:

• 1158: Morimond is in control of the Spanish Order of the Knights of Calatrava (in the fifteenth century, 2,000 knights and six commanderies) and active in the Reconquista;

• 1187–93: the third Crusade is preached by three Cistercian prelates; loss of the Syrian abbeys;

• 1202–4: the abbot of Vaux de Cernay joins the Fourth Crusade as chaplain-general; the founding of abbeys in Romania;

• 1180–1210: during the Albigensian Crusade, Arnaud Amaury, abbot of Cîteaux, commands an army of French and Burgundian knights with Simon de Montfort. The Béziers Massacre;

• 1190: the pope entrusts the Cistercians with the mission of preaching the Gospel to Prussia and the Baltic provinces. Fierce battles and foundation of new abbeys.

THE CISTERCIANS AS DIPLOMATS FOR PEACE

- 1218: the General Chapter calls the soldier monks back to their abbeys. Ever empirical, the Cistercian abbots prefer power through diplomacy, often more effective and generally less cruel.
- 1159: Schism of Anacletus. Twenty Cistercian abbots work on drawing up the Treaty of Venice (1177), intended to settle relations between the "Pope and the Empire".
- 1226–1270: reign of St. Louis, the "Cistercian king". Foundation of the abbey of Royaumont. Cistercian abbots active in all areas of diplomacy.

The move towards scholarship

- 1237: monks from Clairvaux are students in Paris;
- 1245: Clairvaux sets up the Collège Saint-Bernard in Paris.

Changes in organization After a century of existence, the Order continued to grow in fame and power with no serious problems occurring to disturb its internal organization. Its Constitution shows how well adapted it was to the development of new houses and to its political and economic role. However, the number of foundations and activities under the control of the General Chapter was eventually to exceed a critical threshold. The carefully constructed system of shared powers, in which lay the originality and the strength of the Cistercians, was threatened.

In the thirteenth century, the incorporation into the Order of numerous groups of "holy women" was to contribute to the quantitative instability of the institution. The unequally distributed weight of the different houses also contributed to weakening the central authority of the Order, bringing about the first serious questioning of its statutes and its very workings.

Cistercian nuns The fame of the Cistercians attracted not only kings and princes but also women seeking religious perfection. In the thirteenth century these women lived together in more or less anarchical communities in the towns. The extraordinary phenomenon of a growing number of nunneries that chose to follow Cistercian practices is well illustrated by the adoption of the famous royal abbey of Las Huelgas in Castille in 1187.

The end of unanimity The number of abbeys grew so great that the General Chapter became difficult to manage. From the end of the twelfth century, the need for an intermediary stage between the abbot and the assembly was met with the creation of the "definitors".

Their nomination became part of the process of jockeying for power, and it was on this subject that a dispute broke out between the abbots of Cîteaux and Clairvaux. Clairvaux, still as powerful as ever in terms of the number of its daughter houses and its influence in political and economic domains, was bound to challenge the more important role of the abbot of Cîteaux within the general Chapter. After some skirmishes in 1215 and 1238, a serious conflict broke out in 1262. The papal bull *Parvus fons*, known as the "Clementine Bull", signed by Clement IV on 5 February 1265, brought the dispute to an end by changing several of the rules under which the General Chapter operated. Most importantly, it satisfied Clairvaux's desire for a more important role within the definitory.

However, simply to reform the constitution was not enough to resolve the dispute. The great problem for the future lay elsewhere: how to maintain the functioning of this great Order, stretching out in long lines of succession to the four corners of Europe. In the centuries that followed, the only solution seemed to be in the formation of national groupings of abbeys, a process that would lead to the collapse of the Order.

Tisnov nunnery, Czech Republic, also known as Porta Coeli *after its beautiful thirteenth-century door.*

CHAPTER IX

ECONOMIC POWER

The self-sufficiency laid down by the Rule was achieved by the exploitation of the Order's land through the system of granges, under the enlightened management of the cellarer, and using the well-motivated and free labor of the lay brothers, who were helped when necessary by the monks or by waged workers. This arrangement gradually led the Cistercians, who lived a life of poverty, to endow their abbeys with wealth unknown to any other institution of the time. When in the thirteenth century a failure to recruit new lay brothers resulted in the system losing its effectiveness, the Cistercian "economic machine" was in a strong enough situation to be able to continue its successful work of enriching the Order.

These Cistercians, though seeking to flee the world, were in fact essential to it, their products forming an essential part of the economic system. Apart from donations, usually in the form of land, they had—at first at least—no income in coin, neither paying nor receiving tithes. Thus they could not buy those products that they were unable to produce for themselves except by selling part of their harvests. Consequently exchange (selling in order to buy) assumed a particular importance in the Cistercian economy.[1] Very soon the monks, who consumed very little themselves, had large amounts of high-quality produce to exchange. With the general increase in population, the market was booming, and the Cistercian economy flourished, particularly in the period 1150–1250.

The wealth of the Cistercians has often been stressed, particularly with reference to the role played by the White Monks in the revolution in agricultural and industrial techniques that led to the expansion of the towns, in the thirteenth century; a consequence of the over-production occurring in rural areas at that time. Although the Cistercians were at the forefront of progress, they were not generally inventors of new techniques. Their talent lay in their ability to adapt the innovations of the time to a larger scale, setting up a rational scheme of working on the site of production, and initiating medium and long-term policies for supply or commercialization.

LAND OWNERSHIP

The original land holdings of the abbeys derived from donations prompted by religious devotion. This land was essential to the Cistercians, who could only support themselves by growing their own food on their own estates, following the land tenure system of the time. "The monks' natural inclination, in order to increase the number of donations, must have been to encourage the pious

Ter Doest grange, Belgium, interior and exterior.

sentiments of the faithful to turn in this charitable direction. There was also the risk that the monks might use any accumulated wealth to buy new land, rather than using it to help the poor who had a right to their surplus." Indeed, this is what subsequently happened, and it is perhaps significant that the very first of Clairvaux's acquisitions (the fief of Cunfin) was made in 1153, immediately after St. Bernard's death.

It was not long before such transgressions of Cistercian principles became frequent. It was for this reason that the rule against acquiring any mill that was not for the exclusive use of the monks had to be renewed by a statute of 1157. In 1191, the General Chapter recognized "that the Order has the reputation of ceaselessly purchasing and that the love of property has become a festering sore."[3] As a consequence, in 1192 the acquisition of property was forbidden. The decision was withdrawn in 1215, but revived in 1216. It was renewed again in 1240, and then once again suspended in 1248, although acquisitions had to be authorized by the General Chapter. This was changed, the following year, to a simple warning against falling into debt. In 1256, certain abbeys were able to get round a new attempt by the General Chapter by disguising purchased land as "charitable" donations. In 1289, the ban on acquisition no longer appears in the *Livre des anciennes définitions*.[4]

The examples of Clairvaux and Chaalis With its five granges created before the death of the first abbot in 1153, and the ten more established before 1200,[5] by the beginning of the thirteenth century Clairvaux possessed some 5,000 acres (2,000ha) of farmland. Further acquisitions between 1200 and 1280 made it possible to increase the fields around each grange, bringing them to 500 acres (200ha) each. The following centuries brought five granges standing alone in the countryside, and seven in villages, infringing the principles laid down by Cîteaux that forbade establishments in inhabited areas. "At the same time as they were violating the statutes of the General Chapter, they were similarly ignoring the prescriptions of the *Carta Caritatis* that had forbidden Cistercian monasteries to possess certain kinds of property. In 1196, Clairvaux acquired the church of Bologne. In 1231, it

owned three whole villages with their inhabitants. There are examples of the abbey buying single serfs. In 1224, it bought the communal mill of Longchamp from Gautier de Vignory. The number of acquisitions (for payment, after 1221) of tithes and rents would be too long to list."[6]

Examination of the network of granges belonging to the abbey of Chaalis (founded in 1136 by Pontigny) confirms the Clairvaux data. The monks established a group of five granges for agriculture, grazing and forestry, eight for the production of cereals, and three storehouses. The earliest granges were less than 10 miles (15km) from the abbey, while the last to be acquired lay more than 30 miles (50km) away.

As for the importance of the domain, "it seems that the granges built in the thirteenth century corresponded to an existing estate. [...] Nothing like as large as the great monastic estates of the eastern Elbe, it appears that the average dependency of Chaalis was between a minimum of 500 acres (200ha) and around 860 acres (350ha) for the largest, Vaulerent."[7]

A massive acreage The total area of the land holdings of the Cistercians in thirteenth-century Europe will probably never be known, given the difficulty in examining the history of the many abbeys dismantled in the course of the centuries. It is, however, possible to attribute about a dozen granges to each of the 700 monasteries founded before 1300, which gives a figure of 7,000 establish-

ments (or 5,400 square miles [1.4 million hectares], based on an average size of 200 ha. for each grange). These figures should be increased, to allow for:

• forested areas; for example, Foigny owned fourteen granges that cultivated probably no more than 7,400 acres (3,000ha) of fields and pastures; the rest of its properties corresponding to some 25,000 acres (10,000ha) of forest;

• estates belonging to nunneries; not insignificant, even if the nunneries—900 according to modern estimates—only possessed one or two granges each;

• large abbey estates created in "new" areas, such as those of Grandselve in Aquitaine (25 granges), Maulbronn in Swabia (20), Walkenried in Saxony (17), Eberbach in the Rhineland (16), Fountains, Rielvaux, and Waverley in England (26, 20 and 18 respectively), Tarouca in Portugal (30), etc.;[8]

• the lands colonized and owned by the Cistercians to the east of the Elbe (60,000 acres [240,000ha] at Lubiaz in Silesia, or 74,000 acres [30,000ha] in Zinna in Brandenburg), or in reconquered Spain.

Land was not the only source of wealth. To give the full picture, account has also to be taken of the industrial and craft establishments. These represented both complementary property developments and significant capital investments. The abbey of Foigny, for example, owned fourteen wheat mills, a fulling mill, two spinning mills (*tordoirs*), three furnaces, three forges, a brewery, three presses, and a glass factory.[9] Such territorial

wealth could not fail to arouse envy and bitter criticism. Gerald of Wales, as early as 1188, was denouncing the Cistercians' greed, but admitted at the same time: "Their door is never shut and, in their hospitality to strangers, they excel all other religious Orders."

THE END OF SELF-SUFFICIENCY

With the expansion of their estates, the Cistercians needed to develop a large body of lay brothers. During the second half of the twelfth century, the call to conversion was still being heeded by the peasants. Everywhere, the lay brothers, bearded and untonsured, worked in silence, reciting the four prayers (the Lord's Prayer, Creed, *Miserere*, and *Ave Maria*) they had learned by heart during their noviciate, since the rules forbade their being allowed to learn to read.

After 1200, the situation changed: the system whereby the abbeys cultivated their own lands gradually disappeared as the Order found it increasingly difficult to recruit lay brothers.

This change is partly explained by the behavior of the monks. "The inferior status of the lay brothers, the humiliations they were forced to undergo, resulted in revolts: from the end of the twelfth century in Pontigny, twenty such disturbances between 1168 and 1200 within the Order, and another thirty during the thirteenth century."[10] The *Exordium magnum* records the uprising at Schonau, where the lay brothers were infuriated at not receiving new boots as the monks had done. More serious incidents were the murder of the abbot of Eberbach in 1261, and the mass apostasy of the lay brothers that took place in some abbeys.

Another reason was that agricultural progress had improved the standard of living in the countryside. "Apart from spiritual considerations, the certainty of having a roof over one's head, enough to eat, and a more secure existence were not insignificant factors in the decision to become a lay brother. But what was of value in the first half of the twelfth century was of less interest fifty years later."

Furthermore, the Dominicans and Franciscans were offering a new way of living in the faith, in the attractive world of the towns. From 1223, this situation began to worry the General Chapter. As discipline among the lay brothers became lax, particularly in some granges where alcoholism took over, regulations were laid down in 1237, restricting the lay brothers' consumption of beer and wine. Hundreds of incidents resulted, with fights and even some deaths.[11] Almost everywhere the Order was forced to replace the lay brothers with wage-earning workers, more expensive and less motivated. Several abbeys leased out their land, losing all responsibility for the management of their farms. In 1262, certain abbots handed over the running of some granges to lay brothers already living there. They successfully managed their land, providing an example of social promotion that was unique for the period. Granges were also managed by *familiares*, devout lay people living in the monastery, promising obedience to the abbot but without the actual religious status of a lay brother, although in practice they were assimilated by the latter groups that remained in the abbeys until the French Revolution (there were still fifty at Clairvaux in 1667, and ten in 1790).

ECONOMIC STRATEGIES

As good managers, the cellarers were keen to optimize the conditions of production. The specialization of the granges, and even of certain abbeys, began to replace the varied occupations that had hitherto characterized feudal estates. The vineyards and iron-producing granges still reveal in their architecture this system of production that made it possible to select skills and transmit knowledge, thanks to the continuous training process of the young by the old.

The Cistercians were innovative, above all, in their management, not only of the principles of organization in the heart of the abbeys and their productive satellites but also in the initiatives taken to set up economic strategies:

• vertical integration: the abbey of Balerne in the Franche-Comté specialized in salt production, an indispensable necessity for the communities and their flocks, and not yet a royal monopoly; between 1150 and 1267 production increased from three to fourteen *montées*;[12] thus, when self-sufficiency was not possible on the level of a single abbey, it could be on the level of a regional group; this explains why the same clay roof and floor tiles can be found in different abbeys, when only one of them had suitable means of production.

• horizontal integration; long before theories of liberal economics, the Cistercians practised trading agreements, seeking to hold a monopoly, at regional level at least, in order to set prices; it is clear that during the whole of the thirteenth century Clairvaux and those of its daughter houses that were involved in metal production (La Crête, Auberive, Longuay, among others) had no real competition in southern Champagne (the upper valleys of the Seine, the Aube and the Marne rivers).

Facing page:
Tarouca Abbey, Portugal. Lay brothers' range.

Left:
Stove at Salem, Germany. Cistercian monks inspecting their property.

The Cistercians' ability to erect complex legal frameworks to support, protect and optimize their production should also be emphasized. The policy pursued at Clairvaux to guarantee, in both the medium and long term, a secure supply of salt at the best price is an illustration of this. The abbey could supply itself with sea salt from the Channel, or rock salt from the Franche-Comté or from Saulnois in Lorraine. Although distant, sea salt from the Channel was welcome when an unexpected donation occurred. But the abbey had to decide between Lorraine, where it had established a specialized grange at Marsal, and the Franche-Comté, where a large donation at Lons-le-Saunier in 1174 allowed it to enjoy several years of cheap production. Decisions were made according to the time taken for travel (one day less from Marsal), the supply of wood needed for the drying rooms (an eight-year lease for a forest was calculated according to the depreciation of the material invested), negotiated exemptions from tolls, possibilities for lodgings for the lay brothers or employees involved in the operation. When Clairvaux, having used salt from the Franche-Comté, found it advantageous to exploit salt at Marsal, its daughter house of Auberive became the intermediary for the agreement. This was a true group economic policy.[13]

MAJOR CISTERCIAN INDUSTRIES

There was no sector of the economy that the Cistercians were not involved in. Their preoccupa-

Fontenay Abbey, Burgundy. Forest boundary stone.

tion with perfection was applied as much to human activity as to the practices of monastic life, with an unfailing assiduity and a determination to succeed in producing the best results. They desired to be the first and the best in all fields, for the greater glory of the Order. This pride, which placed the Order above all other things, which led to constant challenges, and which justified all that they did, lies at the heart of the founders' success and was to be characteristic of the Cistercians through the centuries.

Wood from the forests The demographic explosion of the twelfth and thirteen centuries ravaged the environment of medieval Europe, destroying thousands of acres of woodland through excessive deforestation, and polluting the rivers. The Cistercians deserve credit for playing no part in this devastation. Their use of watercourses and their efforts to keep the abbeys hygienic are well known. Less well known is the continual care they took not to destroy their forests.

Rather than deforesting their land in order to increase the amount of cultivable land, they systematically set about improving heaths and wasteland, and draining marshy areas. Although the lives of the saints paint a different picture, the monks were more land improvers than woodcutters. On the other hand, they cleared away the undergrowth so as to allow their flocks to find grazing beneath the taller trees. Most importantly, they set up a system of forestry management (over a period of twenty years generally) that allowed firewood to be gathered without preventing the regeneration of the forest that represented their capital. Wood was of course vital for tools, building and fencing, dams and bridges, barrels and carts, cooking fuel and fuel for the forges.

This forestry policy was pursued for centuries in every Cistercian abbey. Its advantage was that it prevented speculative rises in the price of wood. It was used as a model for legislation to protect the forests, such as that passed by Colbert in the seventeenth century. Today the sites of the majority of ancient Cistercian abbeys are still surrounded by forests (in France, often state owned). They are the heritage of a system that respected the wooded environment, and that marked a break with the

thousands of years when the hunter-gatherers and then the farmers of every continent had considered the forest as an inexhaustible source that could be burned and cut with no thought whatsoever for the centuries to come.

Cereals The climate in the twelfth century was warm and relatively dry, between two colder periods. This favored the "agricultural revolution" linked to the increase in population throughout Europe since the year 1000. Easier work and an optimal amount of sunshine for cereal growing resulted in abundant harvests. New production techniques could be tried out without risk. The Cistercians were part of this upturn. Horses, now better harnessed with a rigid collar and shod with protecting iron shoes, began to be used. Except in mountainous regions, they were less slow than oxen in plowing with the new heavy plows that were beginning to replace the lighter scratch plow. It was also discovered that if horses were harnessed one behind the other in a line, they could pull heavier loads—something unknown to the Romans. The Cistercians possessed some famous stables, at Jervaulx in England, or at Otterberg in Germany. Vaucelles and its seven granges owned 200 horses for 1,000 acres (4,000ha) of fields. The speed of the horse made it possible to adopt the new system of triennial crop rotation. By allowing the land to lie fallow only once every three years rather than every two years, but yet not impoverishing it thanks to the planting of well-chosen complementary crops, production was increased by 32 per cent. The huge Cistercian cereal barns, built on a basilican plan with a central space flanked by aisles and with high gable walls at either end, increased in size in order to accommodate the harvests. The cereal barns of Clairvaux are well known.[14] One of them, Cornay, was already in existence in 1194. Like most buildings of this period, the roof timbers were renewed between the sixteenth and the eighteenth centuries (Cornay in 1577), though often reusing some of the original beams. Cornay had five aisles and a ground surface of 16,000 sq ft (1,457m²).

The cereal barns of Chaalis[15] are even more famous on account of the outstanding architectural quality of one of them, Vaulerent, the end wall of which is enlivened with a turret enclosing a spiral staircase ascending to a small guardroom in which three little openings form crenellations. The wooden roof is supported by arcades resting on well-preserved limestone piers (c.1230). It is also one of the largest barns built by the Cistercians, since its floor surface is 17,800 square feet (1,656 m²). It measures 235 x 75ft (72 x 23m).

In these cereal barns the winter and spring harvests, of wheat, barley, rye, and oats were stored. In addition, the harvests of the complementary rotation crops were stored there, oleaginous plants and hemp (for textiles), and also plants used for dyes such as woad, which produced a blue dye.

Wine Wine growing had survived the fall of the Roman Empire thanks to the early Christian bishops. They preserved a vineyard around their episcopal seat to supply the needs both of the eucharistic communion (then using bread and wine) and the Roman ritual of offering wine to important visitors.[16] This tradition was revived by all monasteries, and by the Cistercians in particular. Their vineyards rapidly became famous: Burgundy, the cradle of the Order, enjoyed geological and climatic conditions that favored great vintages. Cistercian rigor found in the cultivation of grapes and wine-making activities worthy of its meticulous quest for perfection.

In the twelfth century, Cîteaux received in donation the vineyards of Clos Vougeot. It was to keep them until the Revolution. The vineyards of Morey, Beaune, Mersault, and Mercurey also belonged to the Cistercians. Pontigny, for its part, renewed the old vineyard planted by the Romans on the hillsides of Chablis. Clairvaux had two important wineries that before 1200 were providing wine (already sparkling, of course) in the two localities of Colombé-le-Sec and Baroville (Morvaux), that today produce the Côte-des-Bar champagne.

Cistercian wine production flourished equally in Germany. In the Rhineland, Baumgarten, Neuburg, Himmerod, and Heisterbach possessed the best vineyards. Eberbach discovered the advantages of terraces for the cultivation of vines. In the fifteenth century, the abbey made a giant barrel, containing 264,000 gallons. (317,000 US galls.; 12,000 hectoliters) of wine, that was to make the

Stove at Salem, Germany. The harvest, sowing, and the wine-harvest.

area famous throughout the world. In Saxony, Pforta and Walkenried also had important vineyards.

Fruit Within the walls of the monastery, the monks reserved for themselves the tasks of gardening and looking after the orchards. In this field too, their influence was important. In an age when fruit could not be transported, the exchange of trees was common between abbeys. In this way the russet apple came from Morimond to Camp and then to the orchards of eastern Europe. Traveling the other way, the "master of the orchards" planted in France apples from his garden in Borsdorf. The Norwegian abbey of Lyse supplied the town of Bergen with fruit, and owned ships to take its produce for sale in England, exempted from taxes under a decree of King John dated 1212.[18]

Fisheries and fishing Every Cistercian abbey had its fishponds, and many dammed their rivers to create one or more ponds upstream of their site. The "master of the fish" bred carp for eating by the monks and lay brothers—since the Rule forbade the eating of meat—and also for sale in the market.

In the Upper Palatinate, the abbey of Waldsassen, that specialized in fish rearing, created installations that were unique in Europe. Almost 200 ponds made it possible to separate the female carp, carp of less than a year old, and carp for eating! Important fishponds were also to be found in England, particularly at Byland and Bordesley.

In Scandinavia, where agriculture was inevitably a somewhat limited activity, the abbeys were involved in sea fishing. The abbey of Gutvalla on the island of Gotland, for example, kept a sizeable fleet of boats.[19]

Top and bottom:
The "cellar", the Clairvaux wine grange at Colombé-le-Sec.

Middle:
Fontcalvy, wine grange of Fontfroide.

Sheep The monks needed sheep for their clothes and for other domestic uses, so they kept their own flocks. Furthermore, the scribes and illuminators needed the sheep skins to make parchment. Every abbey possessing land developed this activity, and the Order soon became the major wool producer in Europe.

It is difficult to estimate the number of animals that made up the Cistercian flocks, but there is general agreement on the following figures: 11,000 animals at Meaux in 1270, 18,000 at Fountains, 14,000 at Rievaulx, 12,000 at Jervaulx. But England did not have the monopoly: Froidmont had 5,000 sheep in 1224, and Clairvaux 3,000. It is interesting to note, however, that all these abbeys were affiliated to Clairvaux. Their most important customers, installed in Flanders and Florence, took several thousand fleeces every year. Flexing their financial muscles, the Cistercians stood together.

When the English Cistercian monks threatened to cut off supplies of wool to the continent, the Flemish textile industry was brought to a halt.

Mills The Cistercians had a systematic policy of mechanizing all those activities that could use water power. The use of camshafts and gearing systems speeded up the work of the lay brothers. Flour mills were mechanized, as were those for oil, fulling, and other activities.

These new machines revolutionized the textile industry. "After weaving, the cloth was placed in a water tank and pounded in order to compress the material and bring the fibers together, making them soft and thick. Originally this process of fulling was carried out by trampling the cloth with the feet, but later wooden hammers replaced the human foot. In a mechanized mill one man could replace forty fullers."[20]

The Cistercians were particularly interested in flour mills. In the thirteenth century, when they leased out their cereal granges, they kept the mill. The lessee was obliged to become a client, paying in kind. In a period when gruel and bread were the staple diet of the peasants, ownership of the mill gave the monks control over the price of grain and the possibility of buying the milled flour cheaply, only then to sell it on to the town markets with a hefty surcharge. The Cistercians were not prepared to give up these advantages. Like Foigny, the abbey of Zinna in Brandenburg had fourteen mills. "Milling developed to the point where it became an industry, and one of which the Cistercians held the monopoly. During the thirteenth century, Reinfeld and Doberan bought every mill they could get hold of, both windmills and water mills. When they could not obtain secure possession of every mill, they still had control over its working, since their water rights allowed them to regulate the flow of water by means of dams."[21]

Tiles and pottery The Cistercians needed tiles to cover the wooden roofs of their many buildings. Concerned that their constructions should last for several generations, they rarely used the traditional thatched roofs of peasant houses. Thatch was less durable and presented too great a fire risk. A number of granges specialized in the production of

terra-cotta, manufacturing tiles for both roofing and for floors. At first confined to the abbey owning that grange, production was subsequently shared out among neighboring Cistercian abbeys. Eventually, tiles and pottery were produced commercially in the towns and countryside in the proximity of pottery kilns.

The chimney of the kiln at the grange of Commelles provides valuable archeological evidence for the production of tiles in an abbey like Chaalis. Referred to from 1198, this activity took place at Commelles because of the deposits of clay there of a quality suitable for the production of roof and floor tiles, close by a sufficiently large forest to supply a regular supply of fuel for the kiln.[22]

Mining and metalworking Numerous recent publications, making good use of a combination of research into documents and archeology, have highlighted the importance of Cistercian mining and metalworking.

Before Cîteaux, the Benedictines had derived income since the ninth century from their mines and forges at San-Miguel-de-Cuxa and Sainte-Marie-aux-Mines. The chief exploiters, however, were the landowning lords.

"The situation changed in the twelfth century. By this time there was a Cistercian metal industry. The model of this industry can be reconstructed from examples found in Burgundy and Champagne, an area rich in wood and ores, and the cradle of the Cistercian Order. The expression "monastic metal industry" is accurate, for the monks worked the mines themselves, extracting the ore and smelting it. Metallurgy could be adapted to the new system of production devised by the White Monks, the grange [...] Wage-earning laborers worked alongside the lay brothers, producing the iron. Their presence is documented from the second quarter of the thirteenth century, but probably began at an earlier date."[23]

For a long time, the monks produced metal for their own use (tools, construction, etc.). From

Above, left:
Sheep at Rievaulx,
England.

Above, right:
Stove at Salem,
Germany. Monks fishing.

Left:
Abbey of Obazine,
Limouain. The fish-stew.

1

2

3

4

5

6

7

10

8

11

9

1188, however, Vauluisant began to sell its products. In this field of activity, the monks met with more serious competition than was the case with agricultural produce. The Carthusians in the Franche-Comté and the Templars in the forest of Othe owned important centers of production. The Cistercians were interested in the income that might come from technical innovations. They were to play a decisive role in the diffusion of the water-powered hammer that marked the first stage in the mechanization of the iron industry.

The Cistercians had a presence in many important pre-industrial areas. In the Franche-Comté, Balerne industrialized the Hérisson valley in cooperation with the Carthusian abbey of Bon-Lieu. There was a forge at Champagne-en-Rouez in the Maine valley; at Orval in Belgium; at Le Valasse, Beaubec, Mortemer, and La Trappe in Normandy; at Fontmorigny in Berry; at Clairvaux, Vauluisant, La Crête, Auberive, Longuay, Fontenay, Morimond, Trois-Fontaines, La Bussière, and Cherlieu in the Champagne-Burgundy area.

Outside France, the White Monks were not content merely to create metalworking sites. The flexibility of their organization enabled them to exploit local resources that had not been available to them before. In Scotland the abbey of Newbattle developed one of the first coal mines in the region (open-cast, and later in galleries). Culross exported its coal, with 170 ships to ensure its transport overseas. Fountains developed lead mines. In Bohemia, deposits of silver were mined by the abbey of Sedlic.

CISTERCIAN TRADE

Since they had to sell those products of which they had a significant surplus, the Cistercians passed new legislation so that this unforeseen activity could be carried on in the spirit of the Order. Only two monks were allowed to go to the nearest market to buy and sell. Important deals were negotiated in the houses that the larger abbeys owned in town. Each of these was managed by a lay brother.

Some abbeys, ahead of their time, had retail shops as early as the mid-twelfth century. The abbey of Rein in Austria sold its agricultural produce, and especially its wine, in a shop in the town of Graz, "At the sign of the Gray Cowl". Already the myth of monastic quality was brought into play to promote sales, just as today with the beer and cheese from the abbeys.

The towns that welcomed Cistercian trade also profited from it, for it attracted many clients, thus increasing sales in the local shops and inns. The monks of Eberbach, on the other hand, were forced to leave Cologne and Ulm, where they had built a shop and a wine cellar. Since their wine was sold retail, but exempt from tax, the local merchants accused them of unfair competition and succeeded in having them expelled.[24]

This anecdote is revealing. Cistercian behavior was ambiguous, in that the White Monks embodied a significant material success that was developed by monks whose own lifestyle was one of austerity. Furthermore, they were among the first to put into practice a style of production that was to anticipate, many centuries in advance, an almost ecological respect for nature.

Facing page and above: Staffarda Abbey, Italy. The covered market where the Cistercians sold their agricultural produce to the local inhabitants (exterior and interior).

Fossanova Abbey, Italy.
A Cistercian
Romanesque nave.

Noirlac Abbey, Berry. A
Cistercian Gothic nave.

CHAPTER X

THE ESSENCE OF ARCHITECTURE

Clairvaux and Fontenay pointed the way and provided the model. From 1150, for a period of just over a century, Cistercian abbeys covered Europe with their new churches. These were enclosed within the solid walls surrounding the monasteries constructed in the heart of cultivated farmlands, only punctuated here and there by granges, storehouses, and mills that marked centers of activity in the great stretches of as yet sparsely inhabited medieval countryside.

The construction of the abbeys founded in the time of Stephen Harding and Bernard of Clairvaux was reaching completion. Cîteaux, the mother house, was finally able to consecrate the abbey, created in accordance with the functional program established by St. Bernard, more than fifty years after its foundation. The daughter houses, richer than the mother houses built in the pioneering years of the Order and numbering some 300 established between 1150 and 1250, no longer delayed for a generation before starting building work. The Cistercians were seen as financially secure and were able to borrow money. Some abbeys helped their daughter houses, and until 1240 donations continued to be numerous and generous.

Established at a turning point between two eras, that of a rural world dominated by Christianity, and that which saw the emergence of the towns and the increasing centralization of power, the Cistercians built at a time of transition between a fully-developed Romanesque architecture and the birth of the Gothic style. Conservative in thought and innovative in action, the Cistercians of the twelfth and thirteenth centuries made their architecture a pragmatic synthesis of these many contradictions.

TOTAL RESPECT FOR THE FUNCTIONAL PROGRAM

All the abbeys followed the functional program defined at Clairvaux and Fontenay by Bernard of Clairvaux. This can be clearly seen from a comparison of the plans of the core buildings around the cloister, the "conventual quadrangle."

The almost dogmatic care with which the abbots and General Chapter, scrupulous overseers, sought to carry out St. Bernard's immutable plan is well documented.

The only notable exception is Belmont in Syria where the chapter house stands apart from the cloister, for reasons that are not fully understood. The inspectors from the mother house (Morimond) were too far away in this case to intervene, but the General Chapter generally showed itself to be uncompromising. In 1235, it reaffirmed that all constructions not conforming with the Rule and the statutes would be demolished. In 1198, the count of Auvergne, who had donated money to the abbey of Bouchet for the establishment of a nunnery there, was instructed by the Chapter "to ensure that the reconstruction of the abbey followed the customary plan, otherwise it would be forced to refuse his offer."[1] Thanks to significant donations in 1221, the plan insisted on by the General Chapter was respected. The rare variations found in the basic plan never affected the general scheme of the monastery, and always resulted from circumstances and the need to adapt to a particular site. At Fontfroide, for example, the choir monks' range, to the north of the church, was built eastwards at right angles in order to allow the dormitory latrines to stand over the river that flowed past

the abbey and passed through a narrow conduit between the east end of the church and the rock face of the mountain sheltering the abbey from the violence of the wind.[2]

ROMANESQUE ARCHITECTURE, GOTHIC ARCHITECTURE

From the point of view of architectural execution, the Cistercian buildings constructed during the most flourishing period of the Order, which saw new sites springing up everywhere, were not all identical. From the same ground plan there arose widely differing interior volumes and spaces, façades and elevations, openings and roofing techniques. Marcel Aubert, in his essential *Architecture cistercienne en France*, written in 1947 with the marquise de Maillé, has drawn up an almost exhaustive inventory of every component, element, and deviation of this architecture handed down to us by the White Monks of the twelfth and thirteenth centuries. And yet the weight of erudition contained in this masterly and indispensable work obscures the essential details that distinguish one abbey from another. By emphasizing the formal analysis to the detriment of a commentary on the significance of the choices made by the Cistercian builders, Marcel Aubert accepted all selection criteria, even the most artificial.

The square east end A whole literature thus emerged that sought to classify the Cistercian churches according to the type of east end. The famous square east ends of Clairvaux II and Fontenay, that provided the model, are not without

Right:
Sénanque Abbey,
Provence. Apsidal east
end.

Below:
Silvanès Abbey,
Rouergue. Square east
end.

Facing page:
Alcobaça, Portugal. The
perfection of early
Cistercian Gothic.

significance given the importance of their position in the church, a protecting wall for the pre-eminent holy place which is the altar. But the apsidal east end, and the so-called Bernadine flat east end which are frequently contrasted with it, are no more than minor variations on the common theme of a sanctuary without ambulatory, with a restricted surface area, and without decoration. To ascertain the truth of this, one only has to look at the three sister churches in Provence, similar in every way in stylistic detail even though the east ends differ (square at Silvacane and apsidal at Thoronet and Sénanque).

Furthermore, as the monastic building campaigns succeeded one another over the years, a number of builders used happy combinations of apparently contradictory architectural vocabulary. At Loc-Dieu, for example, apsidal side chapels are added to either side of the east end of the sanctuary,

without compromising the architectural unity and without in any way causing us to doubt its classification as a Gothic Cistercian church.

The vault as a criterion for classification When the Cistercians began work on their vast schemes, their architects had a great variety of building techniques at their disposal. The latest innovations concerned the roofing of buildings. The reinvention of the vault by the Romanesque architects, between 1080 and 1100, led to the abandoning of exposed roof timbers. The Benedictine builders encouraged the spread of the tunnel vault (sometimes pointed, with or without transverse arches) and groin vaults.

From 1140, the first cathedrals and the great Benedictine abbeys became confident enough to throw intersecting rib vaults across the naves of their biggest churches. Thus it was that the true form of the architecture was decided by the choice of roof. The building abbot and his chosen master of works were forced to commit themselves to a method for roofing the abbey church, the chapter house, and the refectory of their abbey. The architecture that resulted from their choice, the one that mattered, inevitably translated both a reverence for the perfection of the past, and the espousal of a kind of progress, and, furthermore, one that embodied scholastic philosophy and theology.

Their attachment to the canons of the day was sometimes progressive: a number of buildings display a mixture of different roof types, and some abbeys constructed the nave of their churches with Romanesque vaults and their cloisters and chapter houses with Gothic rib vaults, as in the case of Poblet and Maulbronn. Other abbeys, not wishing to be left behind, modified all or part of the roofs of their naves, sometimes leaving in place the groin-vaulted aisles from the first building campaign, as at Pontigny, Noirlac, or Fontmorigny.

In northern France, from 1150, the Cistercians adopted the Gothic vault, and all that that implied, almost everywhere.[3] Pontigny, the only one of the first daughter houses of Cîteaux to have preserved its abbey church, is evidence of the perfection of the mastery of this spectacular technique attained by the Cistercians.

THE SPIRIT OF CÎTEAUX

Together with the bishops and the new Orders, and some of the Benedictine abbeys such as Saint-Denis, the French Cistercians too were wedded to progress in all its forms, spreading the word of the Gothic style to their European sisters. But not all Cistercian abbeys followed them, or if they did, not necessarily immediately. Even in France, local customs remained strong in some provinces, as in Provence, where the "three sisters" of the Cîteaux filiation, through Bonnevaux and Mazan, continued, between 1160 and 1190, to build in an exquisite Romanesque style.

Whether the east end was square or apsidal, the vault Romanesque or Gothic, it mattered little. The spirit of Cîteaux cannot be summed up in a series of technical procedures that are no more than means to attaining the best possible combination of the intended function, and the form that makes it possible for it to happen. The Rule of Benedict of Nursia says that a monastery is a workshop in which to practise prayer (chapter 4), just as Le Corbusier was later to say that the Radiant City should be a "machine in which to live". Bernard of Clairvaux laid down the formal conditions that ensured that this workshop fulfilled its task: a total absence of decoration, so that the design of the architecture could emerge in all its truth (*Apologia*). Under such conditions, all building techniques have equal value if they are used in a "minimalist" spirit, resulting not from a vain and profane search for decorative effect but from a studious and humble attempt to create an architecture that could be sanctioned by usage.

Above:
Léoncel Abbey, Vercors. The typical Cistercian "waterleaf" capital.

Below:
Faithfulness to building materials: in Cistercian architecture (Otterberg Abbey, Germany); in the architecture of the Modern Movement (concrete as used by Le Corbusier at the Dominican monastery of La Tourette, near Lyon).

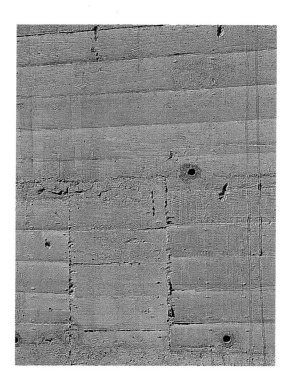

THE EXAMPLE SET BY CISTERCIAN ARCHITECTURE

The "miracle" of Cistercian architecture lies in the White Monks' ability, over a period of more than a century, to build churches and monastic buildings using a variety of different architectural techniques that obeyed the same program and the same aesthetic point of view—both of which were instantly perceived equally by the monks and by outsiders.

Freedom in architecture Every master builder in a Cistercian abbey had to combine the demands of a general program with the particular local situation, adapting the building to the chosen site, the characteristics of the available water source, the possible need for special facilities to be added to the basic layout, the materials available in that region, and even the climate or amount of daylight dependent on latitude. In each case, the result was a specific and unique architectural solution.

This is the essential truth of architectural creation, made up of a succession of reiterations between program and constraints, where the architect attempts to get round the difficulties, assessing, through a permanent dialogue with the builder, the pertinence of his obligations, while at the same time seeking to give the possible solutions a spatial coherence. This was the price of architectural quality, and so it was in every Cistercian abbey.

Thus we see the absurdity of the debate, wrongly evoked by certain architectural historians, that seeks to dwell on the excessive constraints of the Order's program and the lack of freedom given to the designer.

Fernand Pouillon, in *Les Pierres sauvages* has recreated an illuminating dialogue between the abbot and the monk who became master of works at Thoronet, the daughter house of Clairvaux that so closely followed its spirit:[4]

"The fundamental design of our monasteries is laid down by the strict *Rule*, that determines from the start the form of the church, the cloister, and the order of the rooms surrounding it. Did you, who have passed your whole life under this program, find it oppressive? Did it prevent you from expressing yourself?"

"No, Father, quite the contrary. I loved the framework of our plans, which nevertheless allowed the builder great freedom."

A functional architecture If, in the words of Thomas Aquinas, "beauty is the light of truth", then Cistercian architecture is a permanent homage to function, something that is intrinsic to architecture.

"Functionalism is the analysis of the true necessity of an object, a place, a building [...]. It requires imagination to find the most suitable form for a given function that is judged to be essential. For any building, then, functionalism is the analysis of all its parts, of the way in which they are 'inhabited'. Here functionalism takes on a wider and more human meaning, for whether a place is habitable is not just a matter of comfort, but is a more significant expression of likes and dislikes."[5]

Modernity Although contrary to the beliefs of the Cistercians, who did not consider their abbeys as works of art, a contemporary reading of Cistercian architecture, ignoring the religious, economic, and social context of its creation, has led many to admire the elements of its architectural vocabulary. Its striking modernity made a great impact on

Pontigny Abbey, Burgundy. The only abbey church that remains of the four "first daughters". A cathedral in the fields.

Le Corbusier, who was prompted to write a preface to an excellent book on Le Thoronet.[6]

Le Corbusier found in Cistercian architecture a confirmation of his own ideas. Materials should be used in their original state, "with their rough skin", the surface of stone or rough concrete. Captured light should be seen, like shadows, as another form of material. Cistercian architecture is "the intelligent, correct, and magnificent interplay of volumes assembled under light." The true and visible decoration of architecture is to be found in the affirmation of structure, an act of faith in technical progress similar to that which allowed the master builder of Clairvaux to pass without any qualms from groin vaults to rib vaults. Despite the fact that this vault symbolized heaven, for Le Corbusier and the modern movement the orthogonality of Cistercian architecture was a perfect illustration of the "poetry of right-angles".

THE GREAT CISTERCIAN CHURCHES

"'Oh my daughter, you are too beautiful!' St Bernard is supposed to have exclaimed when he visited Hautecombe under construction. How many tears might he have shed at Vaucelles, the plan of which, recorded in Villard de Honnecourt's notebooks, can be compared to the abbey church of Cluny!"[7] As the Order acquired power and glory, and the blessing of Louis IX, king and saint, the temptation grew to compete with the greatest religious buildings of the period. The Cistercians built enormous churches, on the scale of cathedrals, and soon abbots' houses, as grand as the country houses of the local aristocracy, began to be incorporated within the walls of the monasteries.

Clairvaux began the process, by demolishing the eastern arm of the abbey church, immediately following the death of the abbot. This was in order to transform the sanctuary into a vast reliquary, dedicated to the future glory of the abbot once he had been canonized, and requiring an ambulatory with nine radiating chapels set in a curved wall.

The dedication, in 1174, appears to mark the end of the work, and corresponds to the canonization of the saint.

Pontigny too pulled down the square east end of the church, in order to enlarge the sanctuary, between 1205 and 1210. Today it represents one of the most perfect Gothic *chevets* of the Burgundian school.

Following the example of Clairvaux, ambulatories were built at Cherlieu, Savigny, Bonport and Breuil-Benoît (whose two churches have exactly the same plan), at Clairmarais, Vauclair, Bonnevaux, and Vauluisant. The same thing happened at Poblet and Veruela in Spain, Alcobaça in Portugal, Beaulieu in England, and at Warnhem in Sweden.[8]

It was not long before new Cistercian churches began to appear with an east end with apsidal chapels radiating from an ambulatory. Longpont took its inspiration from the cathedral of Soissons, completed in 1212, and in its turn influenced

to surround its presbytery by a rectangular aisle opening into twelve chapels. This solution, more suited to the spirit of traditional Cistercian architecture, was also used at Morimond, Ebrach in Germany, and at Fontainejean, a magnificent church of which little remains today. However, the richer abbeys were already beginning to commission work from the most famous craftsmen of the day, to whom the fame of cathedrals and wealthy town-houses was indebted. Neglectful of the spirit of Cîteaux, some abbey churches acquired historiated stained glass windows, richly carved choir stalls (Marienstatt and Maulbronn), and sculptured retables.

Above:
Cîteaux Abbey. The classic "definitory" where the General Chapters of the order were planned.

Above right:
Villard de Honnecourt. Two sketches of east ends with ambulatories and apsidal chapels. The famous architect may have been involved at

Vaucelles, since the design of the abbey church is found in his Album.

Facing page:
Santes Creus Abbey, Spain. Decorated capitals in the Flamboyant cloister, c. 1340.

Royaumont. The church of Ourscamp imitated Noyon cathedral. Altenberg in Germany and Valmagne in Languedoc have many similarities.

Particular mention should be made of Vaucelles, an important daughter house of Clairvaux. In 1216, the church dedicated by the archbishop of Reims was 433 feet (132m) long. It was the largest Cistercian building of the thirteenth century.

Cîteaux too was enlarged at the beginning of the thirteenth century. However, it remained faithful to its original square plan, choosing instead

CENTURIES OF TRIAL

---

*While the Cistercians, in the depths of their secluded valleys, by the still waters of
their tranquil lakes, were prospering, embellishing their abbey churches which were
increasingly filled with statues, retables, and sculpted tombs, the townsfolk were
listening to the preaching of mendicant Orders in the churches that they had built
for them: these were spacious, practical, accessible to everyone, and as simple as
those of Cîteaux. Everywhere they were creating a kind of void around the white
monks, so well situated away from towns, people, and the restless secular life.
In turn, the great name of Cîteaux began to decline, and the history of the
Cistercian Order was synonymous with the waning of the Middle Ages.*[1]

Preceding page:
Orval Abbey, Belgium.

Right:
Loc-Dieu Abbey,
Rouergue. A monastic
site that was first
fortified and then
transformed into a
summer residence.

CHAPTER XI

THE TRIALS OF THE LATER MIDDLE AGES

(1265-1453)

THE LATE THIRTEENTH CENTURY–A PERIOD OF UNCERTAINTY

Cîteaux had taken over responsibility from Clairvaux for the Collège Saint-Bernard in Paris, while the General Chapter henceforward oversaw discipline and the program of studies. The Cistercians were concerned more than ever before with the intellectual education of their best monks. Their colleges multiplied. The General Chapter of 1281 obliged the greater abbeys to establish philosophy and theology courses. And yet, doubt had begin to grow in the very heart of the Church about the doctrine to be taught. The papacy was suspicious of the synthesis that sought to bring Aristotelianism and Christianity closer together. It was in a Cistercian abbey, Fossanova, on his way to the Council of Lyon where he was to defend himself, that Thomas Aquinas died in March 1274. Three years later the bishop of Paris roundly condemned "the detestable errors which certain have the temerity to study and discuss in the schools." More fortunate than Abelard, Thomas Aquinas was soon rehabilitated.

The White Monks were also uneasy about their involvement in temporal affairs. They had been zealous supporters of the Crusades, and the final blow of the last Crusade, after the loss of Acre in 1291, was the forced abandonment of Belmont, the only abbey they still possessed in Syria.

The Cistercians had been equally enthusiastic about the development of their enormous estates. Now, in cases where the management had not always been prudent, several abbeys were in deep financial trouble. Less and less was heard about abbeys working their own estates.

This situation prompted Benedict XII, the second Cistercian pope and former abbot of Boulbonne, then Fontfroide, to promulgate in 1335 the so-called *Benedicta* Constitution, which was intended to take over the administration of the abbeys. The abbot would lose his financial autonomy, and controls were to be exercised over his management at the level of the community, the General Chapter, and even at the level of the papacy.

The women's abbeys affiliated to the Order, often short-lived, but which flourished in large numbers in Germany and the Netherlands (Béguine convents), became increasingly little more than pious homes for the unmarried daughters of the petty nobility and the richer bourgeoisie. These houses, though often edifying were places where the mystical essence of the thirteenth century was no more than a memory.[2]

TRIALS AND MISFORTUNES

It is hard to imagine what sins had been committed by God's people to deserve the misfortunes that befell Europe from the mid-fourteenth century. To the folly of kings and lords, perpetually at war for over a hundred years and causing untold suffering to the ordinary people who lived in the middle of these battlefields, was added a number of major calamities of a kind never seen before.

In the autumn of 1315, following a poor harvest, famine began to make itself felt. When the two following summers proved equally disastrous, it took on dramatic proportions. Once again, scenes such as those described by Radolphus Glaber three centuries earlier returned: skeletal children, peasants gnawing tree bark, cannibalism.

Worse was to come with the plague of 1347 to 1351, known as the "Black Death". It knew no social barriers. A third of the population of Europe was wiped out and certain abbeys lost all their monks and lay brothers in the space of a few days.

The Hundred Years' War (1328–1453) also hit the Cistercians badly. Their isolation made them particularly vulnerable to attacks and pillaging by the "Great Companies". Some abbeys, including Clairvaux, fortified themselves. Monks from particularly exposed abbeys were authorized to leave to take shelter in strongholds or in their town-houses. In 1360, the General Chapter was held in Dijon. The abbey of Cîteaux was pillaged in 1350, in 1359, and again in 1438. Taxed twice over in order to pay for the expenses of war and then for the ransom to free the king, John II, it lacked the means to pay even for repairs to its buildings. From 1360, the notorious mercenaries pillaged all Clairvaux's granges, one after the other. More than forty abbeys were more or less destroyed during the Hundred Years' War.

Dundrennan Abbey, Scotland. The art of the "picturesque ruin", removed from its historical context and made pleasing to the eye.

CHAPTER XII

THE BREAKING UP OF THE ORDER
(1453-1597)

THE CONGREGATIONS[1]

Even before the beginnings of the idea of the nation appeared with the Renaissance, the Great Schism (1378–1417) caused a deep unease in the western Church for a period of almost forty years, troubling the unity of the Cistercian Order. The cardinals, unable to agree, had elected two popes. The pope in Rome suspended the abbot of Cîteaux, who was taking his orders from Avignon and was therefore considered to be a schismatic. The abbots were now obliged to meet in national General Chapters. Each of the popes showered those abbeys loyal to him with privileges and dispensations, the effect being to destroy any uniformity of observance. When the Schism came to an end with the election of a single pope, the temptations of separatism did not disappear with it. The regular meetings of the General Chapter had been one of the basic principles of the *Carta Caritatis*, as a way of preserving unity in all things. By now geographical distance, wars, schisms, and slack discipline made it impossible for the abbots to maintain this tradition of the annual journey. This was to prove disastrous for the Order. Congregations appeared all over Europe: Castile (1427), Lombardy and Tuscany (1497), Portugal, Poland, Aragon, Calabria. In 1586, the congregation of the Feuillants began its experiment with extreme ascetic practices.

THE DESTRUCTION OF THE ABBEYS

The lack of active abbeys in some countries meant that there was no move by congregations to inde-pendent organization. Destroyed by populations in revolt or by royal decree, in the space of a single century hundreds of abbeys became those rural ruins that still arouse the enthusiasm of tourists and archeologists today.

Bohemia The death of Jan Hus was the signal for a bloody popular uprising (1419–34), aimed particularly at the Cistercian abbeys (especially Sedlec, Osek, and Vyrsi-Brod).

Germany Luther's Reformation (1517) represented a direct attack on the monasteries. From 1520, many German monks and nuns left their monasteries and convents. The peasants rose up and attacked the Order's houses. The property of the abbeys was confiscated by the princes newly converted to the Protestant faith.

England With the feeble pretext of divorce, Henry VIII succeeded in gaining control over the Anglican Church, suppressing the religious Orders and filling the royal coffers with their confiscated wealth (the "Dissolution" of 1536–39).[2]

Ireland Even more destructive than the Dissolution, the systematic demolition of the monasteries was the work of Oliver Cromwell and his Ironsides who subdued the island in 1649 with a particularly ferocious fanaticism.

France Fighting between Catholics and Protestants did not spare the French Cistercian abbeys. Cîteaux suffered more than any other monastery. In order to pay for the reconstruction of their abbey, the monks were forced to sell their Pommard vineyards.

The situation in 1597 (Edict of Nantes) Even including the abbeys with independent congregations in Italy and on the Iberian peninsula, the Order now only controlled 400 monasteries. It had become once again an essentially French Order, though with a significant presence in Germany, Austria, and Poland. Many abbeys, including some of the most famous (such as La Ferté), had fewer than ten monks. Cîteaux had gone from eighty monks (and thirty lay brothers) to twenty monks (and five lay brothers). Clairvaux had lost hundred of residents, but remained the most populous abbey with 130 monks and a similar number of lay brothers and employees.

BENEFICES IN COMMENDAM

It was Pope Gregory XI (1370–78) who originated the institution that "in the last analysis, caused more harm, both to material and to morale, than all the wars, disasters and the Reformation put together." Under the pretext of his role as guardian of the monastic Orders, he claimed the right to appoint abbots. The kings (such as François I, with the *concordat* of 1515) then claimed to assert their feudal rights of nomination. "From that moment, the system of free election, the glory of monastic reform in the Middle Ages, was replaced by appointments, where political considerations took precedent over the vital interest of religion."

Many of the new abbots were chosen from within the ecclesiastical hierarchy and some

Fontfroide Abbey, Languedoc. The "Louis XIV" courtyard, so-called because of its classical style, but built in the mid-eighteenth century.

became excellent monastic leaders. But frequently clerics from court or even laymen were appointed. Few of them lived on the spot. They were concerned above all with collecting the monastery's revenues, shared between the abbot (who awarded himself the greater share) and the community, a division laid down in law.

Cîteaux, Clairvaux, and Morimond were exempted, but the greater part of the Cistercian abbeys in France were subjected to this system of commendatory benefices *in commendam*, anti-economic by definition and obviously incapable of

dealing with any truly religious feeling (of the 228 monasteries still existing in 1789, 194 were *in commendam*). The most damaging effects could be seen in southern Italy (the Papal States and Naples). The Order's visitor in 1551 reported that of the 35 abbeys *in commendam*, sixteen no longer had any monks, and the nineteen others totaled only 86 monks, living in extreme poverty.

CHAPTER XIII

SWANSONG

The seventeenth century saw the opening up of a period of reform in the Church, in the spirit of the conclusions of the Council of Trent (1545–63). The Cistercians fell in behind the movement in all those places where they still had active abbeys and where the prior of those abbeys *in commendam* had been able to retain some freedom of action and sufficient material means. For a century, spiritual inquiry flourished in a sort of febrile atmosphere that led to new forms of observance but also to new divisions within the Order. A significant split also opened up between those abbeys that had remained rich and powerful, despite the difficulties of the past, and those abbeys reduced to poverty and few monks. In the end, they were all to disappear in the face of the attacks of the Age of Enlightenment and the revolutionary violence of the end of the eighteenth century. Nevertheless, in a return to that feverish desire to build that had inspired the first Cistercians, the White Monks of the eighteenth century left to future generations a considerable architectural inheritance, steeped in classicism in France, but sumptuously Baroque in other parts of Europe.

THE EFFECTS OF THE COUNCIL OF TRENT IN THE SEVENTEENTH CENTURY

Pastoral activity Protestantism disputed the very principle of traditional monasticism, the contemplative life having neither pastoral nor social usefulness. In response to the new expectations of the faithful, the Cistercians became increasingly involved at parish level, particularly in Germany.

Almost all the Cistercian houses allocated monks to pastoral duties, and the General Chapter of 1601 established the legal status of parishes managed by the Order. Everywhere abbeys were opened up to visitors and even to pilgrims.

Jansenism Of the spiritual movements that arose in the seventeenth century, Jansenism was the most famous on account of the celebrated names of its followers (such as Pascal) or its sympathizers (such as Racine). The Order remained outside the development of this doctrine, although adversaries of Jansenism regarded the once Cistercian nunnery of Port-Royal-des-Champs as a hotbed of heresy. The famous Mother Angélique Arnaud and her brother Antoine were unable to prevent the expulsion and dispersal of the nuns by royal troops. The abbey was demolished in 1711.

The dispute over observances Throughout the seventeenth century, the French Cistercians fought one another bitterly over the question of the degree of ascetiscm needed for a return to the usages in practice at the time of the founding of Cîteaux.

In 1666, the pope intervened, noting the division of the Order into a variety of different observances, but recommending the holding of a General Chapter the following year. It was the stormiest meeting ever held, because of the intransigence of the abbot of Rancé, the new abbot of La Trappe, a supporter of "Strict Observance", as opposed to "Common Observance".

THE FINAL CENTURY

In France, the decline of the Order, before its disappearance during the tragic years of the Revolution, seemed inevitable. But in the countries of eastern Europe its vitality endured. Nevertheless, to the east of the Rhine the split between the modern philosopher kings and the old Cistercian Order widened.

The example of Austria As in the heyday of the Order, demolished abbeys were successfully revived and new houses founded in central Europe. However, Joseph II, a man of the Enlightenment, could not allow the Austrian Cistercians to follow decisions made in the Order's General Chapter in another country. He forbade the abbots to travel to Cîteaux. In 1782, the contemplative Orders were declared useless "to society and to religion" and

Heiligenkreuz Abbey, Austria.

dissolved, with their possessions confiscated. Thanks to their parishes, the Cistercians were in part able to escape the tidal wave that overwhelmed and suppressed 738 of the country's monasteries. Rudy in Silesia, Zirc in Hungary, and Heligenkruz in Austria became famous schools, giving the Cistercians a new status as academics.

Decline in France It is often forgotten that in France the influence of the Enlightenment was felt even by the monarchy. In 1766, Louis XV set up a monastic commission, the obvious task of which was to diminish the influence, though in any case much weakened by this time, of the monastic institutions. It suppressed 450 religious houses. The commission played an important part within the Order in the eighteenth century. The conflict between Cîteaux and its four first daughter houses, almost as old as the Order itself, had not grown any less acute. In the last few General Chapters of the Order, peace had to be kept by the commission! When, in 1766, the commission sought the opinion of the bishops as to the future of the Cistercian abbeys, the majority declared themselves to be against their preservation.

The French Revolution The freedom of religion instituted on 23 August 1789 preceded the abolition of monastic vows on 13 February 1790. Religious property was confiscated in November 1789, and put up for sale on 17 March 1790. The monasteries were permanently suppressed on 4 December 1790.

So inevitable did these events seem, that few voices were raised in protest. On the other hand, the civil constitution of the clergy, voted through on 26 December 1790, was accepted by only approximately a third of the former Cistercians who had attached themselves to the secular clergy. Some monks joined Cistercian monasteries outside France, including the famous Augustin de Lestrange who managed to take with him a group of Trappists to the former Carthusian abbey of La Valsainte in Switzerland (1 June 1791).

The monks who had taken refuge abroad did not find a lasting home in their new country. Revolution soon swept over the rest of Europe, bringing with it the same policies as in France, but under conditions that were much more violent, because of the resistance to it. Apart from a few monasteries in areas ruled by the Austrian Habsburgs, no Cistercian abbey was able to carry on its monastic life in peace.

A NEW FLOWERING OF ARCHITECTURE

During the two centuries of reform and attack that preceded its extinction, an inexplicable fever of projects and building seized the Cistercian Order. Never, since the first two hundred years of its existence, had so many monastic buildings been planned and, in some cases, at least partially realized. It seemed is if, intuitively aware of its imminent demise, the Order wanted to build new churches to the greater glory of God—as did the Cistercians in eastern Europe—or that it wished to assert its continuing ability to dominate the technical world—as the Cistercians of the great French abbeys seem to have done.

Everywhere the medieval buildings, considered to be "barbaric" (Gothic), were pulled down or remodeled. The desire to embrace the new appeared in every one of the building workshops, busily occupied in altering abbeys that were often at crisis point through lack of recruits, and yet seized with the same crazy enthusiasm for building, common to abbots and to bishops. "Yet neither time nor material resources were sufficient to carry out the complete execution of these magnificent projects. As the Revolution drew closer, in the majority of cases work was unfinished and unpaid for."[8]

Cistercian Baroque in central Europe In the eighteenth century, the Cistercians of central Europe, like their medieval predecessors, had to obey a set building program. The Council of Trent had given architecture a new mission, expanded on in a number of writing by St. Charles Borromeo and encouraged for two centuries by Rome.

"The desire to please the multitude, touch the feelings more than the intelligence, to show through architecture the grandiose restoration of the Roman Church—these were the intentions that finally carried the art of the Counter-

Reformation far from the spirit of "Strict Observance" [...] The Council had justified the use of lights, censers, and ornaments, and recognized the cult of images under attack from the reformers." In the light of this, the Jesuits emphasized the need for the Church to distinguish itself from the Reformation, whose religion was "impoverished in every way and whose churches resembled tennis courts," preaching instead the use of luxury in churches, recalling that Christ had accepted the precious perfume from Mary Magdalene.

The response of the architects and artists of central Europe was the Baroque style. Art should inspire emotions not aroused by the ascetic purity of forms and materials (that Luther too had praised) but by the ravishing of the senses, dazzled by a "superabundance of images, the emotive power of statues, vertiginous painted ceilings, the wonder inspired by a nave overloaded with ornament, the beauty of rare and precious materials, the shimmering of marble, and the prestige of gold." It is no accident if the most beautiful of the Baroque churches, Cistercian and also Benedictine, were situated as if lined up in battle order from southern Germany to Bohemia, where the double threat of

Lutheran Saxony and Calvinist Switzerland was a constant threat.

The majority of Cistercian churches were given the Baroque treatment, without, however, concealing their original Romanesque or Gothic architecture. They were merely embellished with the addition of traditional attributes of the decorative arts. The sanctuaries were furnished with large retables, incorporating the altar, made of marble or wood and furnished with statues of St. Benedict and St. Bernard. The tabernacle was given an important place in the scheme to glorify the dogma of the presence of the body of Christ. In the choir reserved for the monks or nuns, exquisitely carved choir stalls were added. Everything was adapted to highlight the grandeur of the liturgy. The spoken words of the liturgy were uttered from imposing thrones that became a focal point of the nave. The musical accompaniment to the liturgy was provided by organs painted in gold and silver, the music of which—played by the abbey's own organist—filled any silences. The side aisles were furnished with confessionals, each one a work of art. Pews, generally of warm wood, rather than cold stone, and always carved, were installed in the nave. Small altars reserved for the cult of the saints whose relics were displayed there were added in the transepts. These too were mounted on retables, gener-

ally with an oil painting, representing an episode from the life of the saint, framed by twisting columns (like the screws from a wine press, where the bunches of grapes, in relief, were a reference to the earth's abundance, a gift of God).

There were other constructions that were entirely new, coming directly from the essence of

Facing page:
Kaisheim Abbey,
Germany. The church
dating from the end of
the fourteenth century
was given a Baroque
appearance in the
eighteenth century.

Above:
Zwettl Abbey, Austria.
A triumph of the
decorative arts,
particularly of wood
carving, sculpture and
gilding. Beginning of the
eighteenth century.

Baroque, with an interior space arranged like a theater, so that the religious services unfolded like a play in a stage set resembling the antechamber of Paradise. From raised plinths or side balconies, huge, gesticulating, life-size statues of the Church Fathers or the Evangelists proclaimed their sacred words. Walls, ceilings and cupolas were handed over to painters who brought the art of trompe-l'œil to a peak of perfection in scenes from the Bible or the history of the Church suggested by the theologians for the edification of simple souls, for the Cistercians were now managing pilgrimages, such as the famous ones at Vierzehnheiligen near Bamburg and Birnau on the German side of Lake Constance. The whole ensemble of this paradise of forms and refined colors, where even the smell of the waxed wood and the burning incense delighted the senses, was bathed in light that flooded in through great windows of plain rather than stained glass. At the same time, the Baroque architects could, when they deemed it necessary, produce a more sober style.

This more sober style was used almost always in the treatment of space and in the external façades. The Baroque buildings of the eighteenth century would often have been of an extreme banality if it were not for the way in which they were integrated into an ensemble of courtyards and forecourts, that little by little, as the spectator advanced, opened up to reveal the façade of the abbey church and the tower or dome that completed the composition. The outer courtyards where outbuildings were located, low buildings with white, plastered walls in which only the door and window frames were highlighted in bright colors, are as characteristic of the Cistercian abbeys of the Baroque period as the retables of their sanctuaries. Good examples are the abbeys of Zwettl and Furstenfeld.

Another shared characteristic of these newly

Facing pages:
Schlierbach Abbey,
Austria. The library,
decorated as a temple to
knowledge in the spirit
of the Enlightenment.

remodeled Baroque abbeys was the presence in the complex of vast libraries, conceived as the "treasury" of the community. Here cabinet-makers and gilders were encouraged to give expression to all the refinement of a social class that was unashamedly passionate about art and literature. The libraries were generally divided into three rooms, a history library, a science library and, lastly, a library of theology and patrology. Though an innovation in Cistercian abbeys, such an arrangement could also be found in the beautiful libraries of the Benedictine abbeys (Saint-Gall or Melk). Waldsassen in Germany and Vissy-Brod in Bohemia are good examples.

Abbots' palaces in the French abbeys The motives behind the new constructions undertaken in the eighteenth century in the French abbeys were less noble than those of the Baroque buildings carried out by the Cistercians of central Europe. Those few French communities still rich in property and income were eager to abandon the medieval buildings in which they had always lived, to have more comfortable accommodation, more adapted to the new usages of the Order. These included the general introduction of individual cells (1666), the installation of kitchens where meat could be cooked on certain days of the week, and the setting up of libraries.

More prosaically, it was obvious that a number of building projects were initiated purely to allow the abbots, whether absentee or not, to have their own palace at the abbey, suited to the tastes of the refined society of the Age of Enlightenment. The largest abbeys, despite the successive disasters of the preceding centuries, had retained the means for embarking on major building work. Furthermore, Colbert (in 1667) and then the Prince Regent called on the richer monastic communities to provide work for the poor, following a "policy of public works". These various needs resulted, architecturally speaking, in buildings of a very pure form of classicism *à la française* which retained a simplicity appropriate to the heirs of Cistercian asceticism.

Financial means It is clear that Aiguebelle with its two monks and 1,700 *livres* of annual revenue

in 1768 was not in a position to undertake work of the magnitude of that started by Clairvaux the same year. Clairvaux had 54 monks and an annual revenue of 78,700 *livres*. Such financial means allowed the abbey to borrow. Furthermore, its 50,000 acres (20,000ha) of forest—in addition to its 12,000 acres (5000ha) of farmland and its string of ironworks—could, to some extent, be called upon each year. Only twenty abbeys seem to have had the financial capacity to undertake major works with the certainly of finishing them.

The architects One good thing to be said about the Cistercian abbots is that they knew how to choose good architects. The names of some have been preserved by history. Claude Louis d'Aviler, son of the great theoretician of classical architecture Charles d'Aviler, was involved at Auberive, Molesme, and Valuisant. Jean Aubert, protégé of Jules Hardouin Mansart and designer of the great stables of Chantilly and probably also of the Palais Bourbon, was the architect of the abbot's palace at Chaalis, dating from 1736. Lenoir rebuilt the nunnery of Saint-Antoine-des-Champs in 1770, and began work on the great guest-house at Cîteaux. Between 1785 and 1789, Louis Lemasson built the interesting abbey building of Royaumont. The church of Valloires deserves special mention. Rebuilt in 1738 to the plans of Raoul Coigniart, it is the only Cistercian Baroque church in France. The grills and metalwork were made by Jean Veyren, known as "Vivarais", while the woodcarvings (the organ case, in particular) were carried out by the Austrian Simon Pfaff of Pfaffenhoffen.

Clairvaux In 1708, Clairvaux was still a medieval town, surrounded by nearly two miles (3km) of walls. A large number of buildings, corresponding to the most various of uses, had grown up over the course of the centuries, in "lower" Clairvaux (where the outbuildings were located) and "upper" Clairvaux (the main part of the monastery). Pierre Mayeur, elected abbot in 1740, was aware that his abbey no longer corresponded to the spaces needed for daily life in the eighteenth century. He had no hesitation in drawing up plans to reconstruct a new modern abbey on the same site. The abbey church was preserved, of course, together with the lay

brothers' range, which had by now become a huge warehouse. The rest was progressively demolished.

The "Great Cloister" was to be the new focus of abbey life. Pierre Mayeur managed to complete the greater part of the work (enclosed and covered) between 1753 and 1774. It is a considerable building, of a single storey, with inhabitable attics over a ground floor with a covered cloister walk surrounding a garth measuring 165 feet square (50 x 50m). The exterior façade, on the south side, was 460 feet (140m) wide.

There has been much discussion about the reasons for building such a large space. Was it intended that Clairvaux should become a kind of central novitiate for the entire Order? Or was it that Pierre Mayeur succumbed, as did many others in charge of monasteries, to the temptations of building on a grand scale, thus emphasizing their importance? It is clear that the refectory and

kitchen, forming part of the south side of the cloister, take up a disproportionate amount of space. Decoration in carved wood and stucco medallions give an indication of the role of this ensemble as a reception area.

Facing page, top:
Royaumont Abbey, Île-de-France. The abbot's palace. Between Palladio and Bouillée, architecturally very avant-garde for its time.

Facing page, below and left:
Clairvaux Abbey. The great cloister of Clairvaux III, an immense palace with long corridors, but retaining a Cistercian austerity. Napoleon made it into a prison, thus saving the abbey from destruction. Today neglected, this exceptional group of buildings is overgrown with bushes and brambles, and may one day become the most beautiful ruin of the 21st century.

Orval Abbey, Belgium. Although perhaps excessively monumental, the intention of this architecture was to mark the revival of the Cistercian Order after the anti-congregation movements and legislation of the period 1880–1910.

YESTERDAY, TODAY, AND TOMORROW

After the French Revolution, nothing could be as it was before. The Church had lost its traditional political allies, and anticlerical sentiment was fed by both the memory of the Church's past alliances with Rome and its new alliances with the conservatives. Furthermore, the surge of nationalism felt throughout Europe could not coexist with a supranational Church or with the large presence of internationally-minded religious Orders within national frontiers. This explains in part why the revival of Cistercian abbeys in the nineteenth century was the result of localized initiatives, with little coordination over a period of years, and why the old splits between the two types of observance were able to persist. Thus, when the White Monks redefined their statutes in the early years of the twentieth century, they had no other reason for existence except a religious one. The ambiguity introduced by political or economic interests was no longer a part of their religious commitment. If we look back at the history of the Order from its earliest years, it is clear that this is something new.

NINE HUNDRED YEARS OF CÎTEAUX

On the brink of the 21st century, an impartial observer will notice that the Cistercians, although still divided into two Orders, since the inheritance of history is slow to disappear, now appear in the eyes of the world to live in a unanimity rediscovered through the application of the Rule of Benedict of Nursia, in an atmosphere of spirituality unknown since the time of the founding fathers. They are to be found today in the four corners of

the globe (Himmerod in Brazil, Schlierbach in the United States, Lérins in Indo-China, etc.).

But, like the secular Church and other monastic institutions, the Cistercians are faced with a serious fall in numbers, after a period, following the Second World War, when there was a relative upsurge in vocations. The aging population of the communities is a weight on the dynamism of the abbeys. Because of the need for self-sufficiency, in accordance with the Rule, every monastery possesses considerable numbers of buildings, presenting severe problems of maintenance. Cistercian monks still support themselves by their work: light industry at Acey, cheese making at Cîteaux, distilling at Aiguebelle, brewing at Orval. The way forward for them is certainly to continue these activities, taking on workers as necessary. In this way, they are continuing to work within the spirit of development of rural areas—one of the innovations introduced by the Cistercians long ago.

The question of the future of the Cistercians is being addressed. In his recent book of *Souvenirs et réflexions*, the abbot of La Trappe concludes: "In the aftermath of the decisions made by the Second Vatican Council, our generation has put an enormous effort into carrying out a far-reaching renewal. What is to be the task of those whom we have trained and who will tomorrow take up the torch? [...] Most obvious will be the diminution in size of the communities [...] and the unsuitability of the accommodation, intended for much larger numbers. Of course, no community can expect to last forever. [...] Our successors will see further than we can, like the apostles depicted in the stained glass windows at Chartres, perched on the

shoulders of the prophets, and so able to see ahead where their predecessors could not."[1]

THE CULTURAL INHERITANCE

Very few of the Cistercian abbeys of the past have been revived as monasteries. At the time of the Revolution, many became convenient quarries for entrepreneurs from the nearby towns. Others became factories (Fontenay was turned into a paper mill) or were used for administrative functions (Clairvaux was turned into a prison). This change in use partially saved them. No traces at all survive of some abbeys (Signy, for example), but others have left considerable remains.

In the nineteenth century, these historic places began to interest, first of all, the local academic historical societies, which produced many monographs, and then the universities, where a huge upsurge in interest in medieval studies and the world of the Cistercians has become evident.

At the same time, tourists were discovering the abbeys, and the sites began to be appreciated, thanks to the efforts of the owners (whether public or private), captivated by the *genius loci*. Today these abbeys are wonderfully preserved, restored with great care under the auspices of the architects of the *Monuments historiques*, or their equivalents outside France, taking on a new status as museums. We forget sometimes that in these places monks once worked, worshipped and constructed. Today's cushioned environment shows an idealized monastic life. It is for this reason that some of those abbeys converted to other uses (hotels, retirement homes, cultural

Above:
Benedictine abbey of Maredsous, Belgium. This masterpiece of Belgian Gothic-revival was carried out, in the spirit of Viollet-le-Duc, according to a typical

Cistercian plan, modeled on Villers-la-Ville.

Above right:
Fountains Abbey, England. The visitors' center: cultural tourism and themed gift-shops.

The English have become expert in this kind of presentation. Broken columns or stretches of wall pieced by glassless windows, covered with just the right amount of ivy, stand on immaculate lawns like so many gigantic sculptures. Fountains receives 300,000 visitors a year, and the French abbeys more than two million. Paradoxically, it is the guides on these tourist sites, more than the monks committed to the cloister, who answer the public's questions about monastic life and Cistercian spirituality. The ways in which culture is communicated are often unexpected!

Cistercian architecture, in terms of program and functional organization, remains the most admired model. In the nineteenth century it was, as a matter of course, revived by the new communities, who found themselves without ancient abbeys to occupy and having to build from scratch.

Famous architects, too, looked to this model. When, in 1872, the Belgian Benedictines of Maredsous entrusted Béthune with the task of building their new monastery, in the purest "Gothic revival" style, he took as his inspiration the plans of the former Cistercian abbey of Villers-en-Brabant. Le Corbusier did not confine himself to writing the preface to Lucien Hervé's photographic study of Le Thoronet.[2] Asked by the Dominicans in

centers, etc.) still retain an animation that is not out of keeping with the respect owed to the inheritance from past generations. Those sites that have become detached from the majority of their other buildings have been allotted the role of romantic ruins, as artificial as the hermitage in the eighteenth century "desert".

1952 to design their abbey at La Tourette, near Lyon, he too adopted the basic Cistercian plan, although the functions of a monastery of friars, working outside in the world, might have benefited from a different treatment than the one that spontaneously imposed itself on the architect.

This continuation of the image of the Cistercian abbey, a symbol of an extraordinary human adventure, reveals the unchanging cultural posterity of the Cistercians and that of the abbeys that they set up throughout Europe.

Left:
Fountains Abbey, England, Greenery within the ruins.

Below left and right:
Dominican convent of La Tourelle. Cistercian architecture was also a point of reference for Le Corbusier.

PART TWO

THE CISTERCIAN WORLD IN EUROPE

ACEY

Aceyum

location: Vitreux (Jura), Franche-Comté, France

founded: 1136, by Cherlieu (filiation of Clairvaux)

dissolved: 1791 (French Revolution)

present use: OCSO monastery

See also pp. 47, 88, 135.

Bibliography
P. GRESSER, R. LOCATELLI, M. GRESSET, E. VUILLEMIN, L'Abbaye N.-D. d'Acey, CETRE, Besançon, 1986.
Hubert Bonal, "Électrolyse Abbaye d'Acey ou l'ascétisme managérial", in MCS No. 523, 5 January 1998, p. 8

The abbey of Notre-Dame d'Acey stands in an isolated position on the banks of the river Ognon in the Franche-Comté region. The broad valley is cultivated and the monks who moved back into the monastery in 1937 are following tradition by breeding livestock as well as keeping an orchard and a vegetable garden.

These activities are not enough, however, to allow the community to be self-sufficient, as the Rule of St. Benedict intended. The same problem is faced by the majority of present-day Cistercian monasteries. To supplement their work, various crafts are carried out (pottery, distilling, cheese-making, brewing, etc.), continuing decades of production of traditional fare, promoting the image of the monk as guardian of the old ecological recipes—a useful marketing ploy. Acey, by contrast, has for the last thirty years run an industrial business that is very much a part of the needs and constraints of the modern economic world. "EAA (Électrolyse Abbaye d'Acey) is a PME (Small and Medium Enterprise) carrying out subcontracted work for the car industry, and the electrical, electronic, and aeronautical industries. At Acey, metal parts are electrolytically plated with tin, nickel, gold, silver, etc.). EAA, certified ISO9002, has a fully automated factory whose products are of a quality acknowledged and appreciated by its clients."

EAA has twenty employees, wage-earning workers who work 35 hours a week in two teams, and monks who work in the factory between the religious offices. The latter have adjustable timetables, allowing for maximum flexibility in production. The chief executive is one of the brothers, obedient to the spiritual authority of the father abbot, but holding full powers within a system of "communal capitalism". It represents an experiment that is full of paradoxes; finding the right balance between the pressure from the clients who see the abbey's product as an integral part of their economic strategy of a "last-minute" production schedule, the social demands of a business that needs to be exemplary in its human relations, and the practice of a liturgical life that makes heavy demands on the minds and the time of the monks. It can be seen as one way of testing out both monastic asceticism in our modern world and today's system of values.

Over the centuries the abbey has lost many of its buildings, and the electrolysis factory is not housed in an ancient forge or historic mill, dating from a time when architecture glorified the workplace. The church, on the other hand, is still there (1168–1260). Six bays of the nave vault collapsed in the seventeenth century but have recently been replaced by a structure with reinforced concrete diaphragm arches. Today we see the great narthex, before entering a cruciform church of beautiful simplicity. The groin-vaulted aisles, round-headed windows, and square-ended chevet with apsidal chapels are typical of Romanesque architecture in its maturity. By contrast, the internal decoration is entirely Gothic to a height of 65 feet (20m), giving a three-stage elevation: an arcade of pointed arches, a stark, plain wall, and a clerestory of numerous small windows, allowing plenty of light into the building. Recent stained-glass windows add a note of modernity that is appropriate in an abbey such as this: embracing the world of today during working hours, the presence of the modern world is not forgotten during the hours of prayer.

The two bays of the nave
from the south transept,
all that remains of the
twelfth-century church
after the fire that
ravaged the abbey in
1683. The north wall
opens on to monastic
buildings reconstructed
in the eighteenth
century.

ALCOBAÇA

Alcobaça S. Maria de Alcobaça

location: Alcobaça (Estremadura), Portugal

founded: 1153, by Clairvaux

suppressed: 1834

present status: parish church, hospice, and municipal social services

See also pp. 12, 40, 47, 72, 75, 97, 114, 118.

Bibliography
Dom Maur COCHERIL, *Routier des abbayes cisteriennes du Portugal*, Fondation C. Gulbenkian, Lisbon-Paris, 1986.
Dom Maur COCHERIL, *Alcobaça*, Imprensa nacional, Lisbon, 1989.
Dom Maur COCHERIL, Note sur la décoration de l'église de Santa Maria de Cos, Alcobaça, *Alcobaciana*, Alcobaça, 1983.
Anselme DIMIER, *L'Art cistercien*, vol. 2, Zodiaque, La Pierre-qui-Vire, 1971.
Maria A. LAGE PABLO DA TRINIDADE FERREIRA, *Mosteiro de S. Maria de Alcobaça*, ELO, Lisbon, 1987.

Alcobaça, which received its foundation charter on 8 April 1153, was the last abbey founded by Clairvaux during St. Bernard's lifetime, just four years before the famous abbot died. This was the furthest west that the Cistercian Order expanded in southern Europe, standing as it does at the confluence of the rivers Alcoa and Baça (which gave their names to the ancient Roman town of Helcobatia) on land given by Alfonso Henriquez, the first king of Portugal. Legend has it that the king's gift was a thank-offering for his victory over the Moors at Santarem in 1147. "The truth is more simple and more striking. Because of St. Bernard's influence and prestige, the donation to Clairvaux of territory recently captured from the Moors was imbued with political significance. Portugal was only just emerging as a nation and had a population of under a million inhabitants. They therefore called in one of the most important civilizing forces of the day and in so doing re-affirmed their faith in the future" (Dom Maur Cocheril).

In 1195 the Moors returned, pillaging the abbey and killing a number of the monks. Nonetheless, work on the abbey begun by master craftsmen sent out from Clairvaux continued until 1223, when the conventual buildings were finished. Work on the church went on until 1252 and construction of the Gothic cloister did not terminate until well into the fourteenth century. At the same time the monks, their conversi or lay brothers, and a large number of hired laborers set about revitalizing land which had long since been depopulated by the ravages of military campaigns during the reconquest from the Moors. The estate covered approximately 170 square miles (44,000ha), from the Atlantic coast in the west to the Serra dos Canduiros in the east. Lying at the heart of a well-situated basin, the abbey could grow cereals as well as supporting vineyards and olive groves. Before long the monks had set up smithies and were working the mines and salt deposits. The salt was shipped for export on vessels belonging to the abbey itself. The monks drained marshes to reclaim new land and built a road network which facilitated the growth of population centers. Always more estate managers than enclosed monks, the Alcobaça Cistercians set up agricultural colleges, opened a pharmacy and a print works (in the sixteenth century), and even played a role in establishing Lisbon University. The abbots were behind the creation of the military Orders of the Knights of Christ and the Knights of Avis, both of which were engaged in the fight against the Infidels and the Castilians. They sat in the Cortes and were members of the Royal Counsel.

Against the wishes of both Cîteaux and Rome, Alcobaça created an independent Portuguese Cistercian congregation. There was therefore nothing to stop its decline once the abbey became a sinecure for commendatory (absentee) abbots. One in particular rode roughshod over the interests of the monks and flouted ecclesiastical law when, in 1475, he sold the abbey to the Archbishop of Lisbon, "the biggest grabber of church property that Portugal ever knew!".

In 1755 the monastery was hit by an enormous earthquake, followed by terrible floods in 1772. Then came its dreadful pillage by the Napoleonic forces in 1811, and finally during the 1833 Revolution Louis-Philippe's troops once again sacked the abbey, which was only saved from total destruction when the State quickly annexed it for itself. Restoration was

then able to get under way. Today Alcobaça is classified as a World Heritage Site by UNESCO.

Once through the church's sumptuous Baroque façade, flanked by two ranges running over 600 feet (200m) in length, the visitor is struck by the majesty and austerity of the huge Cistercian nave, a "hall church" 348 feet (106m) long and 66 feet (20m) high. The piers are grouped and their multiple shafts stand on chamfered bases, giving the impression of a royal path leading to the sanctuary, which is flooded with light from the nine wide bays of the semi-circular east end. Apart from the aisles, which are almost as high as the nave itself, what we have here is a replica of the church at Clairvaux II, where the newly canonized St. Bernard was laid to rest in 1174. It is laid out on the same plan, has the same dimensions and doubtless even the same colored limestone! The church has changed little over the centuries. King Pedro I ordered his tomb to be built here, next to that of Inès de Castro, "his dead queen". They contain some of the greatest funerary sculpture in western Europe (1361). Off the south transept is a chapel dedicated to the father abbot, containing a group of the Death of St. Bernard (1687–1705). Stepping up from the same transept is the Chapel of Tombs, a royal pantheon which is a wonderful thirteenth-century pastiche. Finally, leading off one of the ambulatory bays is the new sacristy (c.1760) in Gothic Manueline style.

The cloister, a square with sides roughly 165 feet (50m) long, is one of the largest the Cistercians ever built. It is roofed in rib vaults supported on consoles with five capitals. The cloister opens on to the inner courtyard through wide arches with twin supporting piers surmounted by traceried oculi. A wide staircase leads to an upper storey promenade dating from 1484. Through the wide three-centered arches the monks could once have looked out over the first orange groves ever planted in Portugal. From here, the visitor also gets a good view of the monks' *lavatorium* or laver, standing in the inner courtyard. Off the cloister walks are the chapter house, the monks' common-room, and the refectory.

Then there are the day stairs leading up to the monks' dormitory. All these rooms are built like three-aisled churches surmounted by rib vaults in the true Gothic style. But this is not all that Alcobaça has to offer. A modern kitchen has an immense central chimney and running water from the stream flowing through a conduit. Where once the lay brothers' range stood, we now have the Sala dos Reis and the clerks' room, where the administration of the abbey was done. There are two more cloisters with workshops as well as a library.

A visit to Alcobaça would not be complete without going to admire the sumptuous decorations in the church that once belonged to the Cistercian nuns of S. Maria de Cos, four miles (6km) away. In the sixteenth century, this abbey grange was turned into a convent, and nuns continued to live there until 1834. In the sanctuary of the church there is a seventeenth-century Baroque gilded wood retable. The walls of the nave and the sacristy are completely covered in seventeenth-century *azulejos*, or glazed tiles, showing scenes from the life of Bernard of Clairvaux. Finally, the church's most splendid treasure is its beautifully painted vaulted ceiling composed of 24 wooden coffers, each measuring 8ft 6ins by 5ft 3ins (2.6m x 1.6m) in five rows.

Previous page:
The south aisle of the nave from the ambulatory. The narrowness of the aisle is a reminder that the Cistercian liturgy—unlike that of the Cluniacs—had no role for processions. Its main function was to support the nave.

Facing page:
This nave, the most majestic ever built by Cistercians, is traditionally ascribed to the monk Didier of Clairvaux.

Above:
The lavatorium and fountain in the cloister.

Left:
The three aisles of the monks' dormitory, like that of Clairvaux.

Above left:
The gable wall of the south transept (with large oculus) and the transept aisle (small oculus).

Right:
The fourteenth-century "silent cloister" and its walk of 1484.

Above right:
Detail of the façade by João Turriano (1725), constructed around the beautiful thirteenth-century door.

Left:
Sacristy door. The most beautiful example of Manueline Gothic. The royal arms are shown above a tree.

Following double spread:
The monks' day-room. The five sections of the floor follow the slope of the terrain.

BEBENHAUSEN

If it is true that monks in general, and Cistercians in particular, have a passion for building, then Bebenhausen provides the perfect illustration of this adage. In 1180 the abbey was founded by the Premonstratensian Order in a beautiful clearing in the Forest of Schönbruck, at the confluence of the Rivers Seebach and the Goldersbach. Its history, however, recounts little else but a series of building works. The Cistercians took it over in 1190 and by 1228 they had consecrated an abbey church in the Romanesque style: basilica layout, square east end, and flat wooden roof.

The monks' range, still in the Romanesque style, was finished before 1250, while a huge outer wall to protect the outbuildings was completed in 1303 after twenty years' work. In 1320 they started on the large Gothic window in the choir, and in about 1335 masons brought in from Salem inaugurated the beautiful refectory then the laver whose fountain was built in the new Flamboyant Gothic style. With the new century, the abbey treated itself to a new tower (1409) with stone battlements which in visitors' eyes must have symbolized the abbot's taste for fine architecture. Over the next two centuries the abbey was completely modified: the cloister was rebuilt, the former lay brothers' refectory was turned into a winter dining room which could be heated, individual cells were created in the monks' dormitory and they built a guest-house for visitors.

Following the Reformation, the abbey's fortunes were mixed: until 1806 it was a Protestant university; during the nineteenth century it became one of the king of Württemberg's

Bebenhausa

location: near Bebenhausen (Württemberg), Germany

founded: 1190, by Schönau (filiation of Clairvaux)

suppressed: 1802

present status: cultural center

See also p. 110.

Bibliography
Abbaye de Bebenhausen, Baden-Württemberg Ministry of Finance, 1991.
Jürgen SYDOW, *Bebenhausen: 800 Jahre Geschichte und Kunst*, Tübingen, 1984.

Left:
The south side of the
cloister with its half-
timbered upper floor
surrounding the
lavatorium.

Above:
Vault of the east walk of
the cloister at the
entrance to the chapter
house (fifteenth century).

hunting lodges; for a time after the Second World War it housed the Württemberg Parliament.

Both the village and the abbey are now deservedly protected by preservation orders. The half-timbered houses, the large-tiled roofs, stone and carefully executed whitewash imbue the place with character. A stroll through the orchards which dominate the surrounding area quickly reveals how well the conventual buildings meshed with the small town. The tower and east window stand out like little masterpieces.

A walk around the abbey quadrangle is enough to appreciate the perfection of the area leading into the heart of the abbey. Vaulted walkways and little paved courtyards seem to protect it. The cloister is completely cut off from the world. The elegant building over the fountain, the floral decoration in the refectory, the cunning ribbing on the vaults of the cloister walks, the ambitious capitals in the monks' day-room and the chapter house—all these refinements point the way toward the coming of Baroque to the Cistercian abbeys of central Europe, while keeping the structural essence of St. Bernard's plan.

The north walk of the cloister with the bench (warmed by the sun in good weather) for the lectio divina. *Like the* opus dei, *that the monk carried out each time he participated in the divine office, the* lectio divina, *performed twice a day, contributed to the glorification of God.*

Reconstruction of an eighteenth-century cell. Sometimes veritable apartments, cells were created in every abbey where the dormitory had been.

Left:
*Fresco of 1409 on the
north wall of the
sanctuary: Abbot Peter
of Gomaringen presents
the church's new bell-
tower (1407–1409, see
photo p. 150) to the
Virgin.*

Above:
*Sundial on a buttress on
the south side of the east
end of the church.*

BECTIVE

A venerable, 300-year old tree majestically dominates the impressive ruins of Bective Abbey, which is set among pastures where cattle graze along the banks of the River Knightsbrook. The Cistercians bequeathed us a magnificent bridge that crosses to the abbey.

This was the first daughter of Mellifont and, like all its younger sisters, it was founded by the king of the host county, in this case Murchad O'Melaghlin-Sheachlainn. However, he did not survive the Anglo-Norman invasion. The abbey church houses the tomb of Hugh de Lacy, accused by the king of England of conspiring to take his throne (1195). In 1228, when Bective was an acknowledged stronghold, they began to raise huge walls around the cloister, and added towers. Two of these have survived but the one at the transept crossing (whose existence has been deduced from reinforcements to the south transept arch) disappeared along with the nave after the Dissolution when a succession of owners used the abbey as a stone quarry. At the same time, the chapter house with its single loophole window made a very handy blockhouse!

Citadel of faith and military citadel—both required the same constructional rigor which was justified by their functional needs. Both the men who built the crusaders fortresses in Syria and those who built strongholds in western Europe perpetuated this plain form of architecture that centuries later Vauban was to develop further.

Mainistir Bleigthi/Beatitudo Dei
location: near Trim (Co. Meath), Republic of Ireland
founded: 1190, by Mellifont (filiation of Clairvaux)
dissolved: 1536 (Act of Dissolution)
present status: ruins

Bibliography
Roger STALLEY, *The Cistercian Monasteries of Ireland*, Yale University Press, London, 1987.

Left, above and below:
Cloister arcades. As at
Jerpoint, a sculptured
surface stands between
two columns.

Above:
The cloister and fortified
tower above the monks'
day-room. After 1537,
the owners attempted to
rebuild this part of the
abbey as a manor in the
Tudor style!

BOYLE

Mainistir an Buille

location: near Boyle (Co. Roscommon), Republic of Ireland

founded: 1148, by Mellifont (filiation of Clairvaux)

dissolved: 1584

present status: ruins

Bibliography
Roger STALLEY, *The Cistercian Monasteries of Ireland*, Yale University Press, London, 1987.
Anselme DIMIER, *L'Art cistercien*, vol. 2, Zodiaque, La Pierre-qui-Vire, 1971.

It is quite certain that Boyle holds the record for the number of changes of location. It was originally founded by Mellifont at Grelaedinach (1148), on a site known as Ath-da-Larc where an even older monastery doubtless already existed. It was moved first to Dwinconald (1156), then to Bunfinne (1159) and finally to Boyle (1161), just two miles from the famous Lough Key Forest.

A series of attacks and misfortunes led to its ruin. As early as the thirteenth century, at a time when people were still meant to respect churches, the abbey was attacked by English forces (1202 and 1235). The last abbot met a martyr's death in 1584. Even after the Dissolution, the abbey remained a focus of fierce fighting and was finally besieged by Cromwell in 1645!

Despite all this, the church still holds much of interest. The Romanesque architecture of the sanctuary (with a barrel vault), the choir, the transept, and the first five bays of the nave all date from the abbey's foundation. The rest of the church was built in the thirteenth century at the start of the Gothic movement. But above all you are struck by the cylindrical columns surmounted by carved capitals which are of great stylistic importance. These were the work of the Master of Ballintober who was employed by the abbey from 1216 to 1225.

The decorative taste common to Benedictine churches triumphs at Boyle, be it in the scalloped capitals (foliate and non-figurative motifs) or the figurative capitals (especially those decorated with animals).

Left:
Capital by the Master of Ballintober (west face of a pier on the north side of the nave).

Facing page, above:
Cylindrical column in the nave.

Facing page, below:
North wall of the nave.

BUILDWAS

Bildewasium

location: Shrewsbury (Shropshire), England

founded: 1135, by Savigny (Cistercian from 1147—filiation of Clairvaux)

dissolved 1536 (Dissolution)

See also pp. 43, 109.

Bibliography

Henry THOROLD, *The Ruined Abbeys of England*, Wales and Scotland, Harper Collins, London, 1993.
Anselme DIMIER *L'Art cistercien*, vol. 2, Zodiaque, La-Pierre-qui-Vire, 1971.
E. C. NORTON and D. PARK (eds.), *Cistercian Art and Architecture in the British Isles*, Cambridge, 1986.

The abbey of Buildwas stands in the beautiful valley of the Severn. In recent years a nuclear power station has been built nearby. Today, the "wildernesses" that originally attracted the Cistercian monks are rarely what they were!

The monks of Buildwas were not in fact Cistercians in 1135 when a group of local nobles asked the Norman abbey of Savigny to set up a daughter house in Shropshire. This initiative had gained the support of the king of England, Stephen. In 1147, Savigny affiliated itself with Clairvaux and all its monks adopted the Cistercian white cowl of undyed wool.

Unlike the majority of Cistercian abbeys, Buildwas never greatly expanded. It set up no daughter houses, no system of granges, and it limited its building program to no more than what was needed for a small community of monks. Its income was derived from collecting the tolls on the bridge over the Severn.

Their remote situation did not shield the monks from problems. In 1342 a monk murdered the father abbot. In 1377 the nearby abbey of Whitland laid claim to rights belonging to Buildwas, while in 1406 the monastery was attacked by brigands. In 1536, when the community consisted of only twelve monks, it was dissolved and its property handed over to the Crown.

There are considerable remains of the abbey, revealing a construction in line with the "Bernardine plan". The church follows the plan of Fontenay: a small square-ended east end with three windows, a transept with two side chapels, a nine-bay nave with very narrow side aisles. Less traditional are the solid cylindrical columns of the nave. These are more typically English, being found in numerous late twelfth-century churches, both Cistercian (Fountains) and other (Southwell). Nave, transept, and aisles, today roofless, were originally covered with a wooden ceiling.

In contravention of the edicts issued by the General Chapter, the English Cistercians built large stone towers in almost all their abbeys, usually placing them over the transept crossing, giving a nave, transepts, and choir of equal height. The well-preserved tower at Buildwas is wide and low, expressive of the solid serenity of the monks' community.

Because of the sloping ground, five steps lead down to the chapter house, through a door with a round arch and triple roll moldings, standing between two simple bays. The original ribbed vaults are supported by arches resting either on engaged bases or four pillars (two octagonal and two cylindrical) with waterleaf capitals. The neighboring parlor is also well preserved (two rib-vaulted bays).

The other buildings are all ruined, apart from the infirmary that stands to the east of the central monastic enclave, converted into a dwelling house after the Dissolution and now used as a club-house for the employees of the large factory nearby.

Above, left:
The crossing.

Above, right:
The cloister garth seen from the site of the undercroft of the lay brothers' range. In the background the chapter house.

Left:
The "palm tree" in the chapter house.

BYLAND

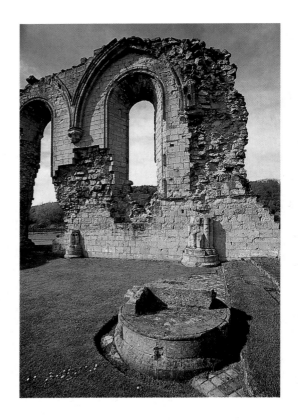

Bellalanda

location: Byland (Yorkshire, North Riding), England
founded: 1134, by Furness (Cistercian order in 1147 through Savigny—filiation of Clairvaux)
dissolved: 1539 (Dissolution)
present status: English Heritage property

See also pp. 54, 57, 107, 109.

Bibliography
Henry THOROLD, *The Ruined Abbeys of England, Wales and Scotland*, Harper Collins, London, 1993.
Anselme DIMIER, *L'Art cistercien*, vol. 2, Zodiaque, La-Pierre-qui-Vire, 1971.
E. C. NORTON and D. PARK (eds.), *Cistercian Art and Architecture in the British Isles*, Cambridge, 1986.

When the site of an abbey was not suitable, the Cistercians did not hesitate to change it. The founders of Byland must hold the record for the number of moves. In 1134, Savigniac monks from Furness set up at Caldra. They moved to Old Byland in 1138 but found that the closeness of Rievaulx was a cause of conflict, and so looked for a new site. They settled at Stocking in 1147, but only temporally. It was not until 1177 that they found a permanent site for Byland "having cleared the woods and drained the marshes" (Marcel Aubert).

The original church was replaced by a large abbey church at the same period as Rievaulx and Fountains were developing, during that great period for Cistercian abbeys in Yorkshire, the early thirteenth century. The beautiful ruins remaining today, spared by the Act of Dissolution, make it possible to reconstruct the plan of a church 328ft (100m) long. Marcel Aubert compares it with Villard de Honnecourt's famous plan, where the nave, transept, and choir are entirely surrounded by an aisle. This huge Cistercian church must have sheltered a large monastic community, since there are traces of altars on the east and west sides of the transepts.

The glory of Byland is its façade. "A beautiful trilobate portal with four archivolts carried on colonnettes; an almost round-headed door opened on to either aisle. Above the main door, a row of three high, pointed windows, surmounted by an enormous rose window that occupies the whole width of the façade between the buttresses. Only the lower portion remains, and all traces of tracery have disappeared" (Anselme Dimier).

At the crossing, and elsewhere, are the most beautiful pavements of glazed tiles anywhere to be seen in England. An interesting feature is the lay brothers' passageway. This segregated corridor, leading to the end of the church, has 35 little niches in the walls, possibly where the lay brothers left their work clothes before going to say the offices.

Left:

The two majestic piers of the chapter house.

Above:

The oculi and triple windows are, together with the corbels supporting engaged columns, the most characteristic features of the architecture of Cistercian churches. The façade of Byland manifestly reveals the signs of its affiliation with the Order.

Above, top and bottom:

• Grave slab of an abbot set in an English lawn.
• Reused stone (with a sketch carved on it).
• Church pavement.

CASAMARI

Casa Marii
location: near Veroli, Latium, Italy
founded: 1140, by Clairvaux
present use: Cistercian monastery, head of congregation
 (since 1929)

See also pp. 57, 91, 97.

Bibliography
Francesca DELL'ACQUA, 'Casamari', published in *Architettura cistercense, Fontenay e le abbazie in Italia dal 1120 al 1160*, Edizione Casamari, Certosa di Firenze, 1995.
Italie Sud, Hachette, 1997.

"Once they had mastered intersecting rib vaulting, Cistercian builders [...] carried the technique with them throughout the whole of Christendom. So dedicated were they to it, that they could well have been dubbed the missionaries of Gothic" (Marcel Aubert). There was no lonelier region than the mountains of Latium, between Rome and Naples, when the "White Monks" arrived at Casamari and started building the purest version of the newly mastered rib-vault technique. They were indeed missionaries of this innovative architecture when they built the cathedral at Sezze or the collegiate church of Sermoneta as well as countless other religious buildings throughout their area of influence.

The earliest settlement on this site was by Benedictine monks. Indeed, Casamari is not

Window from the first cloister, carved by a stone mason and inserted into a rubble wall by a still inexperienced craftsman.

Thirteenth-century narthex of the church. The pieces of fluted column displayed on the ground are Roman.

far away from Monte Cassino. But the Benedictines led a far from exemplary life and the Pope called in his beloved Cistercians to restore order to the house (1140). Their prestige was such that they were also asked to intervene in Sicily (1173) to calm conflicts between local feudal rulers. In gratitude for this, the Sicilian princes showered gifts upon the abbey. Thus it was that the monks of Casamari were able to embark on an ambitious building program.

The architects of Casamari were sent out from Clairvaux—almost certainly the same team that built Fossanova between 1186 and 1208. They were at work on the abbey from 1203 to 1217. The team went from one church to the next, progressing from groined vaults to intersecting rib vaults. Now, at the beginning of the thirteenth century, they built one of the abbey-cathedrals that marked the power of the Order. A much more recent church than many other Cistercian undertakings, at Casamari they incorporated a number of techniques that they had tried out earlier elsewhere, more especially in Clairvaux's daughter houses. The plan used here was obviously the same as Fontenay; the elevation of the nave includes a large main arcade, a middle storey opening into the roof level of the aisles, and a third storey of high-set windows as at Fountains. In the transept there are chapels to the east and west of the crossing as at Byland, while the ribs of the vaults rest directly on the corners of the dosserets as at Noirlac. The façade has two windows, including a central rose window with six oculi as at Hauterive. The porch is like Pontigny (only more refined) and the window panes are of alabaster like those in the abbey churches of Aragon. The list goes on.

The monks came back to live at Casamari in 1929. A museum and picture gallery have been opened in the monks' day-room. The refectory has been turned into a library. They could perhaps get rid of the enormous canopy that clutters the church choir, even though it was a present from Pope Clement XI, given to the abbey at a time when the practice of appointing commendatories, or absentee abbots, had brought the monks almost to ruin.

Facing page:
The cloister garth, south façade of the church and the monks' range.

Left:
Capitals in the cloister. The masons' desire to show off their skill and their sense of humor has triumphed over the rigorous Cistercian principles that permitted only the restrained decoration of a stylized waterleaf.

CHIARAVALLE DELLA COLOMBA

Colomba

location: near Fidenza (Emilia), Italy

founded: 1132, by Clairvaux

suppressed: 1810

present status: parish church and monastery of the Order of Cistercians of the Strict Observance since 1937

See also p. 91.

Bibliography

Anselme DIMIER, *L'Art cistercien*, vol. 2, La Pierre-qui-Vire, 1971.

Marcel AUBERT, *L'Architecture cistercienne en France*, Vanoest, 1947.

The Clairvaux monks who came to set up the abbey called the new monastery *Chiara Valle* in homage to the mother house. There is no question of doubt here. Both the plan and the spiritual regime were strictly inspired by St. Bernard, at least until 1444, when it fell under commendatory (absentee) abbots, and decadence set in.

After its closure in 1810—at a time when relations between Napoleon and Pope Pius VII had worsened—the abbey was occupied by neighboring villagers. The church was turned into the local parish church as we can still see from the organ, pews, and pulpit that clutter up the building. Outside the walls, the land is neglected with many fields lying fallow and the main highway to Rome running just 300 yards (300m) away and making a terrible din! But thanks to the tower, motorists can easily spot the silhouette of the abbey!

Nonetheless, in medieval times Chiaravalle was a flourishing place with numerous monks. In the transept of the abbey church there were three chapels to the east and west of each crossing and a further two chapels at the end of the transept. This unusual layout, which is also found at Pontigny, provides a clear indication of the sizeable number of choir monks who lived there.

The abbey was able to employ excellent craftsmen. The brick buildings are often enlivened by the addition of (white) ashlar. In the same fashion, the wide semi-circular arcades in the nave alternate brick and white stone. A veritable rustic Vézelay! The round-headed doorway to the church is decorated in a similar manner. The large rose window on the façade is set in a circle of white stone which is echoed,

just under the roof, by a sloping cornice with small arches on a white background.

The Gothic cloister (some describe it as Lombardo-Gothic, and why not?) opens into the inner courtyard through eight bays of semi-circular arches grouped in fours, supported by small paired columns in Verona marble whose capitals are decorated with foliage. The paving is in brick and the vaults are reinforced with sturdy buttresses.

The chapter house is remarkable because of the contrast between its Cistercian simplicity and the exuberance of its façade overlooking the cloister. There are also traces of Moorish influence in the way it is decorated. Once again, it is built in red brick and white stone.

Left:

Knot tying the four columns in the south-east corner of the cloister. This masterpiece of the stone mason is found in a number of abbeys, particularly in Bohemia. Its symbolic meaning is uncertain.

Above:

Cloister garth. The oculi in the monks' dormitory are typical of the traditional architecture of the Cistercians. Here they reinforce the appearance of a "citadel of the faith" that every Cistercian abbey was supposed to represent.

*Leaf decoration
(cloister).*

Left:
Chapel in the north transept: St. Bernard as thaumaturge.

Below left:
Night stair (south transept)

Below right:
Opening of the chapter house onto the east walk of the cloister. "Oriental" style.

CHIARAVALLE MILANESE

Clara Vallis

location: Rogoredo, near Milan (Lombardy), Italy

founded: 1135, by Clairvaux

suppressed: 1798

present status: abbey of the Order of Cistercians of Common Observance (since 1952)

See also p. 82.

Bibliography
Commission d'historie de l'Ordre de Cîteaux, *Saint Bernard*, Alsatia, Paris, 1953.
Silvia NOCENTINI, *Chiaravalle di Milano*, in *Architettura Cistercense, Fontenay e le abbazie in Italia dal 1120 al 1160*, Edizione Casamari, Certosa di Firenze, 1995.
Italie, Nord et Centre, Hachette, 1990.
P. ANGELO and M. CASSIN, *L'Abbazia di Chiaravalle*, Moneta, Milan, 1979.

During the second half of the nineteenth century, railroad construction companies never hesitated to demolish any historic monuments that happened to be inconveniently located in the path of their advancing tracks. Cistercian abbeys paid a heavy toll: the church of Freistroff in Lorraine was knocked down and the park surrounding the abbot's palace at Villers-en-Brabant was sliced in two. At Chiaravalle the great cloister was replaced by the Milan-Genoa line, in spite of the fact that the part of the abbey in question had been designed by the famous architect Bramante, responsible for the first design of St. Peters, Rome.

The foundation of Chiaravalle came about under the best possible auspices. It was none other than Bernard of Clairvaux himself who established the abbey boundaries. Already a famous abbot, he had come to take part in the Council of Pisa (June 1135) visiting Milan at the same time. As he approached the city, the entire populace rushed out to greet him. The crowd was jubilant when a madman was healed. The abbot of Clairvaux preached to the people. He was shocked by the luxury of the town's churches, and advocated simplicity in both art and dress. In response to popular enthusiasm, the local city councilors offered him the archbishop's throne. He turned it down and left town with just a few monks to set up a new abbey in the middle of the marshland on the outskirts of Milan (22 July 1135).

The brick-built abbey that survives today is a lovely example of early Piedmontese Gothic, typical of the traditional plan devised by St. Bernard. There is also an interesting succession of decorative additions from later centuries in the pre-Baroque spirit. Firstly, there is a tower rising above the transept crossing. This is a five-storey polygonal construction which was built (starting in 1290) by F. Pecorari. Here we can see the influence of the Torrazzo tower in Cremona and an echo of another brick tower at Saint-Sernin, Toulouse. Then there are the frescos painted on the white plaster of the church; also those of the cupola, attributed to the Maestro della Coronazione. The nave frescos are attributed to a family of fresco painters of Flemish origin. The frescos on the night stairs were painted by Bernardino Luini, one of Leonardo da Vinci's pupils. Finally there are the walnut choir-stalls (1645) with carvings by Caravaglia showing scenes from the life of St. Bernard. Thus the Italian Cistercians were already bringing in the best artists of the day, just as the German and Austrian Cistercians would do at the height of the Baroque period.

Facing page, bottom:
South transept and night stair.

Left:
The small and large bell-towers.

Above:
Cistercian simplicity despite the elegant Lombard frieze. The heavy brick buttresses suggest a poor mastery of the art of building.

CÎTEAUX

Cistercium (Novum monasterium)
location: Saint-Nicolas-lès-Cîteaux (Côte-d'Or), France
founded: 1098
dissolved: 1791 (French Revolution)
present use: monastery of the Order of Cistercians of the Strict Observance (Trappists)

Bibliography
Auguste VINCENT, *Toponymie de la France*, Montfort, Brienne, 1984.
Louis DEROY and Marianne MULON, *Dictionnaire des noms des lieux*, Le Robert, Paris, 1992.
Denis OUAILLARBOUROU, "La restructuration de l'église de Cîteaux", in *Liturgie*, 1996.

"In this place stood the first church of Cîteaux, consecrated 18 November 1106 by the bishop of Chalon, where the founding fathers Alberic and Stephen, together with St. Bernard, devoted themselves to prayer." The commemorative plaque makes it clear: nothing remains of the abbey where the Cistercian adventure started. The monks who returned to Cîteaux in 1898, eight centuries after the founding of the monastery by Robert of Molesme, found no remnant of the old monastery of the first Cistercians. They lived in an immense eighteenth-century building, of no great architectural interest, even though it was designed by the architect Lenoir. On the occasion of the ninth centenary of the founding of the abbey, work began on the restoration of the only two parts of interest remaining from the past: the library, dating from the fifteenth century, built above one of the sides of the cloister of the monastic copyists, and the former definitory, where the monks whose job it was to prepare and execute the decisions of the General Chapter worked. These two reminders of the grandeur of the Order have become part of a "discovery tour" of the site, laid out outside the monastic enclave. It cannot be easy to live in a "wilderness" when it is also a place of such historic significance, attracting crowds of pilgrims and tourists.

The monks of Cîteaux similarly carried out alterations to their church to celebrate, on 21 March 1998, the anniversary of the arrival of Robert of Molesme at the site. Such an initiative is not unusual: the majority of "living" monasteries today occupy monastic buildings put up in the nineteenth or early twentieth centuries according to the architectural canons of the day. It was a courageous initiative for all that, because of the symbolic importance of Cîteaux. It meant that the community, the master of works and his architect had a certain moral obligation to produce something exceptional, from respect for the past and for the edification of future generations. Perhaps the task was too great. Of all the work undertaken, one of the most taxing was the restoration of Cent Fons. The spring is some seven miles (10 km) from Cîteaux, and the water, diverted into channels in the thirteenth century by the monks, still flows down to the walls of the abbey. The well-drained land is no longer marshy as it once was, in the period when the monastery site almost acquired the name of *cistellum*, consecrated in legend as the name of the famous waterleaf sculpted on Cistercian capitals, when in fact it was called *cistercium* ("bread basket"). The mistake in transcription by a copyist created a particularly poetic relationship between Cîteaux and the water that can be found running through every Cistercian abbey.

CISTERCIANS TODAY

Since 1892 two separate Cistercian Orders have been in existence, each with its Abbot General in Rome, its own General Chapter, constitution, and organization. This split goes back to the 18th century and has created different styles of monastic life. In France the Order of Cistercians of the Common Observance (OCCO) is represented by the community at Lérins (see case study on this abbey). As for the Order of Cistercians of the Strict Observance (OCSO), since 1962 it has no longer been governed by the Abbot of Cîteaux as Vicar General. As in the past, the abbeys have agreed to come under the control of an "immediate father", but they are independent enough to be able to decide their own spiritual and material practices (timetable, work, etc.). Today, these "Trappists" comprise some 3,000 monks in 91 "abbeys" and around 2,000 nuns in 60 convents (Trappistines, together with three associated Orders, the Bernardines of Esquesmes, those of Oudenaarde, and those of the Suisse Romande). Sixteen Trappist abbeys are to be found in France, seven of them on historic sites: Acey, Aiguebelle, Cîteaux, Melleray, Sept Fons, Tamié, and La Trappe.

Bibliography
Marcel PACAUT, *Les Moines blancs*, Fayard, Paris, 1993.
La Vie cistercienne hier et aujourd'hui, Cerf-Zodiaque, Paris, 1998.

Above:
The definitory.

Left:
General view of the fifteenth-century library and eighteenth-century definitory. "At Cîteaux there are scarcely any ruins! An ugly building. A few precarious Gothic bays! But all around in the great woods is silence. The fields are calm and the horizon at peace." Gaston Roupnel, *La Bourgogne.*

Facing page, bottom:
The "Burgundian" bricks of the library.

CLAIRVAUX

Clara Vallis

location: Ville-sous-La-Ferté (Aube) Champagne-Ardennes region, France

founded: 1115 (one of the "first four daughters") by Cîteaux

suppressed: 1791 (property seized by the state)

present use: Prison

Bibliography
Histoire de Clairvaux, Conference Proceedings (June 1990), Bar-sur-Aube, 1991.

Straddling the borders of Burgundy and Champagne like a monk's habit, the ancient forest of Gaul still covers the hills and valleys that buttress the Langres plateau. It is a silent land.

It was here that Bernard of Fontaine came to open up the clearing of Val d'Absinthe (Wormwood), so called in reference to the life of bitterness that he came here to seek (Revelation of St. John the Divine, 8:11). Less than forty years later, at the death of the famous abbot (20 August 1153), the abbey consisted of 800 monks and lay brothers. Sixty-nine monasteries and their hundred dependent monasteries depended on Clairvaux.

In a quarter of a century Bernard of Clairvaux had created a political and religious capital, acting as arbitrator between kings and lords, creating bishops and popes, reigning over dogma and faith. Clairvaux was never again to have such a great influence. Nevertheless, although the abbey had to face all the same vicissitudes that others experienced from the fourteenth century onwards, it maintained a constant economic development, its wealth never drained by a beneficed abbot holding the abbey in commendam. In the eighteenth century it became one of the most powerful institutions of the Ancien Régime.

Clairvaux survived the Revolution without too much damage. Under the Empire, the abbey was turned into a prison in 1808. This too became a famous institution, symbolic of the penitential world and witness to many a drama. The church, perhaps the most beautiful of the Cistercian Order, was doomed to be sold as a quarry for building stone in 1812.

Clairvaux remains a mythical place, no doubt because of the continuity between the voluntary enclosure of the monks, and that imposed on prisoners. A place of memories, Clairvaux is today a place of mystery with its 75 acres (30ha) enclosed by interminable high walls, walls within walls, preventing any view of the remains of the splendors of the past.

The Ministry of Justice has handed over the majority of the historic buildings, and these are now undergoing a first campaign of restoration. It has built a modern prison in the former orchard of the abbey. This has made it possible for the Association for the Renaissance of Clairvaux to organize visits to the site, while obeying the conditions of security necessary, given the close proximity of this major prison. The increasing number of visitors has encouraged the opening of a visitors' center in the fifteenth-century guest house for women (*hostellerie des dames*), which stands outside both the monastic and the prison complex. It will, nevertheless, be many years before the prison and the old abbey, each on its grassy site, can coexist comfortably in the Val d'Absinthe.

Of Clairvaux I (the *Monasterium vetus*) there remain only a few stretches of the walls of the fishponds, still supplied from the spring. Excavations of the site would yield valuable information about the early years of the monastery and the life of the pioneer monks.

Clairvaux II was the response to the considerable increase in the size of the abbey. The years 1135 to 1145 saw the construction of the first Cistercian abbey to be built according to the functional program laid down by Bernard of Clairvaux and his cellarers, Geoffrey of Ainai and Achard. The church of Clairvaux II was built in two stages. In the year the abbot died it consisted of an aisled nave of eleven bays, a

transept with four rectangular chapels and a square-ended east end, the whole covered with a Romanesque vault. In the period between the death of the abbot and his canonization the church was given an apse and ambulatory with nine radiating chapels, and a new rib-vaulted roof. A large reliquary was installed for the body of the great saint. Of this second abbey, there remains today only the lay brothers' range, an archetype of architecture in the Cistercian spirit.

Clairvaux III is an expression of the wealth of the abbey in the eighteenth century, by now a great landowner and possessor of many forges. The church and the lay brothers' range are preserved, but the stables in the main courtyard and men's guest-house have been rebuilt. A large classical cloister unites the refectory, living quarters, and the library. Majestic and severe, it reminds us that Clairvaux was one of the upholders of Strict Observance in the seventeenth century.

Clairvaux has been a prison since 1808. The abbey can still be discerned beneath the stone infilling, the path round the battlements, the watchtowers and the long corridors interrupted at intervals by grills. In Blanqui's lock-up it is still possible to see a column from the monks' day-room. The long history of the prison has given historians and sociologists a fertile area for investigation, both into the evolution of styles of incarceration (dormitories, then "chicken coops", then cells), and into the famous prisoners who were incarcerated here—from Communards to members of the Resistance, from Kropotkin to Charles Maurras.

Indeed, Clairvaux—with its history, and the architecture that, with a surge of excitement, we can still discover today—forces us to reflect on the meaning of freedom.

Top:
General view of the monastic town of Clairvaux with its 7.5 acres (3ha) enclosed within a wall more than two miles (3km) long.

Above:
Clairvaux Prison (beneath the great eighteenth-century cloister).

Lay brothers' range of Clairvaux II (c. 1150). The half-buried undercroft (used as a refectory on the south side). Archeological investigations show that the (Gothic) vault of rounded arches may have been made at the end of the building period, after the (Romanesque) pointed groin vault of the storey above.

...rothers' range of ...aux II (c. 1150). ...y brothers' ...itory (see also photo p. 30). Side view looking towards the west wall (unrestored windows from the nineteenth century) of a central bay. The dormitory of three aisles has twelve bays over a length of almost 260 feet (80m).

DUNBRODY

Dun Broith, Portres S. Mariae

location: Dunbrody Abbey (Co. Wexford), Republic of Ireland

founded:, 1182, by St Mary's, Dublin (filiation of Clairvaux)

dissolved: 1536 (Act of Dissolution)

present status: ruins

The guidebooks say that "Dunbrody is one of the most beautiful abbeys in Ireland". And what a wonderful country Ireland is, when visitors wishing to visit the site still have to go and collect the keys from the nearest cottage!

The ruins of Dunbrody lie on a bend in the River Barrow which in the Middle Ages was a major maritime transport route, since its neighbor, the ancient city of New Ross, was for a long while the biggest port on the island of Ireland. In 1175 Hervé de Montmorency donated the Dunbrody lands to the English abbey of Buildwas, which sent out a lay brother to test the site. His report, however, was unfavorable and Buildwas turned the gift down. The property was then offered to St. Mary's Dublin, which opened the "daughter house" in 1182. But the abbey got off to a bad start and had already been partly abandoned by 1536 when, thanks to the Act of Dissolution, Sir Osborne Etchingham built his Tudor manor house in the south transept of the church.

All that remains today is the outer wall of the conventual quadrangle and the tower at the transept crossing. The abbey looks far more like a stronghold with a keep and bailey. Indeed, the dark transepts of the church would have made excellent little forts! In Ireland, the experts talk about the "cavernous transepts of Dunbrody". In the church itself (1210–40), the beautiful triplet in the rectangular east end and the customary night stair have survived. There are also a number of unusual features on the north side of the nave elevation: very wide arches support a wall pierced by windows above the piers, which breaks the symmetry. One of the windows is off-center, the other is twinned, and no clear date has been ascribed to them. These openings seem to owe more to chance than necessity, which always makes for interesting, but never satisfying, architecture.

Facing page, above:
• *Night stair.*
• *South aisle of the church (walled-up transept).*
• *Cloister arcading.*

Left:
Crossing.

Facing page, below:
• *The nave, the tower over the crossing and the square east end.*
• *The monks' door, now walled-up (south side of the church)*

Bibliography
Roger STALLEY, *The Cistercian Monasteries of Ireland*, Yale University Press, London, 1987.

DUNDRENNAN

Dundrena

location: near Rerrick (Kirkcudbrightshire), Scotland

founded: 1142, by Rievaulx (filiation of Clairvaux)

dissolved: Dissolution of 1538

present status: ruins

See also p. 124.

Bibliography
Henry THOROLD, *The Ruined Abbeys of England, Wales and Scotland*, Harper Collins, London, 1993.
J. S. RICHARDSON, *Dundrennan Abbey*, Historic Scotland, 1994.

Do fortunate abbeys have no history? It does in fact appear that despite its name, which means Thorny Hill, Dundrennan never encountered any serious vicissitudes during its long years of existence, even though Scotland never ceased to be torn by the fighting between the new local monarchy and its over-ambitious or over-independent vassals or against the kings of England, always anxious to annex Scotland and absorb it into their own crown.

The abbey was founded in 1142 by King David I (1124–53). At that time there was a truce between Scotland and England during which King David invited monks up from Rielvaux. Almost five centuries later, in 1591, after the abbey had been dissolved, Scotland went through some of the darkest days in its history. Elizabeth I had supported the Protestant revolt against Mary Stuart whom she had executed in 1587. The way was open for James VI of Scotland to become James I of England and Scotland—and for Henry VIII's old Act of Dissolution to be implemented at Dundrennan.

All that remains of the twelfth-century Gothic abbey is the transept, part of the choir (but without the east end), and the truly beautiful thirteenth-century façade of the chapter house. The cloister foundations frame a well-groomed lawn, now a public garden. Dundrennan itself looks just like a magnificent sculpture set in the midst of the most lovely countryside.

Facing page, above:
North wall of the choir triforium.

Facing page, below:
Transept pillar.

Left:
In monastic times the enclosing wall hid the beautiful landscape around the abbey.

FLARAN

Flaranum

location: Vallence-sur-Baïse (Gers), Midi-Pyrénées region, France

founded: 1151, by Escaladieu (filiation of Morimond)

dissolved: 1791 (French Revolution)

present use: regional cultural center

See also pp. 55, 91

Bibliography
Marcel AUBERT, *L'Architecture cistercienne en France*, Vanoest, Paris, 1947. Marcel DURLIAT, *L'Abbaye de Flaran*, Sud-Ouest, Bordeaux, 1994. J. F. LANGEAU and A. GARCIA, *Flaran, ancienne abbaye Notre-Dame*, in Anciennes abbayes en Midi Pyrénées, Addoc, Tarbes, 1991.

In recent years Flaran Abbey has been reliving a cultural life linked to its religious past. It has, in fact, become a focal point in one of rural France's traditional districts, in the heart of the Gers department, renowned for its Armagnac and walled towns.

As soon as the Cistercians from Escaladieu got here in 1151 they started reclaiming land along the River Baïse that had been given to them by local lords. This entailed regulating the flow of the river, so their first task was to dig a diversion canal. The abbey itself was subsequently built on an artificial island

after the first generations of monks, who were fated to live in huts, had collected enough gifts and made sufficient savings from the sale of surplus agricultural products to be able to pay the master craftsmen and workers needed to get large-scale building works under way. It was therefore the second abbot, Étienne, who gave the go-ahead in 1180. Construction took about thirty years to complete.

In the provinces of northern France, the Cistercians were already masters of the intersecting rib vault. This technique, however, had not yet filtered down to the southern provinces. In essence therefore the architecture of Flaran, like its three provincial sisters, was still Romanesque.

Despite turmoils throughout its history, the abbey has managed to preserve nearly all the buildings ever constructed. Of course, it was pillaged by bands of soldiers during the Hundred Years' War (1426), suffered at the hands of fanatical Protestants during the wars

of religion (1569), and was run into the ground by absentee abbots, and its shrunken monastic communities were unable to maintain the buildings in good condition. It was then acquired by the nation (1791) for the sole purpose of asset stripping even at the cost of total destruction. Despite all this, when the abbey was given to the Gers département to administer in 1972 it still represented one of the rare examples of what a Cistercian abbey must have been like at the end of the twelfth century.

The sobriety of the church was in accordance with the spirit of Cîteaux. It has a pleasing elevation with a short three-bay over which rises a pointed tunnel vault supported by three transverse arches. These are supported on shafts resting on corbels elevated 13ft (4m) off the ground so as to reduce the amount of space they occupy. Beyond the crossing,

which is rib vaulted, the pointed tunnel vault extends into the apse as a semi-dome. The three windows that illuminate the sanctuary emphasize the masonry in light-colored stone. Both the south aisle and the transept are still Romanesque, while the north aisle is rib vaulted in order to contain the height of the floor above, which is connected to the nave by means of a narrow staircase built inside the thickness of the wall. The entrance to the stair is half-way up the wall. It was here that the abbey records must have been kept. In the Middle Ages the charters that you possessed (whether real or forged) were the only means of proving rights of any kind, however fundamental to the organization of society.

Since the tower originally planned for the transept crossing was never built, the outside of Flaran Abbey is today as squat and lacking in ostentation as ever it was. The main front is

simple a wall with two fairly plain windows and an oculus. There is no tympanum over the door while two functional buttresses mark the line of the arcades inside. The east end is more attractive, with its five apses. Once more, however, the Lombard band decoration is very plain as is the half-timbered upper part of the sanctuary apse.

Montmorency's Protestant troops destroyed three of the cloister walks. These have been

reconstructed in a simple fashion which suits the place well.

The fourth walk was nearly lost in 1913. The stones had already been numbered and the purchaser "a Parisian antique dealer with a shop in New York" (J.-F. Lagneau) was ready to hand over the money. A local society managed to thwart this last misadventure that the seductive, yet absurd, collectors' passion for cloisters could have caused!

What draws people back to Flaran is that its chapter house is intact. Based on a square plan, four marble columns (one red, one black and the other two white—all doubtless taken from some earlier place of worship in the area) divide into nine Gothic vaults that are charmingly primitive. "The roll-molded ribs penetrating the vaults taper away between the square transverse ribs resting on corbels set in the walls or on shafts. The capitals are decorated with long, flat foliage and the

abacus is cruciform in plan." (Marcel Aubert). The chapter house is lit from the east by plain windows and three bays—one door and two large richly-molded arched windows—open on to the cloister. The sacristy and tiny library were built by the same master mason and are both bigger and more beautiful than the plan laid down by St. Bernard's Rule.

Apart from visits to the buildings themselves, Flaran also organizes other activities aimed at letting people know more about the Cistercians and the surrounding region. Amongst other things, the cultural center at Flaran is wisely playing a part in the renewed interest in the historical study of the Cistercian world. Since their launch in 1979 by the late Charles Higounet, International History Days once a year bring together specialists on the subject, who produce much respected work.

Facing page, above:
The chapter house.

Facing page, below:
Boss in the north aisle.

Left:
The north aisle and
monks' door, the north
transept and night stair,
from the nave.

North aisle of the church.

Side chapels (with rounded apses) in the north transept.

FONTENAY

Fontanetum

location: Marmagne (Côte-d'Or), Burgundy, France

founded: 1119, by Clairvaux

suppressed: 1791 (French Revolution)

present status: Privately owned

See also pp. 12, 34-39, 47, 50-52, 60, 69, 74, 78-81, 85, 88, 104, 109, 113, 135.

Bibliography
Abbé CORBOLIN, *Monographie de Fontenay*, Cîteaux, 1882.
Gérard de CHAMPEAUX and Dom Sébastien STERCKX, *Introduction au monde des symboles*, Zodiaque, 1980.

Angels must have stood round the cradle at the birth of Fontenay. This beloved daughter of Bernard of Clairvaux was singled out for particular attention. He turned it into a family business by naming his paternal uncle, Godefroy de Rochetaillé, as first abbot, to which post he was succeeded by his nephew Guillaume de Spiriaco. The site chosen belonged to Bernard's maternal uncle, Raynard de Montbard. This branch of the family enjoyed a comfortable fortune and contributed on several occasions to the building work, which explains both the quality and the rapidity of the construction. For the abbot of Clairvaux—that great "multinational " builder—the abbey of Fontenay was to be the demonstration model. It was the first to be finished, and the one that adhered most closely to the Bernardine plan and the spirit of Cîteaux. To crown the success of this achievement, the consecration of the church was marked by a special ceremony, on 21 September 1147. Monographs of the nineteenth century continued to perpetuate the legendary accounts of the scene: "The church is crowded with the people that have flocked in from all around. The vassals, the abbey laborers, are at the back, the aisles are full of women and children on their knees, three hundred White Monks in the nave. The abbot of Clairvaux has just spoken, eloquent as always. This man, whom the historians were to call arbiter of kings and people, prostrates himself on the stone floor of the sanctuary. Immediately an old man dressed in white gets up. He wears a tiara, he is one of the successors of St. Peter, Eugenius III, formerly a monk of Clairvaux. Around him stand ten white-bearded men, dressed in red, cardinals; to the right, kneeling, are eight bishops; to the

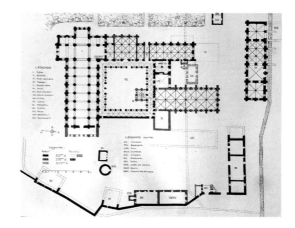

left, also kneeling, all the abbots of Cîteaux, with miters and crosiers like bishops; along the apse walls, on either side of the choir, all the ancient Burgundian nobility, fully armed, who will fall and be extinguished in the Crusades."

Fontenay has preserved almost all its original buildings. In 1359 the English pillaged it but left it intact. Two centuries later, when it was held *in commendam*, it suffered neglect, but only the thirteenth-century refectory collapsed from lack of upkeep. In the nineteenth century it was bought up and used as a factory, but not for building stone. Since 1820 it has remained in the hands of the same family. Louis Élie de Montgolfier and his father-in-law Marc Seguin, inventor of the first locomotives, transformed the abbey into a paper mill. In this century, their descendants have taken on the restoration of the historic buildings and their surroundings with the same energy and passion. Fontenay has been designated a UNESCO World Heritage site.

The abbey represents one of the most complete and most perfect examples of monastic architecture from the height of the Romanesque period. The *raison d'être* of the Roman-

Above:
General view from the
park, to the east of the
abbey. The façades are
as harmonious as a score

by J. S. Bach: the
serenity of the monks'
buildings with its
identical openings,
regularly spaced in a

subtle binary pattern;
the counterpoint of the
east end of the church
with its verticality
echoed in the gable of

the triumphal arch.

Following double spread:
The cloister from the
chapter house.

ply the windows without weakening the building. There were nothing accidental about the number of windows for each set of openings to the light. There were invariably three, four, or five. The three lights in the apse corresponded to the Trinity, to the three days Christ was entombed, the three ages of the Jewish people, and to the three meanings of the Scriptures (historical, allegorical, and moral). Four is the number of the elements, the seasons, the rivers of Paradise, the points of the compass, the Evangelists, and, most importantly for Bernard of Clairvaux, the dimensions of God, "who is at one and the same time length, breadth, height, and depth" (*On Consideration*, V.27). Five recalls not only the esotericism of the Cabala and its five-pointed star, but also refers to the books of Moses, and the dimensions of man for Hildegarde of Bingen. Three plus three in the east end gives six, the number of days of the Creation. Three plus four at the entrance to the church makes seven, the number of the sacraments, while three times four gives twelve, the number of the apostles and the number of monks needed to found an abbey. In this way, numbers became "instruments of meditation", as the light flowed through the windows, fixing their image of the screen of the walls. This light is broken by the rhythm of the nave piers (a square core, with a pilaster on the nave side and two lateral half-shafts with waterleaf capitals of an extreme plainness) as they mark the progression up to the altar.

The presence of the "four elements" can be strongly felt at Fontenay. Earth is recalled in the nearby iron mine, or the humus slowly forming in the immense forest . Fire is the forge, part of the abbey where wood was consumed to produce metal. Water is all around, flowing through the site, as the light (Air) flows through the abbey buildings. These "four elements", always present in the Cistercian world, express a pre-Franciscan pantheism. Bernard of Clairvaux writes more than once in his letters: "We learn more in the woods than we do from books. The trees and the rocks will teach you things you cannot learn elsewhere." (Letter 106)

Above:
The cloister at the corner of the north and the east walks. The central pier is surrounded by twin columns.

Facing page:
Bull of Pope Alexander III (1168) confirming Fontenay's possessions and privileges.

esque style, according to André Malraux, was to "transform signs and symbols, giving them life through the manifestation of a spiritual truth that the universe reveals unconsciously, and which it is man's duty to bring to light". There is a whole literature—excessive perhaps—on the subject of the symbolism of medieval architecture, in which all the signs, for those who can interpret them, reveal the divine mystery. It would appear that the symbolism of number was the one most frequently used in the Middle Ages, following the neoplatonic tradition where numbers translate a "world system". For medieval man, God, the perfect being, obviously possessed the science of numbers. Thus the architects of Fontenay, sufficiently masters of building techniques, were able to multi-

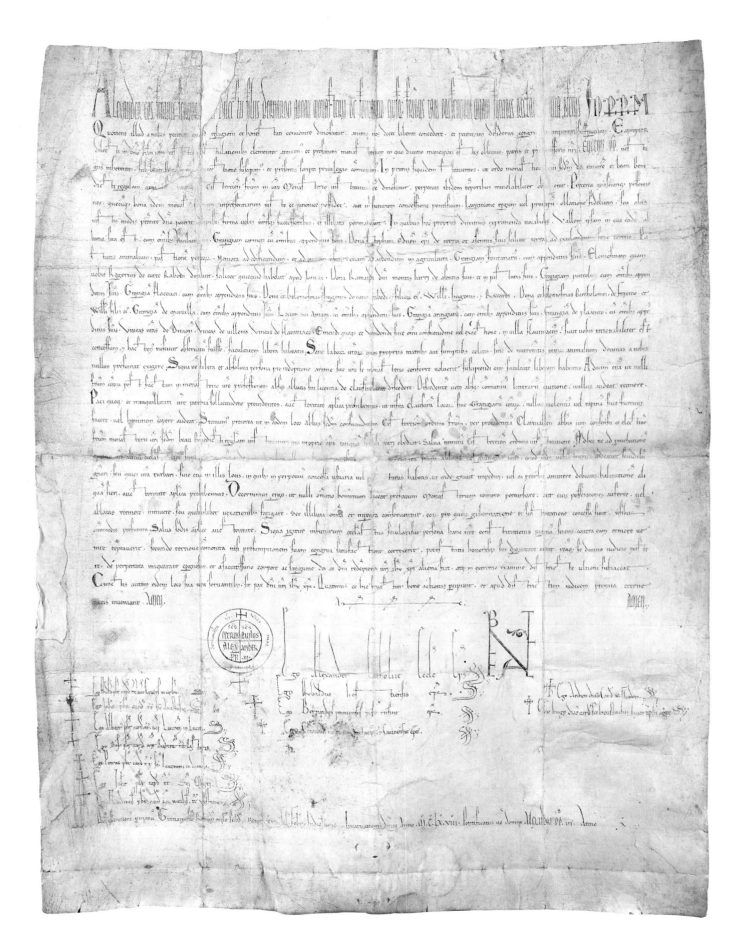

The nave at noon in spring. Night has been swallowed up by the victory of the dawn, the darkness and shadows have disappeared and the true light fills the space, above, below, within, for we are already filled with the morning of His mercy. *Bernard of Clairvaux,* Nativity 3.

St. Bernard's spring and lake. At Fontenay water is everywhere, held back by dams (at the lake) or channeled in the park. It drove the forge and the mill, supplied the kitchens and the lavatorium, and provided ponds for the carp that provided food for the monks' meatless meals.

FONTFROIDE

Fons Frigidus

location: Narbonne (Aude), Languedoc, France

founded: 1146, by Grandselve (filiation of Clairvaux)

dissolved: 1791 (French Revolution)

present status: privately owned; open to the public

See also pp. 47, 60, 63, 79, 106, 113, 123, 126.

Bibliography
Marcel AUBERT, *L'Architecture cistercienne en France*, Vanoest, Paris, 1947.
Viollet-le-DUC, *Dictionnaire de l'Architecture française du XIe au XVIe siècle*, vol. iii (p. 426).
Henri FOCILLON, *Art d'Occident*, Le Moyen Age roman et gothique, Armand Colin, Paris, 1963.
Anselme DIMIER, *L'Art cistercien*, vol. iii, Zodiaque, La Pierre-qui-Vire, 1971.
Nicolas d'ANDOQUE and André MELE, *Abbaye de Fontfroide*, Editions Gaud, Moisenay, 1966.

What can you say about Fontfroide? A few hours' hike up into the Corbières, the limestone foothills of the Pyrenees, was once enough to cut the abbey off completely from the "sound and fury of the world". Even today, when you come to the end of the road and find Fontfroide, it seems "tucked into the hollow of the hills", as if frozen in time...

Nevertheless, some kind of tension within the abbey itself seems to keep the site awake and adds a dimension of expectancy and mystery to its discovery. Can this be the *genius loci* which the weight and might of history has been unable to extinguish? Even the most perfect day here can be brutally interrupted by the noise and fury of mountain streams suddenly flooding, of storms lashing the place or violent winds fanning fires up until they almost lick the abbey walls.

On the other hand, the church at Fontfroide, with its wonderful acoustics, plays host to concerts of Gregorian chant that fill the space with an absolute sense of peace.

Monks first came to Fontfroide in June 1093, thanks to Aymeric II of Narbonne. The earliest here were hermits who then gathered to form a community (doubtless Benedictine) in 1118. From 1144 this grew close to the Grandselve under Gérard de Sales (a disciple of Robert d'Arbrissel, who founded Fontevrault). Then in 1146 Fontfroide became affiliated to the Order of Cîteaux. Bernard of Clairvaux went to Languedoc in 1145 to preach against the apostate monk Henri de Lausanne. He did not get very far with that, but his visit did engender new daughter abbeys. Fontfroide, which came less than four years later, was in turn to found Poblet, the most famous abbey of Catalonia.

The abbey was "a citadel of orthodoxy" in the heart of territory under the influence of Aragon and its liberal attitude to the Catharist sect. Fontfroide was therefore in the front line in the fight against heresy. When Pope Innocent III decided to wipe out the Manicheaens, he chose two monks from Fontfroide as his legates. One of them, Pierre de Castelnau, died at the hands of an assassin. It was a former abbot of Fontfroide, then abbot of Cîteaux, who led the bloody crusade against the Albigensians. Even today, the abbey is still generally thought of as the bastion of the Catholic faith that was aligned against the Catharist forces of Montségur or Quéribus.

The extent of the abbey's influence was marked a century later by the eminent roles played by two of its abbots. Arnaud Nouvel was made a Counselor to Pope Clement V, while Jacques Fournier became pope under the name of Benedict XII. During the same period, Fontfroide grew to be one of the richest abbeys within the Order with 25 farmsteads, to which Foncalvy bears splendid witness. Its real strength lay not in its wines but in stock rearing. Thanks to its rights of transhumance with Aragon, by 1341 it had herds of over 20,000 animals.

Fontfroide managed not only to survive the trials of absentee abbots but actually to do well out of them. Eighteenth-century abbots continued embellishing the monastery but by this time there were not many monks left. Those who were there, however, still enjoyed substantial revenues which they used to live in ostentatious luxury (the abbey accounts show that the cook's wages were higher than the alms given to *the shameful poor*). During the French Revolution the City of Narbonne turned the abbey into a hospice, a decision which preserved it almost

Like the ancient monastery of St. Catherine nestling in the mountain valleys of *Sinai, Fontfroide is hidden in the heart of the Corbière hills, in an uninhabited landscape.* For the Lord's portion is His people … He found him in a desert land, and in the waste howling wilderness." *Deuteronomy, 32:9–10.* (The "Song of Moses").

Right:
The west front, very weathered, but still majestic. Two windows and an oculus refer as always to the Trinity. A single door with a tympanum carved with three bas-reliefs, including a beautiful crucifixion. This door was only opened to receive the mortal remains of the viscounts of Narbonne and other benefactors of the abbey buried at Fontfroide.

Facing page:
The fourteenth-century tower seen through the Romanesque arcades of the west walk of the cloister.

intact. By 1843, Mérimée and Viollet-le-Duc had managed to get the abbey listed. Indeed between 1858 and 1901 a Cistercian community from Sénanque was allowed to move back in. But the state passed a law against congregations and put the abbey up for sale once more. This time it caught the fancy of an American art lover who had the idea of moving the cloister to New York. Gustave Fayet and his wife Madeleine d'Andoque, also art lovers but in their case being of solid Languedoc stock, bought the abbey themselves to save it from being shipped abroad. They turned Fontfroide into an artistic Mecca which attracted famous painters and great musicians. According to Frédéric Van Der Meer, they "restored the abbey in sumptuous fashion".

You need to visit Fontfroide time and time again since it is less easy to decipher than Fontenay, even though it adhered to St. Bernard's plan. It is also more complex than Le Thoronet owing to additions made by abbots during the seventeenth and eighteenth centuries. The abbey church, the cloister (twelfth century) and the chapter house (from the twelfth to the fourteenth centuries) deserve special attention.

Let Henri Focillon describe the place. "At first the general structure of Fontfroide church seems faithfully to follow the Fontenay model. The nave has a Gothic barrel-vaulted ceiling with a string-course of Burgundian type at the springing of the vault. But the piers reveal an admirable and novel interpretation of the Cistercian theme of interrupted supports. The body of the pier, with its engaged columns, of composite type. It appears to be suspended above the level of the ground, from which it is separated by a huge polygonal mass of masonry, totally devoid of decoration apart from a thick quarter-round on the upper part. In the nave, the paired columns are corbelled out from this mass of masonry, the articulation being emphasized by console brackets. The effect is that between the floor and the bases, a powerful abstract area is created, where bare plinths appear to have no other function but to jack up the whole system, the entire church, into the air."

In the last century Viollet-le-Duc already demonstrated the architectural prowess of the

Cistercian master builders. "Even though the plan used (in the cloister) at Fontfroide is, in principal, the same as that used in the cloister at Fontenay, the architectural details are far richer: the archivolts are molded, as are the round windows in the tympana of each bay; finely carved capitals in the arcade; thanks to the materials used, the slender columns are textured and stand out from the rest of the building..."

Viollet-le-Duc also underlined the role that the round windows of the tympana played in lighting the chapter house. This was an area of vital importance to communal life, which is

here treated with real elegance. "The roll-molded ribs with their long voussoirs penetrate the thickness of the vault and taper away between the square transverse ribs. Diagonal and transverse ribs rest on four slender detached marble columns, whose concave capitals are decorated with two rows of flat foliage, and on marble shafts (rather than the usual corbels) rising from on the upper step of a bench which runs all the way round the room." This chapter house was built at the same time as those at Flaran and Escaladieu. Their combined influence can be seen in various Spanish chapter houses.

Right:
Cloister capital.
Below, from left to right:
• Eighteenth-century vine scroll grille (door to the lay brothers' refectory opening into the Louis XIV courtyard).
• Cloister at the summer solstice, evening.
• Fountain in the main courtyard.

Page facing:
Elevation of the north side of the nave. The stained glass by Richard Burgsthal was installed at the period when Fontfroide became an artistic center frequented by famous painters, musicians and writers of the early twentieth century.

Facing page:
Elevation of the south side of the nave.

Left:
South aisle of the nave.

According to Cistercian thinking there was no question of economizing on the quality of the materials, the perfection of the work, or the choice of the best proved types of construction. For them, the act of building was the act of praying. They aimed for the eternal. When I see this architecture, I know that St. Bernard had indeed the highest of conceptions, the Platonic conception, with a taste for pure volume and the harmony of numbers, which comes from the divine.
Pierre Dalloz.

FONTMORIGNY

Fons Morigniaci

location: Menetou-Couture (Cher), central France
founded: 1149, by Clairvaux
present status: Privately owned

See also pp. 47, 109, 114.

Bibliography
Benoît CHAUVIN, *Fontmorigny, abbaye cistercienne en Berry*, 1993.
Claude MANGEOT, *Notre-Dame de Fontmorigny*, 1997.

That the abbey of Fontmorigny still stands amidst its ruins is due to the devotion of its owners. The story of its restoration, over a period of several decades, is part of a more general movement to improve privately owned historic sites, following the English example of historic country houses.

A decision of this kind takes on particular significance in the case of Cistercian sites, that are generally to be found in depressed rural areas (as indicated by the aid they receive from the European Community). To bring an abbey back to life means acting to improve the entire surrounding area, very much as the White Monks did when they first founded their monasteries. In every country of Europe, the State or the local authorities or public associations, owners of the Cistercian abbeys, are becoming aware of this complementary dimension of the protection of their national heritage.

This policy has been acted upon, in varying degrees, for many years by many private owners. In France, such sites include Fontenay, Fontfroide, Loc Dieu, Vaucelles, Valmagne, Vaux-de-Cernay, Val-Richer, Val-des-Choues, and Villiers-Canivet.

"During the summer of 1987, our search for a holiday home led us to visit a Twelfth-century Cistercian church, for sale with a small house'. We had no idea what we were going to find. We were confronted with crumbling buildings overgrown with brambles and ivy. We had the certain feeling that we had been chosen, and we bought Fontmorigny without a second thought.

"This marked the beginning of an adventure that was to turn us into specialists in monastic history, builders, concert organizers, promoters of tourist merchandise, and finally company directors. Very quickly, we were made to realize that to be the owner of a historic monument was a job not a hobby: we would need to change our approach. Firstly, we needed to understand the site, becoming involved in the restoration work. The monument needed to be reinserted in the collective memory, and to contribute once again to local cultural and economic life."

Although Fontmorigny had been in ruins since the seventeenth century and later converted into a farm, the monastery had not been entirely forgotten. In 1923, the State had prevented it from being used as a source of building stone, and Marcel Aubert, in his work on Cistercian architecture, mentions the abbey 25 times! In 1981 the bell-tower over the crossing collapsed. In 1982 the State was persuaded to prop up the nave only following pressure from the recently founded association of "Friends of Fontmorigny".

By the end of 1997, the church had been restored, the water-supply system was working again, the buildings had been cleared of rubble, and the lay brothers' refectory had been brought back into use. There are further plans under consideration for the future.

The historical studies and excavations carried out on the site have proved to be of great interest, particularly in showing that the church was built on earlier foundations. Will we ever know how many religious buildings have succeeded one another on the majority of consecrated sites? At Fontmorigny, there was a Benedictine abbey as early as the eleventh century, part of the reforming movement inspired by the Vita apostolica that saw itself as spiritually being part of the "early communities",

The large rectangular fish pond (263 x 82 ft [80m x 25m]), dug alongside the southern face of the monastic buildings, forms part of the abbey's complex hydraulic system. A channel passes beneath the church.

as described in the Acts of the Apostles. The monk Foulques left the abbey in 1128 to become abbot of Dunes, in Flanders. Attracted by Cistercianism, he attached his new monastery to Clairvaux in 1138. Fontmorigny was to follow this example in 1149. The abbey's architecture was adapted to conform with Cistercian principles.

Like many major historic monuments, Fontmorigny is today acquiring an architectural perfection that it has probably never known since it was founded. The work of restoration has to take into account a whole range of grants and restrictions, including legislation on the protection of the national heritage, and conditions laid down for applications for financial assistance from the public purse. However, it is for the owners to give a social justification to this joint effort that is added to their own contributions of time and money. Fontmorigny can today claim the status of a small business with developments such as: opening to the public with guided tours by trained guides; the setting up of collaborative work with researchers (historians and archeologists) and the University; the organization of local cultural activities (exhibitions, concerts, conferences); participation in the work of the European Charter for Cistercian abbeys and sites; support of the local economy through payment for the work and the services for the restoration, and the employment of permanent staff; the encouragement of local hotel accommodation and restaurants; the production of local specialities and crafts.

Above:
The undercroft of the lay brothers' building, consisting of two aisles divided into four bays by three octagonal central piers.

Right:
Pavement of the church. The building was restored several times, but the floor may be original.

Entrance to the garden.
At the height of the
abbey's prosperity the
walls of the monastery
embraced an area of
some 12 acres (5ha).

FOSSANOVA

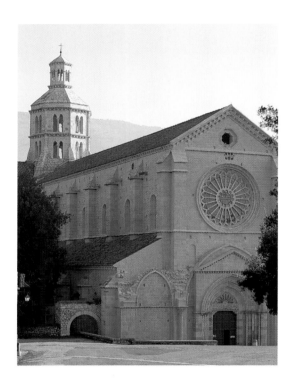

Fossa Nuova

location: near Priverno (Latium), Italy

founded: 1135, by Hautecombe (filiation of Clairvaux)

suppressed: 1795

present status: parish church

See also pp. 112, 123.

Bibliography
Abbazia di Fossanova, Guide Iter.
Marcel AUBERT, *L'Architecture cistercienne en France*, Vanoest, 1947.

How beautiful the abbey church of Clairvaux II must have been! We can tell this from Fossanova. Here, in fact, the monks decided to set about building a replica of the church at their mother house. And it is still standing today as testimony to the perfection of St. Bernard's model. Admittedly, the centuries have added a Gothic portal, a bell tower at the transept crossing and even a large radiating rose window on the façade. But none of these additions, though interesting in themselves, has touched the extreme purity of the space within where pale limestone is softly bathed in light, the long empty nave is given rhythm by the sturdy pillars with their typical Cistercian corbels.

These corbels support transverse arches associated with a groin vault. The Fossanova architects were so at home with this difficult building technique that they used it over and over again, in the choir, the transept, the chapels, and the aisles! The church was built between 1186 and 1208 at the same time as its "three Provençal sisters" were under construction. At the time, the start of the thirteenth century, Mediterranean builders had really come to grips with the Romanesque style, at the cost of ignoring the new northern techniques of rib vaulting.

The church is a moving place to visit, but it was not the first place of worship built in Fossanova. Earlier, a Benedictine monastery dedicated to St. Stephen had been established on the banks of the Amaseno. However, Innocent II, the famous pope whose election was disputed by the College of Cardinals but whose appointment was supported by Bernard of Clairvaux, then made sure it was handed over to monks affiliated to Clairvaux (1135). As soon as they arrived, the Cistercians set about drain-

Facing page, bottom:
The chapter house
supported by two eight-
shafted pillars (c. 1250).

Left:
Entrance to the
"monastic village".

ing the malaria infested swamps of the region. They dug an enormous drainage ditch which in turn gave the abbey its new name, Fossa Nuova (New Ditch). A few years later (1172) they modified the abbey plan to bring it into line with the conventions of the Order. This work continued right up to 1208, when the church was consecrated by Pope Innocent III.

It is not only the church that is interesting at Fossanova. The refectory walkway in the old Romanesque cloister inherited from the Benedictines was modified after 1280 to incorporate a laver and fountain. Here marble workers from Rome demonstrated their carving talents. The chapter house was given a rib vault. The refectory and infirmary, both situated outside the conventual quadrangle to keep it free of rubbish and contagion, were given majestic diaphragm arches. St. Thomas Aquinas died at Fossanova on 7 March 1274. He was on his way to Rome to defend a number of his theses of which the Vatican did not approve, and had asked the Cistercians for shelter. A high relief by Bernini commemorates the event.

Above, left:
The two periods of the cloister.

Above, right:
The north aisle from the transept.

Facing page:
The columns and capitals of the Gothic cloister are reminiscent of Cosmati work.

FOUNTAINS

Sancta Maria ad Fontes

location: Ripon (North Yorkshire), England

founded: 1132, by Clairvaux

dissolved: 1539 (Dissolution)

present status: Privately owned (Studley Royal), managed by the National Trust

See also pp. 12, 39, 72, 77, 102, 107, 110, 136, 137.

Bibliography
Julien GREEN, "La terre est si belle", *Journal 1976–1978*, Le Seuil, Paris, 1992, pp. 137–138 (13 May 1977).
Glyn COPPACK, *Fountains Abbey*, English Heritage, London, 1993.
Anselme DIMIER, *L'Art cistercien*, vol. 2, Zodiaque, La Pierre-qui-Vire, 1971.
E. C. NORTON and D. PARK (eds.), *Cistercian Art and Architecture in the British Isles*, Cambridge 1986.

"In the afternoon, a long walk to the ruins of Fountains Abbey that the king's antipapist fury failed to destroy completely. These Protestants asked themselves: 'While a cathedral might be useful, what is the point of these monks and their monasteries?' So down with these harborers of superstition! To get to the abbey, you have to walk for miles through an entirely deserted park. Would we ever reach the end of these green meadows interspersed with gigantic trees, with here and there in little clumps of trees—the timid intrusion of a futile century—small antique-style temples approaching like curious dilettanti from the eighteenth century? The sky is gray, but it is pleasant to walk on this lush grass, even if one begins to

feel a little tired. Those intent on destroying the abbey must have lost some of their enthusiasm on the way, for the distance is significant. To break the monotony of the walk, stretches of still water appear, reflecting the passing clouds. We arrive at last. That great exercise in theft, the Reformation in its temporal aspect, used this place as it did others elsewhere. Henry VIII's newly enriched supporters took away the stones they needed to build those sumptuous houses that we so unreservedly admire.

What can one say about the abbey itself? It is the biggest I have ever seen. It is Cistercian of the best period, the twelfth century that mysteriously took away with it the secret of a faith without doubts that we have never entirely recaptured. You can still see, up above the massive walls, the tracery of later rose windows. No stained glass windows left, of course. The sky provides all the colors one could want. The stone is white, as white as ivory, and by contrast the trees all around look black. [...] We go down into the store room. A forest of countless columns stretches away beneath these low vaults. Higher up, the imposing refectory, and further off, even larger, inhabited, it seems, by an even more profound silence, the chapel where the day came for the very 'last Mass'. We wander here and there, talking more quietly than usual."

This beautiful passage from Julien Green's Journal sums up the place. Suffice it to add that Fountains was conceived, like so many other abbeys, as a result of the desire of a number of Benedictines—in this case from St. Mary's Abbey in York—to return to the letter of the Rule of St. Benedict (1132). Encouraged by the local bishop, they turned to Bernard of Clairvaux, as the monks of neighboring Rievaulx had done before them. It was Geoffrey of Ainai who came to oversee the building of the new abbey (1135), to ensure that the "Bernardine plan" was scrupulously adhered to.

And so it was, until the early thirteenth century, when the abbot, John of York, had to resolve the problem of the increasing number of monks. He knocked down the east end of

the church, building a new five-bay, aisled choir, terminating it with a second transept containing nine altars against the back wall, subsequently known as "the chapel of the Nine Altars".

Another modification made to the original plan was the enlargement of the chapter house, almost as large as the refectory and, like it, at right angles to the monks' cloister walk. Were chapters held beneath its three aisles and six bays attended by representatives of the fourteen daughter abbeys of Fountains?

The last alterations, carried out by Marmaduke Huby (abbot, 1495–1526), were more spectacular. With the considerable wealth amassed by the abbey from its large flocks of sheep and involvement in the wool trade, the abbot embarked on a restoration of the wooden ceiling of the nave (returning to a Romanesque style of roof), erecting at the same time the enormous Perpendicular north transept tower (a good example of English Gothic). An affir-

mation of monastic power can be seen in the deliberate showiness of the great bay added to the west façade of the church.

The Dissolution broke brutally upon the ostentatious insouciance of the English Cistercians. In 1537 the abbot, William of Thirsk, was hanged for his part in the Pilgrimage of Grace against the Protestant Reformation. In 1539 his successor left the abbey with the promise of a pension.

The abbey first served as a source of building stone for its new owner, Sir Richard Gresham, but in the eighteenth century its still significant ruins began to interest a neighboring estate, Studley Royal. The Romantic era with its cult of ruins had arrived. Fountains Abbey was incorporated into an immense park where centuries-old trees, as fiercely protected as the ancient stones, weave in and out of the walks, giving glimpses of the neo-Classical statues and temples that have been the glory of the English garden.

Thanks to the National Trust, this artificial nature and the wonderful ruins of Fountains Abbey are open to more than 300,000 visitors each year.

The aesthetic success of the whole is indisputable, and there is probably no way of extracting the abbey from the obvious artificiality of its surroundings. Even if monks came back to live here and reconstruct the abbey, as was proposed by the Benedictines some years ago, the artifice would in all probability remain. The Benedictines' proposal was, furthermore, greeted with a howl of protest. It is too late to try to change the strongly held image of the great ruined abbeys, these immense frozen statues standing within unreal meadows.

The great eastern transept, 130 ft (40 m) wide, facing the park of Studley Royal.

The channel beneath the cellar.

Above:
The river beneath the last two bays of the lay brothers' range (two aisles of twenty bays), the largest of any Cistercian abbey. (See photo on p. 76).

Facing page:
The door of the church, in the center of the nave.

FURNESS

Furness

location: Dalton-in-Furness (Cumbria), England

founded: 1123 at Tulket; 1127 at Furness by Savigny (Cistercian Order in 1147—filiation of Clairvaux)

dissolved: 1537

present status: Ruins, in the care of English Heritage

See also pp. 65, 67.

Bibliography
Henry THOROLD, *The Ruined Abbeys of England*, Harper Collins, London, 1993.
E. C. NORTON and D. PARK (Eds.), *Cistercian Art and Architecture in the British Isles*, Cambridge, 1986.

In their search for a remote site, the monks of the Savigniac order had ventured into the peninsula of Barrow-in-Furness, jutting out into the Irish Sea. Here they found a rocky valley with tree-covered hillsides. Even Barrow was not more than a small hamlet, and was to remain an out of the way spot until the coming of the Furness railway in 1846. Today it is a dry dock for nuclear submarines!

When it was founded, in accordance with the wishes of the future king of England, Stephen of Blois, the abbey was Benedictine. In 1147, however, it became Cistercian, affiliating itself with Clairvaux. At this date the church was only half built. Despite changes made in order to conform with the Bernardine plan, it retained several features characteristic of Benedictine buildings, in particular the transepts with staggered apsidal chapels. The same arrangement can be found at Vaux-de-Cernay, a daughter house of Savigny that was also begun in 1147.

The abbey developed rapidly and became almost as powerful as Fountains. The abbot controlled a large area of land, stretching up to the Scottish border. Only the power of the king could stand in the way of Furness's sphere of influence. After the Dissolution there was nothing left but ruins.

But the remains, standing in a wonderful site that even the "unattractive shop of the visitor center" cannot spoil, are considerable. One is struck first of all by the height of the walls of the choir and transepts, and the base of the tower begun in 1500 and never completed. What is left allows us to appreciate the Norman style that inspired the first architects. At the beginning of the fifteenth century, later builders

added windows in the Perpendicular style, and an enormous rose window of which some tracery remains.

Worthy of note is the beautiful and unusual sedilia in the choir, carved by a highly skilled stone carver, and consisting of four seats for the officiants and the double piscina needed for the Mass, the whole placed beneath a Gothic canopy and flanked by two niches.

The east side of the cloister still has an attractive series of arches in front of the well preserved thirteenth-century chapter house. The refectory and lay brothers' building, on the other hand, are marked only by their foundations.

Nearby, the infirmary, with its vaulted chapel, has been turned into a museum. Here can be seen two twelfth-century statues of unidentified knights.

Facing page, right:

Infirmary doors.

Above:

The Romanesque
transept from the nave
side.

*The transept and
triumphal arch opening
into the choir.*

The north aisle, from the transept.

HEILIGENKREUZ

Sancta Crux

location: Heiligenkreuz, lower Austria

founded: 1133, by Morimond

dissolved: Never (one of the twelve abbeys that have remained in use since their foundation)

present use: Cistercian monastery with theological school and parishes

See also pp. 50, 127, 128.

Bibliography
P. Gregor HENCKEL-DONNERSMACK, O.C., *L'Abbaye cistercienne de Heiligenkreuz*, Heiligenkreuz, 1989.

Charlemagne created an "Ostarrichi" in the border area in eastern Bavaria, with the intention of protecting the Empire against barbarian incursions. This semi-State was governed thereafter by the Babenberg family who held on to it until the arrival of the Habsburgs in 1246. At the height of Christianity, princes had a duty to keep a large monastery under their protection and to have their family buried there, in order to legitimize their dynasty. It was for this reason that the margrave, Leopold of Babenberg, instructed his son, a student in Paris, to seek out the most vigorous religious order of the day. The young man had just become a novice at Morimond, so naturally it was this abbey that went on to found the monastery of Heiligenkreuz, first called *Sancta Crux*, in 1133. It was so named because of a donation made to the abbey by the margrave of a piece of the True Cross. The site of Heiligenkreuz suited the prince's need for a Cistercian monastery that

could be a model for the colonizers in this region, where the eastern frontier was still a matter of dispute. Otto was later to become abbot of Morimond and then bishop of Freising. He was one of the most important writers of his time, a precursor of Aristotelianism and recognized as the "father of German historiography".

Never suppressed, the abbey has continued to grow. Today we see a succession of courtyards, the first ones being semi-public while those further in are reserved for the monks (cloister and monastery courtyard). These enclosed courtyards and squares are typical of Baroque urban architecture, a style perfected at the Benedictine abbey of Melk, with its seven courtyards. A French example is the Palais-Royal in Paris.

Although remodeled in Baroque style, like almost every monument in central Europe in the seventeenth and eighteenth centuries, Hei-

ligenkreuz has preserved its original architecture, particularly in the abbey church. Entering by a beautiful courtyard, with its two storeys of arcading and ancient trees protecting two fountains with wide basins (the one dedicated to the Holy Trinity is by Giuliassi), we see the west front of the church, Romanesque but much reworked. Inside, the nave has three storeys (round-headed arches, intermediate plain wall, and row of windows at the top), characteristic of late Romanesque. However, the vault is already ribbed, supported by engaged columns resting on corbels, a solution typical of the Order's architects. The crossing opens into a Gothic choir, square-ended like those of Cîteaux

and Morimond. The Baroque furnishings were removed and replaced by a neo-Gothic altar in the nineteenth century. The monks' stalls by Giovanni Giuliani have panels in relief representing the life of Christ.

The cloister and chapter house seem more like mortuaries. In place of the armarium, the chapel of St. Anne contains the body of an abbot of the eighteenth century. The parlor has been converted into a mortuary chapel, where monks were laid out on a catafalque until they were buried. The chapter house is effectively the family mausoleum of the Babenbergs. Portraits commemorate every member of the family of the founder of the abbey.

Page facing:

The great entrance courtyard. Giovanni Giuliani, who carved the stalls, designed the column to the Holy Trinity.

Above:

The monks' day-room. It will be seen that there is no capital between the arches and the cylindrical pillars, the last cut stone of the arch forming an elegant engaged console.

223

The cloister has lost the refectory, but still has the beautiful structure over its lavabo in a fully mature Gothic style. The fountain, made during the Renaissance and inspired by Italian models, has acquired a rustic air, on account of the picturesque chalky deposits from the hard water that have accumulated over the centuries.

The monks' day-room, known as the "frater" at Heiligenkreuz, brings to mind the medieval copyists and illuminators who worked here. The original builders plastered the stone walls and rib vaults, painting lines representing the stone blocks in red (matching the floor paving). It was common to protect the stone with some kind of coating, and Heiligenkreuz was no exception.

With the development, after the Council of Trent, of a more spectacular liturgy, a new sacristy was built in the seventeenth century, to replace the smaller medieval sacristy. Further embellishments followed: in the nineteenth century, the monastery's lay brothers made the cupboards for vestments and precious objects, with their wonderful marquetry of naïve trompe-l'oeil inlay. Conscious of the quality of their work, and in contravention of the Rule of the Order, they added their signature to the first door of the cupboard on the left.

Visitors to Heiligenkreuz are shown, near the monks' day-room, barrel ends painted with naïve scenes. They remind us that the abbey still owns vineyards at Gumpoldskirchen and in the Burgenland; the oldest of these were donations made in 1146!

Above, left:
Cloister, chapter house walk.

Above, right:
The Gothic lavatorium (1290) and Renaissance fountain. The stained glass, like that of the cloister is nineteenth-century.

Facing page:
The great chapter house. The thirteenth-century architecture was left untouched by the eighteenth-century restoration. The wall paintings depict the Austrian margraves and dukes of the Babenberg dynasty buried in the chapter house.

Following double spread:
The church vaults at the crossing (c. 1290), typical of Austrian Gothic architecture.

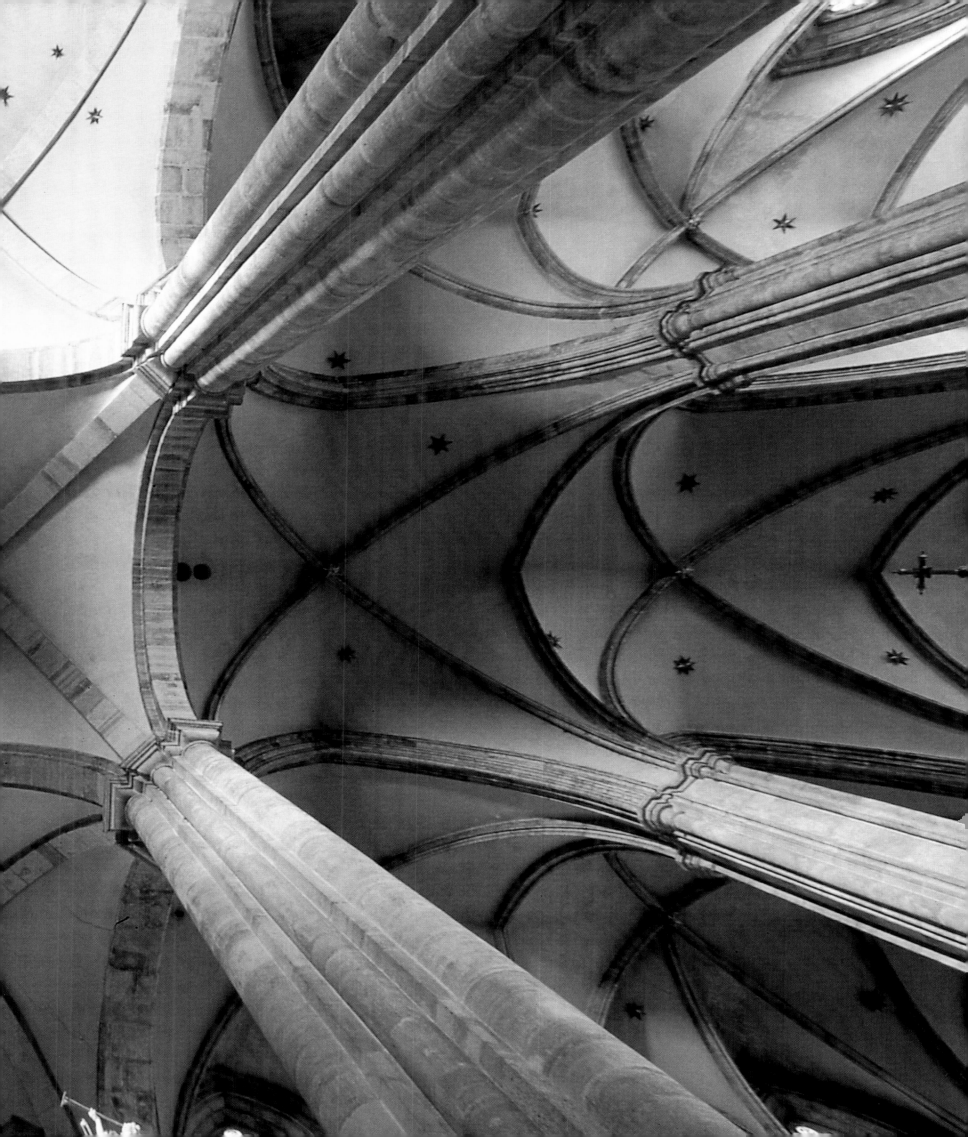

HOLY CROSS

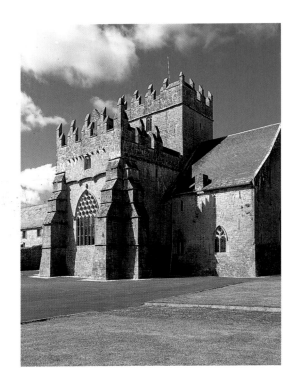

Mainistir na Croise Nasfa, Sancta Crux

location: near Thurles (Co. Tipperary), Republic of Ireland

founded: 1180, by Monasteranenagh (filiation of Clairvaux)

dissolved: 1735

present status: parish church and shrine

Bibliography
Roger STALLEY, *The Cistercian Monasteries of Ireland*, Yale University Press, London, 1987.
Thomas MORRIS, *Holy Cross Abbey*, Eason, Dublin, 1986.

Holy Cross today seems to be the very incarnation of rural Ireland. Even the countryside in which it stands has been shaped by centuries of agriculture and stock raising. An old eight-arched bridge takes you over the swirling waters of the River Suir to the beautiful ruins of the medieval abbey, where you also find a restored church and a pub occupying one of the few domestic buildings of the hamlet. On Sundays the car park fills up, the women go to Mass, the men and old folk go off to the pub, and the youngsters hang out in the cloister chatting away while listening to the service as it is broadcast over loudspeakers.

In fact, Holy Cross has inherited a glorious and eventful past. It was originally founded by Donal O'Brien, king of Thomond, for the Benedictines. But the abbey went through difficult times. When the Cistercians arrived in 1180, they were only able to put things right by turning it into a place of pilgrimage and making a shrine for the relic of the True Cross. Thus by the end of the fourteenth century the monks, now far richer, were able to rebuild the abbey. They used the plans for the original monastery, but carried them out in a particularly graceful late Gothic style.

Holy Cross escaped dissolution thanks to protection from the powerful Butler family, who turned the abbey into a secular college. The Cistercians therefore stayed put until 1735, but not without enduring persecution and pillage at the hands both of Cromwell's troops and of other forces during the Jacobite wars. The monks were forced to live over at Kilkenny for fifteen years and were unable to keep on their novices. In 1685 the flame was being kept alive by just two monks!

Since 1971, after nearly three centuries of neglect, the abbey has undergone a considerable amount of restoration work. This has saved the ruins from irreversible decay and put life back in the abbey itself, which has once more become a place of pilgrimage. It is also a parish church, a cultural center, a tourist office, and so on.

The small two-bay east end of the church is rib vaulted, with liernes and tiercerons. The transept is also Gothic, and the nave comprises six bays, with aisles. There is a wide tower at the crossing. The sanctuary houses a triple sedilia. In the north transept, a fifteenth-century mural painting depicts a stag. There is also a very lifelike owl on one of the choir pilasters. A frieze on one of the flying buttresses of the north transept shows a dog. Clearly in this country the constraints the Cistercians placed on art never totally managed to keep traditional Irish carving out of its abbey churches.

Facing page, bottom:
Corbel on the south-east
crossing pier.

Above:
Remains of the cloister
(north-west corner).

Facing page:

Base of an altar presently attached to the north wall of the church: the Virgin, and Christ on the Cross.

Above:

Unhistoriated corbels with traditional Irish popular figurative elements.

HORE

Mainistir Chaisil, Rupes Casseliae
location: Cashel (Tippperary), Ireland
founded: 1272, by Mellifont (filiation of Clairvaux)
dissolved: 1540 (Dissolution)
present status: Ruined

See also pp. 43, 50.

Bibliography
Roger STALLEY, *The Cistercian Monasteries of Ireland*
Yale University Press, London, 1987.

Hore can be reached only after a walk through marshy fields full of large herds of grazing cows, indifferent to the dramatic site of this Cistercian abbey that seems so isolated, abandoned, and almost forgotten, at the foot of the Rock of Cashel. There, on the rocky promontory that was once a fortress for the powerful prince-bishops, stand the beautiful, romantic ruins of a cruciform cathedral and its surrounding buildings.

The most important of these is Cormac's Chapel, the most remarkable Romanesque monument to be seen in Ireland. As the crowds of tourists flock to visit this Irish version of Mont-Saint-Michel, they rarely look back at the small abbey, lost in the fields, with not even a road to reach it.

The bishop of Cashel had managed to convince Mellifont of the need to send some monks to set up a monastery at the foot of his rock. This was to be the last Cistercian foundation in Ireland, and its site conformed little to the recommendations of the Rule. The monks complained that "from the monastery, the sound of the cathedral bells is too loud". In 1540, the three monks still living at Hore turned the abbey into a parish church and continued to live there. Later the land was "given" to James Butler, count of Ormond. The church, the south transept, and the chapter house were turned into dwellings. Today the abbey is unfenced, open to any visitor. There are no graffiti.

As always, the ruins can be read as a relief plan. Like all Cistercian abbeys, Hore conforms to the standard Bernardine plan. There is something satisfying about visiting a Cistercian abbey, for we know in advance what we will find, whether in Ireland or in Portugal, and we understand the function of each element, admiring the rare variants where the basic principles have been adapted to fit a particular site. It is tempting to speculate on what an abbot might have done if he had changed the basic plan or given his architect a free rein. This is in fact what happened in the fifteenth century, when almost all the abbots had towers added to the abbeys, despite the General Chapter's frequently repeated warning against constructing such ostentatious vanities. But, disappointingly, they almost all follow the same pattern. Hore has one peculiarity, however, being the only Irish abbey to build its cloister to the north, for reasons that are unknown.

Left:
Vault of the crossing, with liernes and tiercerons.

Above:
The square east end with blocked-up triple windows

JERPOINT

Sciriopuin, Jeripons
location: Thomastown (Kilkenny), Ireland
founded: 1180, by Baltinglass (filiation of Clairvaux through Mellifont)
dissolved: 1540 (Dissolution)
present status: Ruined (in the care of the Office of Public Works since 1880)

See also pp. 17, 18.

Bibliography
Office of Public Works, *Jerpoint Abbey Co. Kilkenny.*
Roger STALLEY, *The Cistercian Monasteries of Ireland*, Yale University Press, London, 1987.

It was the king of Ossory, Donald MacGillapatrick, who wanted to set up a monastery in his territory. He approached the Benedictines (1160) who rapidly (1180) adopted Cistercian usages, under the authority of the abbey of Baltinglass. Standing alone in a peaceful country site watered by the beautiful Little Avrigle river, Jerpoint was soon to experience grave problems in its internal affairs. It was involved in the famous "Mellifont conspiracy" (1227), which led to the deposition of its abbot. It was then put under the control of Fountains in Yorkshire, an event that was significant in the policy of Anglicization being operated in Ireland.

In the fifteenth century, the monks no longer practised the early austerity with such enthusiasm. Some anti-papist pamphlets went so far as to assert that, apart from St. Mary's Abbey in Dublin and Mellifont, monks no longer even wore the habit! It is true that, in the early fifteenth century, the abbey built an imposing crenellated tower on the crossing of the church, and decorated the cloister with a beautiful series of column figures. The abbey possessed 14,500 acres (5,870ha) of land and forests, several cottages, mills and, particularly, dams for the creation of fishponds.

The Dissolution did not cause a great upheaval at Jerpoint. By then there were only one abbot and five monks, who all received pensions. The noble protectors of the Butler family of Kilkenny were able to collect the monastic revenues without either having to share it or to pay for the upkeep of the buildings. It was not until the nineteenth century, with the revival of historical studies of the Middle Ages, that the Kilkenny Archaeological Society undertook to restore the site.

The choir of the church, barrel vaulted, is a fine example of late twelfth-century Romanesque architecture. The fourteenth-century windows, replacing the three original oculi, illuminate tomb niches and the remains of wall paintings, on the north side, and the officiants' sedilia, on the south side. The recumbent effigy on a tomb is, according to tradition, the founding abbot.

The transepts both have two little vaulted chapels with square ends. Tombs and burial slabs give evidence of the skill of the Jerpoint sculptors. Two knights in chain mail, known as "the Brethren", repose on a thirteenth-century slab on the south side.

The tower rests on four massive pillars. In contrast the vaulting, Gothic this time, is a delicate stellar rib vault. Under the crossing,

Facing page, right:
North side of the nave.

Left:
The cloister and, in the foreground, a carved figure between two columns of the arcading.

the tomb of Robert Walsh and Katherine Power (1501) bears the signature of its carver, Rory O'Tunney.

The nave has retained its north aisle, very narrow as is usual in Cistercian churches, where the concern was more with providing good abutment for the elevations than space for processions. The columns, alternately square or round, have scalloped capitals. The Cistercian waterleaf decoration is very rarely seen in Ireland, except at Boyle. It seems surprising that Irish art, ever inventive, poetic, and violent, could resign itself to a endless repetition of the same motif.

The most interesting feature of Jerpoint is the arcaded cloister (1390–1400). Partly reconstructed in 1953, the south and west sides are merely remains marked out on the grounds—a solution that archeologists do not recommend often enough. The Romanesque arcade is open to the cloister garth, with a sequence of three round-headed arches resting on pairs of engaged colonettes, linked by panels providing a field for sculpture. The best of Irish art is here, with princes and prelates, peasants and monks, all in clothes of the day. There are also grotesques (in the Irish tradition) and saints, like the fine figure of St. Christopher bearing the Christ-Child.

The monks' range, on the east side of the cloister, is intact. The sacristy and the armarium, the chapter house, parlor, passage (closed nowadays), and the monks' day-room all have fine barrel vaults. Considerable remains of the medieval tiled pavement was found during the restoration work. There are two types of tile: those in two colors, showing a lion's head; and those with impressed lines with four motifs, a lion, a fleur-de-lys, a virginia creeper, and a cross-shaped flower. The subjects are more naturalistic than religious, but very much in keeping with the Celtic tradition.

Facing page:
• *Carved capital on a pillar in the church*
• *The sanctuary*

Above:
• *Carvings between the columns of the cloister. The one on the left represents St. Christopher.*
• *Head of an exhausted man beneath a yoke.*

LÉONCEL

Lioncellum

location: Léoncel (Drôme), Rhone-Alpes region, France

founded: 1137, by Bonnevaux (Cîteaux)

dissolved: 1791

present status: Parish church

See also p. 116.

Bibliography
Les Cahiers de Léoncel.
Léoncel, une abbaye cistercienne en Vercors, special edition of *La Revue drômoise*, Valence, 1991.

No site seems to have been too difficult for the Cistercians! At Léoncel, they tamed a small piece of marshy uplands in western Vercors, overlooking the valley of Valence and Romans and controlling, at the Bataille Pass, access to the citadel of upper Vercors.

The site is majestic, dominated by the cliffs of the Échaillon and the slopes of the Signal du Tourniol. The limestone plateau is densely forested, the trees pieced here and there by rocky outcrops. Oaks and sweet chestnuts grow in the steep valleys, while higher up towards the Ambel plateau beech and fir-trees are found. This vast, synclinal area provides mountain pasture. It is a site that is also eminently Cistercian, for water is abundant. The earliest habitation (cella) was installed on a raised area, so as to avoid flooding from the Lionne (Lioncellum) while at the same time allowing the monks to harness the strong flow of the water of this small river.

However, the abbey could only develop very slowly, because it was exposed to high wind and covered in snow for several months of the year. The climate is particularly harsh in this region, and the monks could only cultivate the fields in the summer, having to collect supplementary provisions from the plain below. It was for this reason that in 1194 they decided to join the small monastic community of Part-Dieu, at the foot of the mountain. The General Chapter authorized the White Monks to live there from St. Andrew's Day (30 November) until Easter.

This dual tenancy allowed the Cistercians to set themselves up in a huge temporal domain, combining the growing of cereals and grapes in the foothills with the forestry and grazing activities of the mountains. The use of the pasture land had been negotiated with the nearby Carthusian monastery of Val Sainte-Marie-de-Bouvante, which meant that a large part of this mountainous region was under monastic control.

The spiritual development of Léoncel kept pace with the development of the monks' economic self-sufficiency. The harsh climate and long distances to be covered meant that life was a constant struggle. One of the first abbots, Hughes de Châteauneuf, was canonized. Nevertheless, after the Black Death and the Hundred Years' War, the abbey never regained the splendor of its first two centuries of existence. Disasters came in plenty: the abbey was destroyed by Gascons in 1390; the community retreated to Roman for thirty years; fire caused further damage during the Wars of Religion (1568); the regular abbots were not at the abbey; there were constant lawsuits with the neighboring landowners; absentee abbots (1681), holding benefices, appropriated all the revenues from the plain, leaving only the mountain pastures for the few monks still living in the monastery; disputes with the Waters and Forests Department over the exploitation of the Ambel uplands; another period when the monks abandoned the monastery in 1726; confrontations with newly hostile villagers (1781). By the time the Revolution suppressed the monastery, it was already dead.

As it comes into view, Léoncel today is still impressive. The old church, that survived the Revolution because it had been the parish church since 1791, appears in all its Cistercian simplicity, standing in the pasture lands and few trees that punctuate the site, surrounded by mountains. The façade has been remodeled: the central portal now opened to the faithful replaces the small side door used in monastic times. There

*General view of the
abbey in the valley,
looking to the east end
from the north-east.*

is a bell tower, of stone to withstand the wind, typical of the two-storey, eight-sided towers found in the Alps. Bernard of Clairvaux, who disapproved of such statements of power, so inappropriate to the monastic life, would have disowned it. He might not have found the three apses of the east end to his taste either—too sensually rounded perhaps?

The interior sticks strictly to the Cistercian spirit, down to the restrained cupola on squinches over the crossing. It is built entirely of the local limestone, as is right and proper. The earliest part of the building (1150–88) is solidly Romanesque: the choir terminates in a semi-dome over a rounded apse, with a smaller one either side; the nave has square piers with quadrant vaults in the aisles. The original wooden roof was replaced by the light and airy architecture of a Gothic vault. The high arched windows illuminate the nave, between the engaged columns that support all the weight, resting on typically Cistercian corbels.

Prosper Mérimée added this church to the list of Historic Monuments in 1840. There are other remains, though, particularly of the former monks' range, now occupied by the Maison Saint-Hughes, where Sister Marie-Françoise Giraud has been looking after the spiritual side of the site since 1974. The Association of Friends of Léoncel, meanwhile, is continuing its important historical research with annual conferences that have resulted in a series of scholarly publications since 1986 (*Les Cahiers de Léoncel*).

Facing page:
Elevation of the north side of the church.

Left:
The blind arcading of the north aisle of the church.

LÉRINS

Saint-Honorat

location: Cannes (Alpes-Maritimes) Provence-Côte d'Azur, France

founded: 1869, by Sénanque

church dating from: 1880–1930

present status: monastery of the Order of Cistercians of the Common Observance

See also p. 135.

Bibliography
Théo Encyclopédie catholique, Droguet and Ardant/Fayard, Paris, 1992.
Bernard PEUGNIEZ, *Routier des abbayes cisterciennes de France*, Editions du Signe, Strasbourg, 1994.
Marcel PACAUT, *Les moines blancs*, Fayard, Paris, 1993.

When in 1869 the Sénanque Cistercians became owners of the Isle of Saint-Honorat they also inherited a rich genealogy stretching back over the whole of monastic history.

An abbey was first founded by St. Honorat on the smaller of the two islands of Lérins in about the year 400. It would still be some years before John Cassien founded Saint-Victor and Saint-Sauveur in Marseilles, and St. Martin had only just arrived in Gaul (Ligugé, 361).

Honorat and his companion Capras came from that part of Gaul which is now Belgium, and initially lived as hermits before creating a monastery that would become a nursery for bishops. In the sixth century, the abbey adopted the Benedictine Rule; it joined Cluny in 978 then the Order of Saint-Victor in 1366. It then passed to the Order of Saint-Maur in 1638 and to the congregation of Monte Cassino in 1645 before reverting to Cluny in 1756. It was then given to the bishopric of Grasse in 1786 and finally sold off as a national asset in 1791.

Of the eleventh-century monastery buildings which over the centuries were fortified to withstand attacks from marauders arriving by sea, we still have a beautiful Romanesque two-storey cloister, which the modern monastery (1880-1930) has incorporated into its general plan.

Today Lérins Abbey is the mother house of the Congregation of the Immaculate Concep-

Facing page:
Aerial view of the island of Lérins.

Left:
Fortified monasticism.

The old cloister (eighth or ninth century).

tion, linked to the Cistercian Order of the Common Observance. This Order groups together twelve congregations of 64 monasteries (roughly 1,300 monks) and five congregations of 86 convents (approximately 1,500 nuns).

Monastic life at Lérins (and at its priory Sénanque) is close to that led by the Order of Cistercians of the Strict Observance (Trappists). It advocates adherence to the basic principles of the Rule (meditation-prayer-work). Almost everywhere else, other congregations follow the direction taken in central Europe during the eighteenth century, which emphasizes the element of service to others (orphanages, board-

ing schools, etc) or pastoral and parish care. An important event in 1998 was the nomination by Pope John XXIII, for the first time in many years, of a Cistercian abbot (the abbot of Lérins) as a bishop.

Left:
The chapel of the Trinity (sixth century).

Above:
The two-storeyed cloister of the fortified monastery.

LOC DIEU

Locus Dei

location: Martiel (Aveyron), Midi-Pyrénées region, France

founded: 1124 (Cistercian Order in 1162) through Dalon (Pontigny)

dissolved: 1791 (French Revolution)

present status: Privately owned

See also pp. 61, 114, 122.

Bibliography
Françoise BAGUERIS, "Ancienne Abbaye Notre-Dame de Loc Dieu", in *Anciennes abbayes en Midi-Pyrénées*, Addoc, Tarbes, 1991.

If the Sleeping Beauty had been a nun waiting for her Prince Charming to return from the Crusades, she would have found at Loc Dieu the perfect site for her story. The Mona Lisa made a wise choice when she chose this abbey, with its high walls—both castle and romantic manor house—for her refuge during the Second World War. Were these swans, floating on the lake that reflects the abbey in its waters, the same as those she saw?

It seems that Loc Dieu became Cistercian through the neglect of its Benedictine founders. In 1134, twenty years after their arrival on the site, they had already constructed several buildings. Too many in fact, because they had to borrow money to lay the foundations of the church in 1159. The only way to avoid ruin was to become Cistercian, associating themselves with the abbey of Bonneval which paid its new sister abbey's debt. This was taking the Carta Caritatis to the letter!

These early misfortunes were quickly followed by others: nepotism in the thirteenth century; abandon after the Revolution. At the end of the nineteenth century its owners embarked on a plan of partial restoration, with a combination of respect for historical monuments and vivid imagination, in the tradition of the great Viollet-le-Duc. The abbey of Loc Dieu may never before have been as beautiful as it was in 1900!

The church has kept its original purity, with a apsidal east end and square-ended transept chapels (twelfth century). The nave was raised in the thirteenth century with broad ribbed vaults, without any change to the narrow aisles with their pointed tunnel vaults.

The cloister dates from the fifteenth century, as does the chapter house of six bays with

rib vaults on two molded columns that, heedless of its function as a place of meditation in the cloister, opens wide on to the park. For several years, at dusk in the summer, Michel Dintrich and Jérôme de Souza performed transcriptions of Bach's keyboard works on ten-string guitars.

Facing page, top:
The south aisle and nave of the church from the choir.

Facing page, bottom:
Oculus in the south transept.

Above:
The chapter house, the later windows giving the appearance of an orangery.

Following double spread:
General view of the abbey.

MARGAM

location: West Glamorgan, Wales
founded: 1147, by Clairvaux
dissolved: 1536
present status: ruins and Protestant church

Bibliography
David H. WILLIAMS, *Atlas of Cistercian Lands in Wales*, University of Wales Press, Cardiff, 1990.
Malcolm Railton ELLIS, *Margam Abbey*, Margam, (no date).

Margam is a difficult place to reach. All the guidebooks, even the most voluminous which claim to describe everything, seem to have overlooked this Welsh abbey tucked away in its secluded valley. Fortunately, the good old *Atlas de l'Ordre cistercien* by Frédéric Van der Meer is always at hand, almost exhaustive in its coverage and definitely indispensable.

Margam nestles in the hills of South Wales close to the sea. Cardiff, where the abbey used to own a town house, lies about 35 miles (56km) to the east.

In the thirteenth century, when Cistercian properties constituted much of the arable land in Wales, Margam featured prominently among Welsh abbeys and was without question the richest of them all. Its property inventory is impressive: twelve granges, eleven watermills and two windmills, five sheepfolds, four fish ponds, five coal mines, two iron and lead mines, four toll roads, five town houses.

The lay brothers were never short of a job! In the thirteenth century revolts among the lay brothers swept through the Order. The Margam revolt of 1206 was one of the most serious. The protesters pulled the cellarer from his horse, then chased the abbot 25 miles from the abbey before barricading themselves in their dormitory. Fountains Abbey was forced to step in to restore discipline. The guilty parties were punished by making them walk all the way to Clairvaux. They were subsequently scattered around a number of abbeys belonging to the Order.

Even today the site at Margam remains very Cistercian, with its valley bottom, meadows, tall trees, and a lovely natural lake. A little way off stand the charred façades of an enormous manor house in the Gothic revival style so popular in Britain. Dominating the abbey from a height of about 300 feet (100m), a bare hillside with traces of a circular enclosure and, at its center, the ruins of a small chapel (Cryke Chapel). Was this an ancient feudal site or an ancient Celtic oppidum?

The church, which is now Protestant, still conforms to St. Bernard's plan. Its façade, however, remains enigma. Above all, there are substantial remains of an unusual chapter house that are well worth a visit. Its round interior is enclosed in an dodecagonal outer wall. You enter the building through an atrium opening on to the cloister which, like the rest of the monastery, has totally disappeared except for a few walls once belonging to the infirmary.

Left:
The great tree at Margam, still much venerated. Bernard of Clairvaux glorified the trees and the forests, as did the Celtic tradition.

Below, left:
The "palm tree" of the central pillar of the twelve-sided chapter house, a masterpiece of the stonemason's art.

Below, right:
The beautiful vestibule leading to the chapter house is unique to the architect of Margam, as are the two astonishing bell-towers on either side of the church façade.

MAULBRONN

It cannot be repeated often enough that a Cistercian abbey can never be reduced just to the "conventual quadrangle" where its liturgical life takes place. An abbey is also made up of outbuildings without which the monks and lay brothers could not do their work. In addition, there were the granges, where the lay brothers and hired laborers produced everything necessary—food and utensils—to tend to the needs of the community, visitors passing through the guest-house, and the poor arriving at the almonry.

Maulbronn is a perfect example of all this. Inside the outer abbey wall we still have all the workshops and service areas contained within a mini-town. This, in fact, is precisely what a Cistercian abbey was, since while it operated in accordance with St. Bernard's Rule, it also enjoyed a great deal of autonomy. On the other side of the fortified gateway, the sole point of contact with the outside world, we find the guest-house and the strangers' chapel (for all those not allowed inside the enclosure, women in particular), the cartwright's workshop, the smithy, cowsheds and stables, a flour mill and bakehouse, a wine press and brewhouse.

The conventual quadrangle itself is even better preserved and, apart from the monks' dormitory, all the buildings conform to St. Bernard's plan. UNESCO has designated it a World Heritage Site along with Alcobaça, Fountains, and Fontenay.

The church was started in about 1150 and consecrated in 1178. It still retains its Romanesque façade with round arches resting on square piers, plain walls, and small, high-set windows from the time when the pitched roof was still

Maulbrunnum

location: Maulbronn, near Württemberg, Germany

founded: 1138, by Neubeurg-en-Forêt (filiation of Morimond)

suppressed: 1557 (Reformation)

present status: Protestant seminary

See also pp. 39, 79, 102, 114, 118.

Bibliography
Anselme DIMIER, *L'Art cistercien*, vol. 2, Zodiaque, La Pierre-qui-Vire, 1971.
Margarete STILLGER, *Allemagne*, Hachette, Paris, 1964.
Marianne BERNHARD, *Abbayes*, IPG/PML, Munich-Paris, 1994.

Facing page, bottom:
The cloister garth and "chapel of the lavatorium", built around 1350 and raised in height two centuries later.

Left:
The beautiful fountain deserved a sumptuous setting. The monks thus gave the lavatorium the character of a baptismal chapel. The design was created by the "Master of the Paradise Door" (so-called after his famous church door) and was the first experiment in the Gothic style carried out by a builder trained in France.

an open wooden structure. A Gothic fan vault was added to the nave only in the fifteenth century, and at the same time they opened up the square east end in the sanctuary to install a huge Gothic window. The raking light softens the austerity of the schist walls.

As a rare witness of the segregation of monks from the lay brothers, the church still preserves the tall masonry screen dividing the nave into two separate choirs.

At the start of the thirteenth century, the church was given a huge porch consisting of three rib-vaulted bays, which opened on to the outbuilding yard through twin bays. This was the "Galilee" toward which the traveler made once he had spotted the church entrance thanks to the spire above it.

The cloister walks open toward an octagonal tower housing the laver, with a beautiful tree standing next to it. The cloister walks still have the original Romanesque bays as well as a few Flamboyant Gothic bays introduced during the thirteenth century. The refectory dates from the later period (1512). Inside it has two aisles in eight bays, supported on seven alternating major and minor piers. The monks entered after washing their hands and faces with water from a fountain comprising three superimposed basins, one of the most splendid ever produced by Cistercian architects. The vaults were most likely the work of a local craftsman named Jorg Largeb. Opening off the east walk, the chapter house contains High Gothic rib vaults, whose elegance is in sharp contrast with the Romanesque groin vaults in the chamber which was used as the lay brothers' refectory, on the west side of the cloister.

Maulbronn thus illustrates the various types of vaulting used in religious buildings. Generations of students must have absorbed this lesson daily just by living here after the Duke of Württemberg turned the abbey into a religious school following the Reformation. The poet Friedrich Hölderlin was a boarding pupil at Maulbronn.

Above:
The chapter house and stellar vaults (c. 1320). The work begun by Master Ulrich in 1424 is still visible thanks to some careful restoration.

Facing page:
The sexpartite vaults of the monks' refectory (c. 1225).

MELLIFONT

Mainistir Mhor, Mellifons

location: Drogheda (Louth) Ireland

founded: 1142, by Clairvaux

dissolved: 1539 (Dissolution)

present status: Ruined

See also pp. 97, 109.

Bibliography
Mellifont Abbey and its Environs, Mellifont Abbey Press, Collon, 1980.
Roger STALLEY, *The Cistercian Monasteries of Ireland*, Yale University Press, London, 1987.
Françoise HENRY, *La Sculpture irlandaise pendant les douze premiers siècles de l'ère chrétienne*, vol. i, Paris, 1933.

The story of the Cistercians in Ireland began at Mellifont in 1142. It was to be a story of unprecedented expansion, for this Bernardine bridgehead went on to found 38 more abbeys. Mellifont was the creation of Malachy O'Morgair, archbishop of Armagh, who became a close friend of Bernard of Clairvaux. It was at Clairvaux that he ended his days and was buried. His life was written by St. Bernard, and this led to a rapid canonization. Like Stephen Harding, who stopped at Molesme on his return from a pilgrimage to Rome, Malachy, journeying to the Eternal City, had made a detour by way of Clairvaux. He was deeply impressed by the perfection of the religious life led by the Cistercians in this large abbey. He wanted to become a monk at Clairvaux, but the pope, like Bernard of Clairvaux, advised him instead to return to Ireland to found a Cistercian abbey there. He chose a wild site in a valley near Drogheda, on the banks of the Mattock, far away from the hunting grounds of the local lords, but close to the territories of the king of Airghialla who promised his protection and donations for the new monastery.

Monks came from Clairvaux to instruct the new Irish novices in the Rule, and to oversee work on the building of the abbey. But it was not long before the atmosphere soured between the locals and the French, as it did later between the Irish abbeys and the Anglo-Norman abbeys created in Ireland after the invasion of 1169. Mellifont had attracted a large number of vocations, and soon established its authority over its daughter houses, cultivating a distinctive local Irish identity that was assisted by the traditional autonomy of Cistercian abbeys. From 1152, the Irish Cistercians met together in a synod. When, in 1200, an abbot of Mellifont agreed to cooperate with the English rulers in an attempt to bring about a reform of religious morals, he was deposed by his monks. Later, the "Conspiracy of Mellifont" (1227) implicated six abbots in a series of "outrageous acts", marking the violent opposition felt towards the visitations of the nominees of the General Chapter. These abbots were deposed by the General Chapter.

Ireland was attracted by the Cistercians, their rigorous architectural model, their strict Rule, their ascetiscm, and their enthusiasm for new technologies, but at the same time the Cistercians upset the old, traditional style of

The most famous building at Mellifont and last bastion of Cistercianism amidst a field of sadly ruined remains is the two-storeyed octagonal lavatorium. *The rough perfection of Irish Romanesque architecture adapted itself without difficulty to the spirit of Citeaux.*

The remains of the cloister seen through an arch of the lavatorium.

monasticism that had existed in the island since the sixth century. It has been noted how Irish art, still very vigorous in the twelfth century, was stopped in its tracks by the new Cistercian principles. Nevertheless, Celtic art was to influence Cistercian architecture in many areas, particularly in the sculpture produced by local craftsmen. The local architects, who built the Cistercian abbeys of Ireland, always retained a fondness for the building techniques of Romanesque architecture (known for generations) rather than Gothic (an innovation imported from outside) that did not become truly established until the period of restoration and improvement in the fourteenth and fifteenth centuries.

Passing through the guardroom that once protected the abbey, the ruins reveal the cruciform plan of the church, inaugurated with great ceremony in 1157, and restored and enlarged several times before the suppression of the abbey in 1539 (when there were still 150 monks). The cloister, partly restored, encloses the grandiose lavabo, octagonal and two-storeyed, where the monks washed their hands before entering the refectory. The chapter house contains a few archaeological remains found in the excavation of the church. There are also the remains of a large stone tower. The Irish monks could never bring themselves to obey this stricture of the Rule!

Facing page, and left:
Ruins of the chapter
house: the vault (early
thirteenth century), floor
tiles and small columns
on a corner pier.

MELROSE

Melrosa

location: near Melrose (Roxburghshire), Scotland

founded: 1136, by Rielvaux (filiation of Clairvaux)

dissolved: 1560

present status: ruins

See also pp. 50, 55.

Bibliography
Henry THOROLD, *The Ruined Abbeys of England, Wales and Scotland*, Harper Collins, London 1993.
Richard FAWCETT, *Scottish Abbeys and Priories*, English Heritage, Batsford, London, 1994.
Richard FAWCETT, *Scottish Medieval Churches*, Historic Buildings and Monuments Department, Edinburgh, 1985.
Marguerite WOOD and J. S. RICHARDSON, *Melrose Abbey*, Historic Scotland, 1995.
E. C. NORTON and D. PARK (eds.), *Cistercian Art and Architecture in the British Isles*, Cambridge, 1986

Melrose was founded in 1136 by David I, King of Scotland. It was near the site of an earlier monastery, which had been run since the seventh century by a succession of saintly monks, nearly all of whom had been canonized (at the time canonization was not done in Rome but by the local bishop!).

The period of peace which allowed David I to invite English monks to come up to Scotland did not last long. The almost permanent state of war between the two countries proved fatal to the abbey, which was always right in the path of their battles. The English sacked the monastery three times between 1300 and 1385. It was later rebuilt and the abbey you see today is a prime example of Scottish architecture from the period when the Perpendicular Gothic style was emerging. It was this style that produced the most glorious of the large churches of Britain.

At Melrose today, only the church remains, but what a wonderful abbey church it is! It is the same size as the major churches the Cistercians built at Vaucelles or Royaumont at the start of the thirteenth century. But coming as it did a century later (1385–1550), the architects had complete mastery over the full Gothic architectural repertoire, and Melrose was to reap the benefits of Flamboyant Gothic technique. This led to enormous bays on the four façades (three of which survive) as well as elevations with an openwork triforium, flying buttresses and abutment piers. In the white northern light, the pink sandstone of the plinth adds a sensuous note to the architecture.

Visiting the abbey throws up some interesting points. For example, you can still see the tall stone screen that separated the monks'

choir from that of the lay brothers. Only a very few of these have survived in abbeys belonging to the Order. You can also see further evidence of the segregation between the two monastic populations from the remains of the lay brothers' passage, which ran along the west side of the great cloister. We know that about 300 lay brothers worked at Melrose (compared to 100 choir monks) and that a special cloister was built for them. How many men became lay brothers in the 750 abbeys that the Order possessed when the Cistercian economic system was at its height?

And how many hired laborers and oblates helped the lay brothers in their work or replaced them in specialist fields? We know that at Melrose the sanctuary was the work of stonemasons from Yorkshire, while credit for the transept belongs to a Frenchman, Jean Moreau ("John Morrow"), who was born in Paris but spent much of his life in Britain. Verses engraved on one of the abbey walls remind the visitor that master mason John Morrow had also helped build St Andrew's and Glasgow cathedrals as

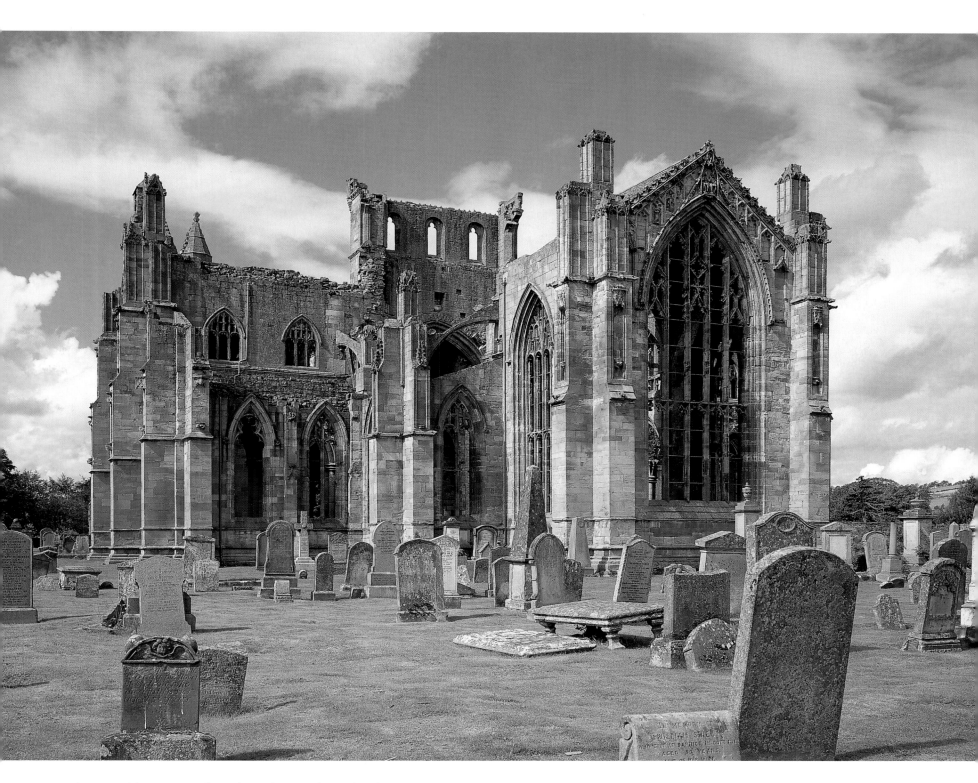

Facing page, right:

A complicated pattern of bosses and ribs decorates the vault of the sanctuary. The abbey was rebuilt at a period when the master masons were eager to show off their talents. The time of the anonymous artisan was almost over, issuing in named architects and artists.

When distant Tweed is heard to rave,
And the owlet hoot o'er the dead man's grave,
then go—but go alone the while—
Then view St. David's ruined pile;
And, home returning, soothly swear,
Was never scene so sad and fair!

Walter Scott, Lay of the Last Minstrel

well as monasteries at Paisley, Nithsdale, and Galloway.

An the edge of the abbey site stands the house of the commendatory abbot, which was built in the sixteenth and seventeenth centuries, partly with stone taken from the abbey itself. It now houses an excellent little museum.

North aisle of the nave from the transept, worthy of a cathedral. The south aisle had eight chapels where patrons of the abbey were buried, following Benedictine custom despite the fact that it had been rejected by Cistercians.

The end wall of the north transept with the door of the sacristy and traces of the night stair. The door to the monks' dormitory today frames a view of the beautiful leafy landscape, such as a Japanese architect might spontaneously suggest in a desire to bring the viewer to reflect upon nature.

The powerful architecture of the pillars in the nave. In the fourteenth century the monks still lived in poverty, but the abbey was wealthy, with a flock of several thousand sheep, setting the rate for wool in the European market.

MORIMONDO

Morimondus

location: near Abbiategrasso (Lombardy), Italy

founded: at Coronago in 1133, by Morimond

suppressed: 1799 (under Napoleon)

present status: parish church

See also p. 79.

Bibliography
Silvia NOCENTINI, *Morimondo*, in *Architettura cistercense, Fontenay e le abbazie in Italia dal 1120 al 1160*, Edizioni Casamari, Certosa di Firenze, 1995.
Paolo CALLIARI, *L'Abbazia cistercense di Morimondo*, Morimondo, 1991.
Padre MAUROLOI, *L'Abbazia cistercense di Morimondo*, Fondazione Abbazia, S. Maria di Morimondo, 1993.

The very name of this abbey declares whose daughter it is. Morimond's task was to establish daughter houses in eastern Europe, but this Italian exception clearly exemplifies the independence enjoyed by abbeys (while respecting the Rule and the Carta Caritatis). This lay at the root of the Cistercian Order's strength.

The name of the abbey also sums up the spirit of Cistercian monasticism, for Morimondo means "dying to the world"! But self-sufficiency and land ownership did not impede growth within the cloister walls. Morimondo was home to almost 300 monks in the years following its foundation.

The abbey, which moved to its current site in 1136, was built between 1141 and 1158, while church construction lasted from 1182 to 1296. The church building marks the zenith of Cistercian architecture in Lombardy. Brick triumphs in the massive columns and the high rib vault with whitewashed panels. The cloister, chapter house, and conventual buildings all demonstrate the complete mastery of brick, the basic material used north of the Alps.

Like so many northern Italian abbeys and cities, Morimondo was caught up in long centuries of conflict between neighboring city states and princedoms. On the border between Milan and Pavia, Morimondo was attacked by the latter in 1237, 1245, 1266, 1273, and 1290.

Some of the greatest names in history crop up in the chronicles of Morimondo: Frederick Barbarossa, St. Charles Borromeo, Pope Gregory XII, Napoleon Bonaparte. There were periods of unrest among the lay brothers and abuses by commendatory (absentee) abbots. And we should not forget the arguments over matters of dogma and even liturgy that frequently upset monastic life. Following the Council of Trent, Morimondo fell out with the Bishop of Milan over whether to pray using the Ambrosian or Roman rite!

Nowadays, Morimondo is used for large-scale cultural events, while plans are in hand to turn part of it into a museum dedicated to the agricultural history of the Ticino Valley.

Above and left:
A triumph in brick, the first material to become standard in those places without a source of building stone. Roman and Italian architects used it with great skill, making the architecture "sing" (in the words of Paul Valéry).

Facing page, right:
The cloister.

NOIRLAC

Niger Lacus

location: Bruere-Allichamps (Cher), Central France

founded: 1136, by Clairvaux

church dating from: 1150–1200

dissolved: 1791 (French Revolution)

present use: cultural center

See also pp. 59, 88, 112, 114

Bibliography
Anselme DIMIER, *L'art cistercien*, Zodique, La Pierre-qui-Vire, 1971.
Émile MESLE and J. M. JENN, *L'Abbaye de Noirlac*, C.N.M.H.S., 1980

Today Noirlac sets one thinking about the way historic buildings are perceived by France's "general public": those people who swell the crowds at Mont-Saint-Michel while being quite unaware of a masterpiece like Noirlac. This is a typically Cistercian abbey, as complete and well restored as Fontenay or Le Thoronet, yet it welcomes only 50,000 visitors a year, one-third of the figure for Fontenay, half that for Fontfroide. True, restoration began only in 1949, and the site, not then open to the public, did not benefit from the huge volume of tourist books written in the early nineteen-hundreds,

which established an influential hierarchy of "places to visit". True, also, that the abbey's setting lacks the emotive power of a forest clearing (Fontenay) or a deserted valley (Fontfroide). True, also, that the most visited abbeys are near to holiday locations. Nevertheless, Noirlac is a beautiful, moving abbey.

Its history, however, scarcely explains its architectural perfection. Have only the charters, archives, and evidence survived which involve the long series of difficulties which the abbey encountered? They started with the choice of site, which did not follow Cîteaux's directives. Settling between the banks of the Cher, then a navigable river, and the main road was hardly fleeing the world. And the monks were not able to suppress a legend (undoubtedly false, but significant) that the river flowed into stagnant creeks ("black lakes", hence Noirlac) where a child had drowned. Why did they abandon the initial name of Maison-Dieu-sur-Cher?

The first abbot designated by St. Bernard was his nephew Robert, who had fled Clairvaux for Cluny. He had been forgiven, but was he capable of such a responsibility? Ten years after its foundation the abbey was unable to survive without help, and the king had to provide the bread ration. In around 1175 the personnel was decimated by plague. Later an abbot was deposed for disobeying the General Chapter. Another abbot ravaged the abbey in a search for gold in the cellars (1234). Then the military ravaged Noirlac and the Berry region. In 1476 a monk was murdered by one of his fellows. In 1506 the monks rebelled against the abbot. In 1510 a commendatory abbot took over, as elsewhere. In 1562 the Huguenots sacked the establishment. In 1654 only four monks remained.

The church, north side. An architecture which is closed to the world. "If you desire to know what is inside, leave outside the bodies that you brought from the world: only souls are aloud inside" (Bernard de Clairvaux, Address to the Novices).

After the Revolution a porcelain factory was set up there, with their kilns in the church! In 1890 the buildings were taken over by an "industrial and agricultural orphanage". The orphans were followed by a group of nuns who proved too mystical, and were condemned by Rome. Then a children's holiday camp. Then Spanish refugees from the Civil War. Then a hospice.

Despite all this, Noirlac still possesses one of the finest monastic ensembles in France, a perfect example of Cistercian architecture of the second half of the twelfth century. It bears witness, perhaps, to Cîteaux's flexibility when it came to forming a living community.

Noirlac is, with Fontenay, one of the two daughter abbeys of Clairvaux which were most faithfully inspired by their mother church. The church of Fontenay (1137–47) was completed very rapidly, thanks to the generosity of the English bishop Eberard of Norwich, who had

taken refuge there. Noirlac did not benefit from this good fortune. Work on the sanctuary, with its square east end, took place in 1150 and 1160, which explains why it is tunnel vaulted and lit by a triplet of Romanesque windows and an oculus. At the same time the transept and four chapels for ordained monks were constructed; groin vaults were attempted for the latter. As for the transept, initially intended to support a traditional vault, it was raised in order to

Facing page:
Fan vaulting of one of the chapter pillars and capital with waterleaf ornament, the only one that the Cistercians allowed in their monasteries. The variations on this theme rapidly became exuberant.

Left:
North side of the ,elevation of the nave.

achieve Noirlac's first rib vaults. After a break of ten years work resumed on the nave. It would be Gothic, but lack of money meant that only two bays of the monks' choir could be completed, together with the south wall against which the cloister would be built. The six bays of the nave were not completed until the thirteenth century, together with the façade (two small doors within a porch which has now vanished, and a hexafoil rose window. Yet, the unity of the church has not been impaired by the length of these works, for St. Bernard's influence was stronger still.

The Bernardine program was also respected, despite the vicissitudes of time, in the buildings of the conventual quadrangle. The present cloister is not the original one. Its west walk was rebuilt after the lay brothers' passage was suppressed. The east walk dates from the fourteenth century, but the chapter house (six square bays) is original (late twelfth century). The south walk gives access to the refectory. This remarkably restored room is divided into two aisles in four bays. The vaulting ribs rest on engaged columns supported on corbels. The south gable wall has four large windows and two rose windows: Jean-Pierre Raymond's clear glass here proves wonderfully adapted to Cistercian architecture.

The lay brothers' range retains a fine cellar from the late twelfth century. In this room, as in all the restored rooms of the abbey, various cultural activities are always going on, allowing a site which deserves to draw larger crowds in future to be shown to best advantage.

Facing page:
Flying buttresses and
buttresses, north side of
the nave. "The simple
flying buttresses en
quart-de-cercle without
ornament which
contrebutent the vaults
of the nave were added
afterwards" (Marcel
Aubert). It was meant to
reinforce the structure of
the nave around 1190.

Left:
Noirlac's refectory is one
of the most elegant of all
cistercian architecture.
The white on white
stained-glass windows
from J. P. Raynaud
emphasizes the
perfection of the whole.

271

Right:

"Still almost intact, Noirlac's cloister is more recent. Its construction began in the fourteenth century and probably continued until the middle of the next century. The details are simple and elegant. The arches are remarquable for their lightness and the elegance of its diagonal ribs." Prosper Mérimée, Notes of a journey in Auvergne, 1838.

Facing page:

The bicentenary linden cloister.

OBAZINE

Obazina

location: Aubazine (Corrèze), Limousin region, France

founded: 1147, by Cîteaux

church 1156–1190

dissolved: 1791 (French Revolution)

present status: Parish church

See also pp. 20, 25, 47, 54, 107.

Bibliography
Bernadette BARRIÈRE, *L'Abbaye cistercienne d'Obazine en bas Limousin* (Origines-Patrimoine), Tulle, 1977.
Bernadette BARRIÈRE, *Aubazine en bas Limousin*, Association histoire et archéologie en Pays d'Obazine, Limoges, 1991.

Perched halfway up the slope, between the plateau and the valley of middle Corrèze, the abbey of Obazine does not fit the principles of the Cistercian Order in the matter of siting monasteries. But the General Chapter and Bernard of Clairvaux were able to set aside dogmatism at times when a large abbey and its daughter house came to seek their support. Such was the case for Obazine, attached to Cîteaux in 1147, or for Savigny and its 29 daughter houses attached at the same date to Clairvaux.

From 1142, Étienne de Vielzot had begun to gather around him, in the forest of Obazine, men and women who lived as hermits in poverty and prayer. As numbers grew, he was forced to create two cenobitic monasteries, one for men on what was to be the site of the abbey,

and one for women at Coyroux, a third of a mile (600m) lower down. So as to safeguard the future of his congregation, Étienne was able to attach the communities to Cîteaux at the same time as preserving their status as a double monastery. The men's community had authority over the spiritual and material life of the female community, who were committed by their founder to total enclosure.

Nevertheless, Cîteaux intervened, in order to ensure that the liturgical and economic life of Obazine conformed with Cistercian usages. In less than a century, the abbey had accumulated a patrimony of more than twenty granges, of remarkably diversified types. Cereals were cultivated in Lower Limousin and Upper Quercy; grapes were grown at Donzenac; forestry and

Facing page, photo on the right:
The church without its first six bays and its pastiche façade (eighteenth and nineteenth centuries).

Left:
The romanesque church tower is a masterpiece due to Aubazine's carpenters, contributing to the perfection of Obazine's abbey church.

pasture were the activities in the Auvergne; even salt-production was carried on at the island of Oléron. But the main contribution of the Cistercians was in the hydraulic arrangements at the abbey. Obazine had no supply of running water, and the type of work advocated by the Rule required it. The monks diverted water from the Coyroux, nearly a mile (1500m) from the monastery, by means of the famous "monks' canal" built into the side of the mountain. This work of art represents a series of technological miracles, such as "St. Stephen's Gap" (La Brèche de Saint-Étienne), corbelled out over a drop of more than 150ft (50m).

The abbey church, reached from the little square of the village of Aubazine, lost six of its nine bays in 1757. The central nave, between groin-vaulted aisles, is covered with a slightly pointed tunnel vault, supported by reinforcing arches descending to engaged columns with undecorated capitals of an extreme simplicity. The same vaulting system is used for the transepts, each with three square-ended chapels. The choir, apsidal with three sections of plain wall and three windows, has a lower roof; the resulting diaphragm arch also has three windows. As always, an assertion of the Trinity, at a time when it was still being hotly debated.

Three elements of great interest attract attention. Firstly, one or two remaining windows in grisaille, almost white, that retain original elements (in the bays of the north wall), providing evidence about early Cistercian windows. Then there is the famous liturgical armoire dating from the end of the twelfth century, one of the few pieces of medieval furniture still in a good state of conservation. Lastly, the cupola on pendentives, built of dressed stone, over the crossing, a rare intact example of this type of construction. It is covered by an unusual bell tower, too imposing to be Cistercian but which achieves the transition from the square crossing to the octagonal tower by means of a "hyperbolic paraboloid", occasionally imitated by other church builders, but never successfully. The Obazine tower remains unique to this day.

Also worthy of mention is the very modern-looking statue of a beautiful Mary Magdalen, found among some remains of a fifteenth-century Deposition during excavations in the nearby monastery of Coyroux.

Facing page:
The nave and the sanctuary with its two bays. The second bay forms a three-sided apse lower than the first one, which allows a diaphragm arch and three small windows. Each side of the apse has a "limousine molding" (a molding situated beyond the arch of the bay and falling on to small columns of the same diameter).

Left:
Interrupted engaged column in the south transept.

ORVAL

Aurea Vallis

location: Villers devant Orval, Luxembourg province, Belgium

founded: 1132, by Trois Fontaines (filiation of Clairvaux)

suppressed: 1797

present status: monastery of the Order of Cistercians of the Strict Observance (since 1926)

See also pp. 68, 109, 122, 134, 135.

Bibliography
Abbaye d'Orval, Orval.
La Belgique selon Victor Hugo, Desoer, 1978.

Orval stands apart as, unusually, it houses two monastic complexes side by side. On the one hand, there is the modern abbey, whose monastic quadrangle is laid out on the traditional plan; on the other, there is the old abbey which has been built and rebuilt time and again since the Middle Ages and of which today only beautiful ruins survive.

Visiting the ruins is a moving experience but not an easy one if you are trying to work out which remains belonged to each of the successive abbeys that once stood on a spot too well beloved of monks and armies alike.

Originally, in 1070 Benedictine monks arrived from Calabria and settled here in the heart of the Gaumais forests, to the east of the Ardennes. Legend has it that Countess Matilda of Tuscany, their patroness, lost her wedding ring in the abbey spring but that a trout from this "golden valley" fetched it back for her. Too far away from home, the founders went back to Italy and were succeeded for a few years by secular canons until Bernard of Clairvaux dispatched the abbot of Trois Fontaines to take possession of the place. By the end of the twelfth century the buildings in Gothic style were finally ready for use by the Cistercian community.

In 1637, during the Thirty Years War, the abbey was torched by Maréchal de Châtillon's troops, only to be rebuilt in 1680. During the eighteenth century, once the Jansenist crisis was over and prosperity recovered, the monks pulled part of the buildings down to make way for a new construction commissioned from Dewez, the architect, in 1759. The monks got little benefit from this because revolutionary troops demolished the abbey in 1793. It was sold as a quarry in 1797 and had to wait until 1926 to return to its original vocation, when monks from Sept-Fons settled there once more. The modern abbey opened in 1938.

Orval adheres to every archetype you can think of when it comes to Cistercian abbeys. Firstly, it is located in the midst of forests, in a secluded valley which has been dammed to create peaceful lakes full of water-lilies and water fowl. Then there are the ruins which bear witness to the long and often dramatic place the Cistercian Order held not only in religious history but in political, economic, and social history too. It is in this spirit that the architecture of Cîteaux came here, passing from one abbey to the next, right on down the centuries. It must be said, though, that the monumental Virgin Mary on the façade and the towers clearly break the Cistercian Rule, while the new building displays a neo-Fascist aesthetic that is not in keeping with the style of life adopted by its present-day Cistercian occupants. Orval has, perhaps, benefited more than it deserves from the image of the ascetic Trappist supplying the world with gastronomic delights. Here, however, they also produce medicines, as can be seen from the medicinal herb garden and the pharmacy museum, both open to visitors.

Victor Hugo was a precursor of the tourists who now throng to Orval. He visited the abbey on 29 August 1862 when he painted a watercolor, obviously Romantic, showing a young girl in the midst of the ruins.

Small chapel on the south side of the east end of the first church.

Basin of the first cloister and traces of the western gallery.

South aisle of the first church.

Trefoil doorway to the "porte des morts", north transept of the church. This door was only opened for the burial of monks or lay brothers. The cemetery formerly extended to the north of the transept and the sanctuary.

OSEK

Ossecum

location: Osek (Northern Bohemia), Czech Republic

founded: 1193, by Waldsassen (filiation of Morimond)

suppressed: between 1420 and 1624, and again between 1945–90

present status: monastery

See also p. 125.

Bibliography
Katerina CHARVATOVA and Dobroslav LIBAI, *Ràd Cistercià*, Prague, 1992.
Marianne BERNHARD, *Abbayes*, P.M.L. Editions, Munich, 1994.
Vaclav VENTURA, "Les cisterciens en Bohème et Moravie", in *Oculus* No. 10, 1997.

The town of Osek has a beautiful Cistercian abbey, returned to the monks after the "Velvet Revolution" of 1990. It had been equally ignored by travelers and guidebooks, for the north of Bohemia is better known for the scars it bears from a century of intensive industrialization carried on in the iron-ore bearing mountains of Krusné Hory that form the frontier between Germany and the Czech Republic. Today, the landscape has changed little: coal mines, power stations, iron works, and chemical factories still alternate with polluted industrial towns, and forests whose trees are dying from the effects of acid rain.

The abbey went through a long initial building period under the protection of the Hrabysice family who wanted to use it for their family mausoleum. The three-aisled Gothic church, inspired chiefly by the Burgundian churches (with a square east end as at Cîteaux), was built between 1207 and 1280. Abbot Slavko, son of the founder of the abbey, built the east wing of the cloister with a chapter house (1225–50). The other sides of the cloister were not finished for another century. Today, this venerable cloister with its fountain and chapter house are all that remains of the original abbey.

At this period, the abbey controlled a small area of farmland, including about ten granges and fifty villages. It founded no daughter houses, preferring to live peacefully in the shelter of the surrounding forests and mountains.

But frontier regions are never peaceful, as Osek was to find to its cost more than once. In 1248 the monastery was damaged in the fighting between the king, Wenceslas II, and his son and heir, Premysl Otakar II. In 1278 Rudolph of Habsburg sacked the abbey. In 1341 a fire reduced the church to ashes and the abbey had to seek the patronage of the king, John of Luxembourg. This did not prevent the destruction of the monastery by the Hussites in 1420.

It was not until 1624, when Catholic Bohemia was withdrawing from the Thirty Years' War, that Osek returned to the monastic life. New protectors enabled it, in the Baroque period, to become the most important Cistercian abbey in Bohemia.

The architect Ottavio Broggio, in charge of restoring the church, involved numerous artists in its transformation into a manifesto for Baroque, to the glory of Our Lady of the Assumption. The generosity of Baroque leads to an accumulation of talent. Marianne Bernhard has drawn up a list of these often minor "talents", but ones that brought to Osek, as to other parts of eighteenth-century central Europe, a fertile

Incited by political power to undertake social tasks (parish apostolate, youth education, etc.), the Cistercians of Central Europe were quick to adopt Baroque architecture for its potential ability to seduce the faithful. Thus art came back in triumph for the glorification of God.

inventiveness, a novelty of form, and an imagination that brought changes to architectural space, introducing a sense of movement, bringing a freedom that announced new discoveries for the future.

The main façade, with its three storeys, white portico, and heavy volutes, was decorated by Franz Anton Kuen with statues of the Cistercian saints, the Evangelists, and the patron saints of Bohemia. Edmund Johann Richter added a statue of St John the Baptist surrounded by angels in 1713. The richly decorated interior is the work of Giacomo Antonio Corbellini. The paintings were executed by a number of well-known artists: Wenzel-Lorenz Reiner, of Prague, painted frescos of a thoroughly Italianate nobility; Johann Jacob Steinfels, known for his illusionistic style, carried out the paintings and stucco work, representing scenes from the life of Jesus, on the ceiling. The altarpiece, depicting the martyrdom of St. Sebastian, was painted by Michael Willman. Reiner was also responsible for the altars of St. Bernard and of the founder of the Order.

In 1945 the German monks were expelled from the abbey, and the remaining community, too small to be viable, let out the monastery to the Salesians. In 1950 the totalitarian government closed down all religious houses in the country, interning their occupants in camps. In 1953 the abbey of Osek was turned into a retirement home for nuns. The buildings, belonging to the State which did little to maintain them, began to fall into a state of disrepair. The monks returned to Osek in 1990 after the "Velvet Revolution". A small community of six is attempting to revive the old monastery.

The small and large organs. The use of the organ in the liturgy dates back to ancient times (the Hebrews already had a portable organ). The organ was familiar to the medieval Cistercians but we do not have evidence of them using it for their psalmodies. During the eighteenth century music was very successful in the liturgy and was used to emphasise emotions along with incense during the services. The organ cases became a pretext for magnificence. They were made of rare woods and precious metals, and covered with sculptures and paintings that were meant to evoke Paradise. Bohemia excelled at this sumptuous art.

Chapter house of the Gothic monastery. The knot that ties the two small columns together is a journeyman's "chef-d'oeuvre"—here a sculptor in stone. We find this kind of achievement—some would say coquetry—in other Cistercian abbeys (eg. Chiaravalle della Colomba, p. 167).

The cloister gallery was probably closed with ornate Gothic windows at the time of its construction because of the rigors of winter.

OTTERBERG

Otterburgum

location: near Otterberg (Palatinate), Germany

founded: 1145, by Eberbach (filiation of Clairvaux)

suppressed: 1560 (Reformation)

present status: twin-denomination church (Catholic and Protestant)

See also pp. 105, 116.

Bibliography
L'Église cistercienne d'Otterberg, Otterberg Protestant and Catholic Presbyteries, 1990.
Otterberg, Kirche Konfessionen Geschichte, 1993.
G. GLAPA and R. WESTRICH, *Otterberg (Pfalz)*, Deutscher Kunstverlag, Munich, Berlin, 1995.

"Anyone who has not seen Otterberg cannot fully understand the Cistercian spirit." This is what Georg Dehios wrote in his work on the German abbeys. It is quite true that the church, which is all that survives of the ancient abbey, is neither purely Romanesque nor particularly Gothic, but it is totally Cistercian. Building techniques harnessed in the service of an architectural ideal and not of a style is precisely what the Cistercians taught us!

In 1143 the Erbach monks were given the land on which they could found a new monastery and they set about the task in 1145. But the site proved full of difficulties and, after consulting Hildegarde of Bingen, they moved to another one in about 1160. The new site was near the River Otter and work on building the abbey got under way. The Romanesque choir and transept were the first to be finished. There was then a pause lasting several years, during which fresh funds were collected. Work started again in 1230 and by 1254 the Bishop of Mainz consecrated the now rib-vaulted church. A lovely radiating rose window adorned the façade but, in accordance with Bernard of Clairvaux's teachings, it had clear glass, and the interior of the church was left totally plain.

Following the Reformation, the monks were turned out of the monastery in 1560. A few years later Johan Casimir, the Prince Palatine, allowed the Walons family to use the (empty) abbey. The first demolition began. But the Spanish occupied the Palatinate in 1621 and restored the abbey to the Cistercians in 1629. The country was then invaded by the Swedes and in 1648 the White Monks were thrown out for the last time (Treaty of Munster). It was not until the Peace of Ryswick (1697) that the church became "twin denomination", with the Catholics occupying the east end and the choir, and the Protestants the nave. A wall was built across the church to separate the faithful of different confessions. Under French occupation at the end of the eighteenth century, the church was turned into a hayloft

The wall was demolished in 1947 and today work is underway on renovating the church. There is little doubt it is now more beautiful than it has ever been. Excavation work has also revealed part of the chapter house beneath a neighboring house.

Transept crossing. The full-centered arch and the rib vault create a purely Cistercian architecture. However, the stylistic qualification of the monument is less important than the signification of the construction by those who planned it and those who use it.

Variations on the aisles.

POBLET

Populetum

location: Vimbodi, Catalonia, Spain

founded: 1150, by Fontfroide (filiation of Clairvaux)

dissolved: 1835 (repayment of national debt)

present status: monastery of the Order of Cistercians of the Common Observance (since 1940)

See also pp. 27, 39, 44, 65, 91, 114,118

Bibliography

Emilia ALTARRIBA and Joseph BALUJA, *Poblet*, 1988.

Jesus M. OLIVER, *Abbaye de Poblet*, Escudo de Oro, Barcelona, 1997.

Anselme DIMIER, *L'Art cistercien*, vol. 2, Zodiaque, La Pierre-qui-Vire, 1971.

Over the centuries even the most war-hardened or life-weary lords must have been moved when in the distance they saw the monastery-palace that is the abbey of Santa Maria de Poblet. They rode towards it through a sea of vineyards that sweeps right up to the ochre walls of the monastery. One of the twelve watch towers in the walls houses the gatehouse—*Benedicamus domino—Deo gratias*. A long avenue leads up to the Golden Gate. "Here it was that kings dismounted and kissed the relics of the True Cross brought to them by the abbot, who came out to greet them accompanied by the entire religious community" (Anselme Dimier). Then another long avenue lead up to the narthex of the church and the Puerta Real

which opens like a chasm between two towers. The very architecture of Poblet demonstrates the power of the Church at the height of Christianity. It exudes a haughty confidence which does much to explain why when revolutionary fever gripped the people they were able to destroy its statues, break its glass windows and tear down all that symbolized the grip of religion over their everyday lives.

The abbey was founded by monks from Fontfroide on a site among hills covered in holm oaks and almond trees. Their job was to exploit a very large gift made by Raymond Béranger IV, the new ruler of the recently formed state of Catalonia-Aragon which had been created by his marriage in 1137 to the only child of the

Facing page, right:
The western façade of the church looks on to the narthex. The pilgrim is welcomed by Mary of the Mystery of Assumption, patron of the monastery and the Order, Benedict of Nursia and Bernard of Clairvaux.

Left:
Vault of the sanctuary apse and the upper part of the large altarpiece by Damia Forment (white alabaster, 1527).

Above:
The proud lantern of the transept is a remarkable sign of the magnificence of the Cistercian Order in Calalonia in the fourteenth century.

Facing page:
The lavatorium, seen from the inner courtyard of the cloister. In the foreground, a clump of acanthus, the eternal ornament of the Corinthian capitals.

king of Aragon. The monks needed to build a large abbey for it was also to house the tombs of this new dynasty. Furthermore, as happened when the neighboring abbey of Santes Creus was founded, the Cistercians were expected to sustain the *Reconquista* through the force of their prayers and the depth of their coffers.

Poblet ran into a few troubles at the start of the thirteenth century when Pope Innocent III appointed Arnaud Amaury, the abbot of Cîteaux (later Archbishop of Narbonne), and Simon de Montfort to head up the all-too famous crusade against the Albigensians. As the "crusaders" reached Languedoc, Pedro II of Aragon, nicknamed the Catholic, felt unable to leave his vassals unprotected. He took up arms against Simon de Montfort and died at the Battle of Muret in 1213. On that occasion, the abbot of Poblet was to discover just how much the multi-national dimension of the Order could clash with the interests of individual states. The abbot was a Cistercian and a friend of Arnaud Amaury, but he was also Catalan and a friend of Pedro II of Aragon. He himself was assassinated in 1214!

In the following centuries the abbey met with both difficulty and success, just like every other Cistercian abbey in Europe. Along with all the other Spanish monasteries, its existence was brought to a brutal halt in the nineteenth century (1835). But after a period of pillage and destruction, restoration work was started in 1883. The church was opened for worship once more in 1935 and the Cistercians took the abbey back in 1940.

The church (1166–1190) is a fine example of Romanesque architecture built faithfully in the spirit that ran permeates the Order's first major constructions. The tall nave has a pointed tunnel vault, whose transverse arches rest on engaged shafts which are supported on corbels ten feet (3m) above the ground. The nave achieves a rare perfection. The aisles, crossing, and ambulatory are all rib vaulted.

During the fourteenth century many innovations were made to the church. The tombs of the royal family of Catalonia-Aragon are in the abbey. Each tomb rests on a depressed arch standing at the entrances to the transept arms. Almost as proof of the abbey's ability to withstand misfortune, when the Black Death raged at its worst they built the famous open-work octagonal tower above the crossing, which sits atop the church like a lace cap. Work on embellishing the abbey started again in the eighteenth century: the west front was given a Baroque make-over; the fine burial place in the chapel of the Holy Sepulchre in the narthex was shown

off to advantage; and a new sacristy was built off the south transept. When the dome was raised by the addition of a lantern higher than the transept tower, the shape of the abbey was completely changed, making it look ever more like S. Geminiano! But even before the Baroque architects were tempted to interfere with the place, the Valencian sculptor Damia Froment had already made a huge alabaster retable which was installed in the church (1527–29).

Next comes the wonderful Gothic cloister which serves all areas of abbey communal life. Its plan is strictly faithful to St. Bernard. Finally, sheltered from the midday sun by the nave of the church, the cloister garth with its cypress

trees adds a note of humble humanity to the abbey. Here the silence is broken only by water trickling in the fountain. A few acanthus plants grow in front of the arches along the east walk. You can admire the fine barrel-vaulted walk, the monks' common-room which is now a library after being used for some time as a writing room, and the calefactory, or warming room. Next there is the refectory, which is also barrel-vaulted with a corbelled lectern set into the wall. Then there is the old kitchen with its chimneys and what used to be the lay brothers' refectory. But you must not miss the perfection of the chapter house where four slender columns support nine wonderfully elegant ribbed vaults.

You get the true measure of Poblet by going up to the first floor of the monks' range where the huge dormitory stretches for nearly 300ft (90m). As at Santes Creus, it has a double-pitched roof supported by nineteen diaphragm arches resting on finely carved corbel capitals. The room is flooded with light from a double row of windows. There are two low windows in each bay, which cast light on the beds, and one high window every other bay to let light and air into the room. This is the same arrangement as at Notre-Dame-du-Val or at Longpont.

Facing page:
The lavatorium and its
fresh water bowl.

Above:
The chapter house.

*The north aisle of the
church. On the right, the
"porte des morts" (door
of the dead). On the left,
tomb of the Princes of
Aragon (the "Royal
Pantheon").*

PONTIGNY

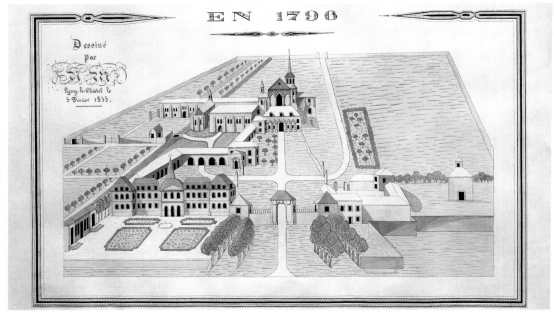

Pontiniacum

location: Pontigny (Yonne), Burgundy, France

founded: 1114, by Cîteaux

church built: 1140–70 and 1185–1205

dissolved: 1791 (French Revolution)

present use: parish church and training center

See also pp. 28, 37, 46–8, 74, 95–7, 102,103, 106, 114, 117

Bibliography
Claude WILNER, *Pontigny*, Zodiaque, La Pierre-qui-Vire, 1964.

A great ship marooned in the fields. Before you do anything else, just take a walk around it. Keep your distance. Then, in turn, walk down each of the roads that lead toward Pontigny. You get the most lovely view, of the *chevet*, when you approach along the Tuilerie from the direction of Ligny-le-Chatel. Only after you have done this should you walk up the avenue that leads to the porch of this unique abbey church. This is in fact the only one that remains of Cîteaux and its first four daughters.

And inside it is even bigger! And taller! And wider! 390ft (119m) long and 65ft (20m) high. The aisles are groin vaulted: they were built first they provided buttressing for the nave. Intersecting ribs were not yet used by the Cistercians but this changed just as soon as they saw how great a saving they afforded in terms both of stone and weight compared to the traditional Romanesque vault. Thus it is we find

a Gothic nave, where the decision to switch style was only taken after work had got under way. Archeologists, including the Pontigny specialist Terryl N. Kinder, have proved that the building evolved organically in this fashion. Later on the Order of Cîteaux got carried away with building and started constructing churches of cathedral proportions. Then the Pontigny monks demolished the rectangular chevet of the original sanctuary and replaced it with one of the largest Gothic sanctuaries ever built with eleven radiating chapels. The tall rib-vaulted *chevet* is elegantly supported on a corona of monolithic columns. The nave is divided in two by choir stalls which date from the end of the seventeenth century (1676). However, they replaced others that were already there and are sited almost at the crossing, a good position for a lovely acoustic. It is also the best position to be in during the services. The lay brothers, way

Facing page:
General view in the eighteenth century.

Left:
The south aisle. Why do the aisles of the Cistercian churches seem to impose a stronger feeling of ascetism, purity and silence specific to the monastic ideal than the naves?

down the far end of the church, had to listen hard and put up with seeing nothing!

As a mother house, Pontigny did not spread itself very far, leaving it to Clairvaux and Morimond to set the records for spawning daughters. Pontigny was rich but without ever attaining the income levels of the more powerful abbeys (in 1765 the Royal Commission of Assessors reckoned it had 25 monks and 27,000 pounds worth of net resources each year, in other words three times less income than Clairvaux and half the number of monks).

Perhaps Pontigny's greatest riches lay in its friendships which, during the Middle Ages, were English. The abbey's main claim to fame was that it gave refuge (from 1164 to 1166) to Thomas Becket, the English prelate exiled for his opposition to King Henry II, who finally returned to his diocese only to fall victim to the "murder in the cathedral". When another archbishop of Canterbury, Stephan Langton, was also exiled, he followed in Becket's steps and went to Pontigny (from 1208 to 1213).

Later still the future Saint Edmund, also an archbishop of Canterbury, was on his was to Rome to seek justice when he stopped at the monastery, where he died (1240). His tomb can still be seen in the sanctuary of the church, but more specifically for centuries it was a place of annual pilgrimage where people came at Whitsun to venerate the saint. It is still on that date that the Friends of Pontigny now organize excellent concerts of ancient English music in the abbey church. Mary Berry and the Cambridge Schola Gregoriana have often taken part…

Pontigny's "lay" period was distinguished for its visiting intellectuals. The pacifist Paul Desjardins used to hold the famous Decades of Pontigny here every year and among those who attended were Gide, Malraux, Martin du Gard, Mauriac, Bachelard…

Above:
The north aisle seen from the sanctury ambulatory. On the left, the grills of the sanctuary (eighteenth century).

Facing page:
The elevation on the south side of the nave. This view shows the Cistercian corbels, allowing the stalls to back directly on to the piers.

Following pages:
Built directly on the thick clay of the Valley of Serein (which is used to make the famous handmade Pontigny tiles), without a crypt and foundations, the great abbey nave seems to have run aground in the middle of the harvest, as if it came from somewhere else. For the peasants of the twelfth century, the Cistercians did indeed come from elsewhere, with their mysticism and their Order, founded on combative faith and progressive colonization.

PORTALEGRE

São Bernardo de Portalegre

location: Portalegre (Alentejo), Portugal

founded: 1518, by Alcobaça (filiation of Clairvaux)

suppressed: 1854

present status: barracks

See also p. 36.

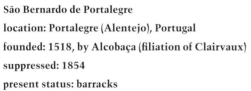

Bibliography
Dom Maur COCHERIL, *Routier des abbayes cisterciennes du Portugal*, Fondation C. Gulbenkian, Lisbon-Paris, 1986.
Portugal, Hachette, Paris, 1989.

In no other European country did the Cistercians exert so strong an influence as they did in Portugal. The enormous fame of Alcobaça overshadows the role played by the eighteen monasteries, fourteen nunneries and two military Orders which represented Cîteaux in this new nation. The founder of the Portuguese monarchy, Dom Alfonso Henriquez (1128–85), called in the White Monks to organize the territory. Later on it was a Cistercian, a Master of the Knights of Avis, Dom João I (1385–1433), who was to found a new dynasty.

Among all the Cistercian establishments, one nunnery stands out. This is Portalegre, established in 1518 in a hamlet in the depths of Alentejo province. The surrounding countryside is covered in beautiful holm-oak forests and is thinly populated. Eagles still fly high over the hills of the Serra de São Mamede. The tiny town is steeped in history and within its ramparts it still preserves countless memories of a rich past and is still deservedly renowned for the tapestries its craftsmen produce.

The founder of the nunnery, Dom Jorge de Melo, was a very colorful character. He was Bishop of Egitane and commendator (temporary or absentee abbot) of Alcobaça before being appointed abbot of Portalegre. Here, he wanted to take in young women without a dowry not, as tradition would have it, as *conversae*, or lay sisters, but as choir nuns. Extremely wealthy in his own right, he was able to provide for the day-to-day expenses of the abbey which he gave to his sister to run. On his death, the inheritance was divided between his mistress, his son, and the religious community!

The abbey at Portalegre was inhabited by fifty to sixty nuns until 1854, when Portugal

Facing page, right:
The abbey of Portalegre has two multistorey cloisters which link together through a covered passage.

Left:
Open windows towards the sky. These remnants of the demolished building are exemplary of the exterior decoration of Portalegre's architecture.

Above:
The narthex of the church.

passed decrees ordering the closure of all monasteries.

The entrance to Portalegre is unusually elegant. The white marble portal is surmounted by the royal coat-of-arms as well as that of the congregation. Then comes a large, enclosed courtyard with a beautiful Baroque fountain in the middle. The church doorway opens on to a pavement of *azulejos*, or glazed tiles, running below Manueline rib vaults springing from corbels decorated with twisted strings, a typical motif found in all local monuments. Once stripped of its furnishings, all that survives of the early church are the screen grills and Dom Jorge de Melo's tomb in Estremoz marble. Two choirs, built one over the other, allowed the nuns access to stalls at dormitory level where they could say Matins. Galleries on both storeys connect the church to the nunnery's two cloisters.

The *azulejos* in the church and galleries depict a mixture of religious and secular subjects. They date from 1739 and have been attributed to a Lisbon workshop. Some of the most beautiful scenes they show are of the famous episode of the infant St. Bernard asleep at the door of the church while awaiting midnight mass, the death of St. Benedict, and that of Bernard of Clairvaux, and the two legendary episodes from St. Bernard's hagiography. One is St. Bernard before Christ where Jesus's left arm, which has come away from the cross, is resting on Bernard's shoulder and the blood gushing from the wound in Christ's side spurts on to the lips of the abbot of Clairvaux. The other is the Lactation of the Virgin where Bernard kneels before the Virgin and Child, reciting the hymn *Ave Maris Stella*. In the moment that he utters the words *Monstra te esse Matrem*, the Virgin bares her breast and a jet of the milk that Christ himself suckled covers the saint's face.

The church decoration includes an altarpiece (north wall of the nave), azulejos, tombs, a nice pulpit, the tomb of Dom Jorge de Melo and two nuns' choirs.

RIEVAULX

Rievallis

location: Helmsley (North Yorkshire), England

founded: 1132, by Clairvaux

dissolved: 1538 (Dissolution)

present status: Privately owned, managed by English Heritage

See also pp. 74, 102, 107, 109.

Bibliography

Glyn COPPACK and Peter FERGUSSON, *Rievaulx Abbey*, English Heritage, London, 1994.
Peter FERGUSSON and Stuart HARRISON, "The Rievaulx Abbey Chapter House", in *Antiquaries Journal*, vol. 84, 1994.
Anselme DIMIER, *L'Art cistercien*, vol. 2, Zodiaque, La Pierre-qui-Vire, 1971.
Philippe BAUD, *La Ruche de Cîteaux*, Cerf, Paris, 1997.
E. C. NORTON and D. PARK (eds.), *Cistercian Art and Architecture in the British Isles*, Cambridge, 1986.

Rievaulx was the first Cistercian abbey in northern England, and benefited from the help of Clairvaux. William, former secretary to St Bernard, was the first abbot. The abbey soon became autonomous and was rich in numbers (140 monks and 500 lay brothers), daughter houses (eleven abbeys), and property (more than ten granges).

The architecture closely reflects the two phases of the abbey's history. Its site, on the banks of the river Rye, in a narrow valley, follows Bernardine principles, although the narrowness of the valley meant that the east end of the church had to be turned slightly to the north. Building started in 1135, at the same time that Bernard of Clairvaux was beginning work on his second abbey. A square-ended presbytery, short transepts, each with three chapels, a Romanesque nave, no decoration: the abbey followed to the letter the spirit of Cîteaux

as defined by Bernard of Clairvaux. All the more so, since it was under the influence of a monk with a strong personality, Aelred of Rievaulx, who was to be abbot from 1146 to 1166. Author of numerous religious works, his influence on the Church in England and the English Cistercians was as great as that of the abbot of Clairvaux on the Latin Church of his time. In 1141, in *Speculum Charitatis*, he had returned to the themes of Bernard of Clairvaux's *Apologia ad Guillelmum*: "Why in the monks' cloisters are there these cranes and hares, these deer and stags, these magpies and crows? These are not the instruments of [hermits like] Anthony or Macarius, but merely women's amusements. None of this is suited to monastic poverty, serving only to feed the eyes of the curious…".

But in 1230, a new six-bay choir with a rectangular ambulatory was built to replace the

Facing page, right:

The five remaining
arches of the original
cloister. They are still
Romanesque, as in
Fontenay, but owe much
of their elegance to the
skill of the master
builders and
stonemasons who used
to work for the
Cistercians abbots.

Above:

External elevation on the
north side of the nave.
The ruins show the real
structure of the
construction. The large
arcades, the openings in
the triforium gallery and
the high windows are
logically arranged to
bear the load.

earlier sanctuary, the nine bays of the nave were raised (the difference can be clearly seen in the masonry of the side walls). The total length of the enlarged building was more than 335ft (104m). The three-storeyed choir (pointed arcade, triforium, and high clerestory) is a good illustration of the perfection of English Gothic in the thirteenth century. Despite much destruction after the Dissolution, the ruins of the church are impressive. Everyone should, once in a lifetime, walk through the nave of Rievaulx Abbey, with the roof open to the sky, the arcades stand-

ing out against the green fields of the surrounding countryside, straight out of a painting of the Romantic era (farmers even keep sheep here, reminding us of the flocks of sheep that made the fortune of the Yorkshire Cistercians). We cannot fail to be impressed by these massive columns that withstood so many vicissitudes, as we cross ground once surrounded by walls, where exquisite glazed tiles emerge from the lawns neatly manicured by English Heritage.

The foundations of a chapter house can still be seen that was unique of its kind, having a

semi-circular end contained within an aisle. A few round-headed arches remain of the cloister arcade, supported on twin colonettes, alternately round and hexagonal. The dimensions of the very large refectory are marked out, while a fine hatchway to the kitchens is still visible. There are ruined remains, too, of the small infirmary cloister—something built by only the largest and richest abbeys.

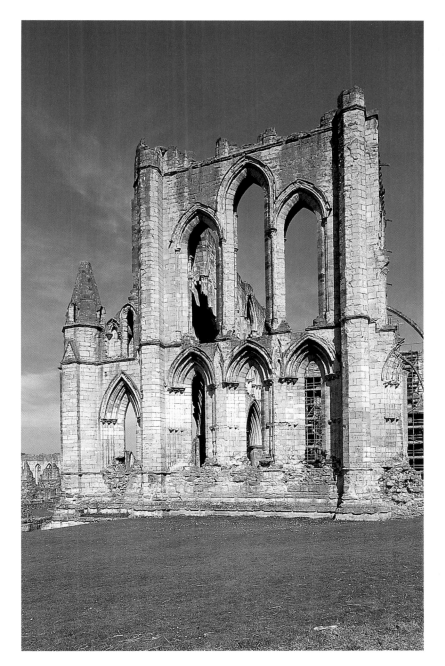

Facing page:
*The square east end of
the sanctuary.*

Above:
*The square east end of
the sanctuary seen from
the outside. The force of
this metaphorical
repetition of the
openings in triplets of
the first Cistercians east
ends reveals a genuine
desire for
monumentality.*

*Opening into the nave
triforium.*

ROYAUMONT

Regalis mons

location: Asnières-sur-Oise (Val-d'Oise), Île-de-France, France

founded: 1228, by Cîteaux

church dates from: 1229–1235

dissolved: 1791 (French Revolution)

present use: cultural center

See also pp. 64, 98, 100, 118, 133.

Bibliography
Henri GOÜIN, *L'Abbaye de Royaumont*, CLT, Paris, 1967.
Christine LAPOSTOLLE, "L'Abbaye de Royaumont", *Ouest-France*, Rennes, 1968.

St. Louis' passion for Royaumont, his own abbey, is well known: "We have deemed it proper to erect, in honor of God, the Blessed Virgin, and all the saints, an abbey of the Cistercian Order in the place named Aulmont, which we decree shall henceforth be known as Royaumont." A true Cistercian site: no houses, a forest, a river, a spring. But already at the beginning of the thirteenth century (1228) the Rule was under pressure. In their foundation charter the monks accepted important means of existence: tithes of wheat, tolls on bridges, taxes on wine presses: things were going back to the Cluniac habits that St. Bernard had condemned!

Royaumont was close to the royal residence of Asnières-sur-Oise and was soon invaded by the court. People admired the speed at which work progressed thanks to royal bounty. They prayed much, too, under the watchful eye of Blanche de Castille. The king's practised an asceticism which would come back into fashion during certain period of mystical reform in the Cistercian Order, notably the "feuillants" and Augustin Lestrange's nineteenth-century Trappists. After confession the king demanded to be flogged with a "discipline" incorporating small iron chains, which "greatly wounded his flesh". The Founding Fathers had not worn hair-shirts and had advised abbots not to receive the royal court or to provide room for the family mausoleum. At Royaumont the whole of St. Louis family was buried, and great men continued to find a tomb there over the centuries. In the fourteenth century the monks begged the royal house "to stop lodging men and horses in the abbey precincts while traveling in the district." Amongst the long list of commendatory abbots is to be found Mazarin. Richelieu stayed at Royaumont while Louis XIII was in residence at Chantilly. The house of Lorraine managed to remain commendatories for several generations. The last abbot *in commendam* in 1781, Henry Éléonore le Cornut de Balivière, Louis XVI's chaplain, who received many crowned heads, endowed the abbey with a new abbot's palace (1785–9) designed by Louis Le Masson. He was never to live there.

At the time national assets were sold off, another nobleman managed to buy the monastery. Joseph Bourget de Guilhem, formerly Marquis of Travaner, began to destroy those parts which might serve as a model factory and lodgings for the workers. This was the start of the Industrial Revolution, already under way

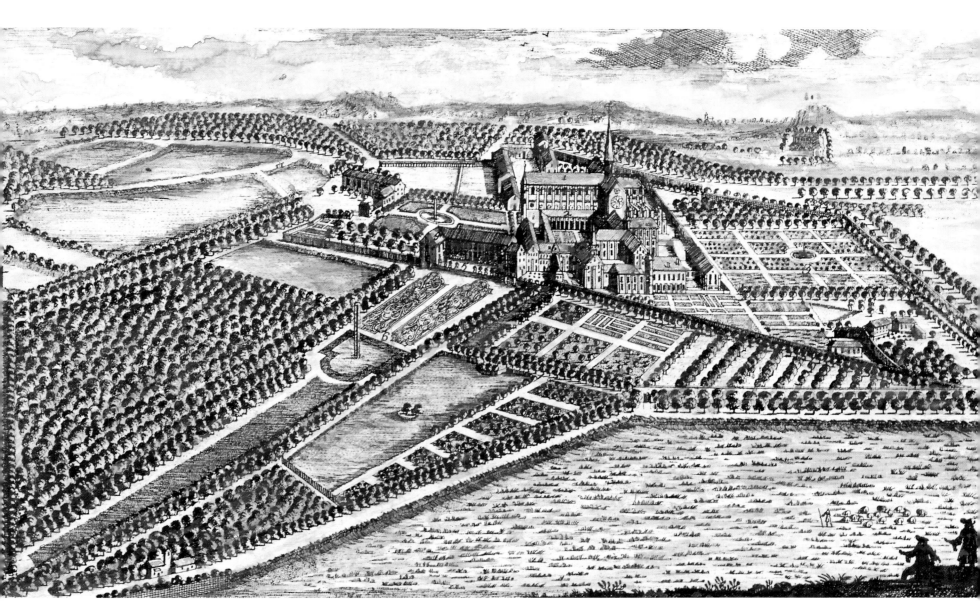

Facing page:
In the foreground, ruins of the church apse. Views of the monks' range and of the south wall of the nave.

Above:
General view (seventeenth century).

West walk of the cloister and remnants of the lay brothers' passage. On the right, ruins of the south wall of the church.

in England, where the god Industry justified both exploitation of the workforce and iconoclastic demolition. Royaumont lost its church, and the rest of the abbey became a cotton-mill with English workers. A great paddle-wheel may still be seen in the latrine block, which provided energy for the 300 factory workers.

At the time of the July monarchy with its frivolity, Parisian society frolicked in the abbey ruins. Plays were staged in the gothic rooms of the factory, against the noise of steam engines! But under the Second Empire monks and nuns everywhere in France bought up the old abbeys. Royaumont played a part in this development until in 1905 the law concerning religious congregations compelled the nuns of the Holy Family to leave their monastery.

Today the abbey "château" is separated from the rest of the domain, and over a long period has been restored by the Goüin family to provide an international cultural center where intellectuals and artists may come together. This utopian dream of 1937 became a reality when the Fondation Royaumont for progress in the Humnanities came into existence; since 1964 it has organized research programs, courses, colloquia, and notable musical events.

Emblematic of Royaumont, the remnants of the staircase of the church's north transept. In the foreground, the bases of the sanctuary columns.

The sanctuary retains traces of the radiating chapels. "As soon as he had control over his kingdom and knew more about life, Louis started building churches and religious houses. Royaumont is the most beautiful and the greatest of all." Jean Sire de Joinville (Book of Holy Sayings and Good Actions of Our Holy King Louis, 1309).

*The large Gothic monks'
refectory. It is used
today as a concert hall
for the Royaumont*
*Foundation. A small
organ was installed in
1983.*

SALEM

location: **Salem (Baden), Germany**

founded: **1134, by Lucelle (filiation of Morimond)**

suppressed: **1804**

present status: **parish church, cultural center, museum, school**

See also pp. 42, 43, 67, 74, 75, 103, 105, 107.

Bibliography
Le Château de Salem, Salemer Kultur und Freizeit, GmbH, Salem.
Margarete STILLGER, *Allemagne*, Hachette, 1964.

Is this huge château of Salem, which sparkles like a new pin and is as prestigious as some kind of provincial Versailles, still an abbey? When you visit it, you can take a long walk beneath its long, high white walls dotted with hundreds of those yellow-framed windows so beloved of Baroque architects. But once you go inside, you will make some unexpected discoveries.

What you find is an abbey church and a monastery buried in the heart of the complex. The church is laid out on a basilical plan and built in the late Gothic style. It was commissioned in 1297, more than 150 years after the White Monks first arrived in Salem under the dual auspices of empire and poverty. A strong religious presence was needed in the Linzgau area, between Lake Constance and the moun-

tains of Heiligenberg and Höchstein. The Lucelle Cistercians were invited to provide it and the abbey swiftly became one of the great centers of Christianity.

But armies also tend to haunt the border country and the Thirty Years' War proved fatal for Salem. When this ended, no sooner had the abbey been rebuilt than it was once more razed to the ground by fire in 1697. In the century that followed the abbots—and in particular Stephen I (1697–1707) and then Anselm II (1746–78)—redoubled the building work and in so doing first opted for the Baroque style (monastery, gate-house, stables) and later embraced Neo-Classicism (treasury). It was with this work that the abbey reached the height of its splendor. It celebrated by erecting a 200-foot (60m) tower with sixteen bells above the crossing in the abbey church. But the tower was so heavy that hardly had this manifestation of vanity gone up than it had to be demolished. Napoleon gave the abbey, which had been secularized in 1804, to the margraves of Baden as compensation for the loss of their lands on the left bank of the Rhine. They set about embellishing the place and opened a well-respected school within its walls.

Despite all the decorative additions that have been made over the centuries, the sobriety of the Cistercian architecture remains. This can be seen in the huge choir with its square east end, the pure lines of its lofty vaults and aisles down the nave, separated by walls resting on arcades. The Baroque remodeling is sumptuous without being invasive, even allowing for the 27 alabaster altars in the nave, the 94 stalls adorned with bas-reliefs showing scenes from the Old Testament, three tribunes—includ-

Left:
The ceremonial room,
which was reserved for
distinguished guests.

Above, left:
Choir and sanctuary of
the church.

Above, right:
South aisle of the nave.
A baroque altar stands
against each pier.

Right:
Like every "lively" abbey in the eighteenth century, Salem was equipped with an large library.

Facing page:
Tile stove of the former refectory, adorned with scenes of the daily life of the Cistercians.

ing the organ loft, four pyramidal monuments in honor of the founding fathers plus twenty quite large statues!

The conventual buildings were big enough to house the monks' ranges and the abbot's parlor and offices as well as enough extra rooms to accommodate two visiting princely courts at the same time! Now one can understand why one of the conventual buildings is 590 feet (180m) long.

It is impossible to imagine Baroque without stucco. Salem offers the most famous stucco decoration in the whole of Germany and illustrates the historical development in the art of plasterers belonging to the eighteenth-century Wersobruun school. It is hard to choose which is the most ambitious between the cloister gallery dedicated to St. Bernard, the summer refectory (later an oratory), the library, the Emperor's state room, the numismatic room, and the abbot's private apartments (where you can admire the famous green Rococo cabinet with the swan motif).

The outbuildings contained within the walls of the monastery include a number of interesting eighteenth-century buildings, such as the stables, which again illustrate the history of Salem. To pull in modern tourists, the abbey has created a range of attractions including a fantasy garden, a toy house, a craftsmen's village complete with blacksmith and master glass-blower as well as an adventure trail! Below the tithe barn, a huge winery still produces the local Salem brew which can be drunk in a bistro housed in the former prison block.

But can you look at Salem without thinking of the shrine in the church at Birnau which belonged to the abbey and which, from the thirteenth century onwards, contributed to its fame and fortune. The church that you see today was the work of Peter Thumb, one of the masters of the Vorarlberg school of Baroque. It stands on a secluded site close to Lake Constance and includes a retable dedicated to Bernard of Clairvaux, flanked by a cherub tasting honey: an allusion to the reputation the great Cistercian abbot and doctor of the church as a "the honey-tongued doctor".

SAN GALGANO

S. Galgani

location: Chiusdino (Tuscany), Italy

founded: 1201, by Casamari (filiation of Clairvaux)

suppressed: c.1600

present status: ruins

See also p. 95.

Bibliography
Vito ALBERGO, *San Galgano*, Andrea Pistolesi, Florence, 1990.
Italo MORETTI and Renato STOPANI, *Toscane romane*, Zodiaque, La Pierre-qui-Vire, 1966.
Italie, Nord et Centre, Hachette, 1990.

Did the Cistercians from San Galgano Abbey help build Siena Cathedral, as legend says? Perhaps not. But their mastery of Gothic architecture would have allowed them to play a major part. The large church (1224-88) belonging to the monastery founded in 1201 still bears witness to the enormous technical abilities of their master craftsmen. All that survives today, however, are the walls, since the roof collapsed in the seventeenth century. The splendid nave in travertine and brick is buried in the depths of unspoiled countryside. It is one of the most beautiful ruins that you can find anywhere in Europe. The façade, built like a fortress, is one of absolute purity. The nave itself is rigorous in design, the rhythm being provided by sturdy cruciform piers between arcades bearing large windows surmounted by oculi, or circular openings. In the true Cistercian tradition, the east end is square with two triplets of windows surmounted by one small and one large oculus through which the blue Tuscan sky shines like stained glass!

How could such an important monument have been abandoned? The reason lies in a mixture of attacks by mercenaries in the pay of the Florentine Republic, revenues pillaged by commendatory abbots and the fact that after the Renaissance the number of people answering the calling dropped off sharply. By 1550 only five monks were left while by 1600 there remained just one, reduced to living as a hermit!

In fact, the abbey had always been in competition with a pilgrims' chapel, the shrine dedicated to St. Galgano, that stood on a small hill just a few hundred yards away. Indeed the shrine was the reason for the monastery.

Galgano Guidotti (1148–81) was a nobleman from Chiusdino. When the Archangel Michael bade him to become a hermit, he obeyed despite the entreaties of his mother and his fiancée Polissena. One day, his sword stuck in a crevice of the rock and no one was able to pull the blade out again, but the scabbard and hilt formed a cross. Galgano could do nothing else but worship before it for the rest of his short life. After his saintly death, a round chapel was dedicated to him (1182–85). The number of pilgrims it attracted prompted the local bishop to build an abbey next to it and invited the Cistercians to run it.

The centrally-planned chapel is still in use today, although a small apsidal sanctuary has been added and you enter through a square narthex. The sword in the stone stands in the middle. The adjacent sacristy is decorated with wonderful frescos by Ambrogio Lorenzetti.

The central portion of the building is covered by an exceptionally fine dome with concentric stone and brick rings. The way the walls are built, layers of brick and white limestone over a base of stone, adds a sense of rigor to the chapel's round form.

Facing page, right:
*The square east end of
the church. Oculus and
two triplets, in a
characteristically
Cistercian style.*

Above:
*Exterior elevation of the
church (south side) and
remnants of the cloister.*

*Interior elevation of the
church (south side).*

South aisle.

North aisle.

The chapter house (thirteenth century). San Galgano perfectly illustrates the Cistercian spirit and its original canon. At the same period, the French "white monks" had already forgotten its principles.

SANTES CREUS

Sanctae Creus

location: Aiguamurcia (Catalonia), Spain

founded: 1150–58, by Granselve (filiation of Clairvaux)

dissolved: 1835 (repayment of national debt)

present use: cultural center

See also p. 95.

Bibliography
Emilia ALTARRIBA and Joseph BALUJA, *Santes Creus*, 1988.
Eufemia FORT I COGUL, *El monestir de Santes Creus*, 1987.
Anselme DIMIER, *L'Art cistercien*, vol. 2, Zodiaque, La
Pierre-qui-Vire, 1971.

Along with Poblet, Santes Creus is one of the "Cistercian citadels" of Catalonia. But it is a citadel full of charm, which over the centuries has allowed itself to be invaded by new buildings. When you walk around it, it feels like a town. You move from one find to the next until in the end, deep in the heart of the monastic city, you discover the ever-present conventual quadrangle laid down by St. Bernard's plan.

The abbey was founded in 1150 at Valdaura del Valles by monks from Granselve (diocese of Toulouse) who had been given land by sev-eral of the great Catalan families. This was at a time when the famous state had been incor-porated into Aragon and the *Reconquista* had mobilized local feudal ties. The monks' sup-port was needed to pray for the "crusade" against the Moorish Almoravides. On the other hand, Valdaura del Valles was still close to the front line that divided Christians from Muslims.

The monks took close on ten years to find their ideal site. At first they set up an estab-lishment at Ancosa (which later became one of the abbey's farmsteads), then at Santes Creus

The seventeenth century "beautiful Gothic cloister" (1332–41) and its inner courtyard with orange trees. A creation of English master Raynard Fonoyll, who introduced the Gothic style into Catalonia.

which is like a platform dominating the Rio Gaya and surrounded by hills. Shepherds grazed their flocks there and, at night, set fire to the crosses that marked out their camp so that they had some light. Hence the name of the monastery.

For many years the white monks played an important political role by imparting their technical skills to local peasants who had returned to the territory that had been reconquered from the Almoravides. Some of the abbots were coun-

selors or chaplains to the royal family of Aragon-Catalonia which had the abbey fortified (1375–78). Nobility wanted to be buried at Santes Creus while men of letters were continuously attracted by its well-stocked library (now in Tarragona).

The inheritance of the French Revolution shaped nineteenth century Spain. Until then, monasteries had managed to hold on to their privileged—indeed over-privileged—position in society. When Napoleon's troops invaded Spain, they made pillaging monasteries a top

priority. In 1823 French troops came back to pillage once more when King Ferdinand VII appealed to the "hundred thousand sons of St. Louis" to re-establish the monarch. For decades to come Spain was to know nothing other than a succession of revolutions followed by repressions. Following a law selling church property passed in 1835 in order to pay off the national debt (known as the de-amortization law), monastic communities in Spain were disbanded. Nevertheless from 1844 onwards, Santes Creus was

paid zealous attention by the Provincial Monuments Commission. For a number of years the abbey was a hospital and then a prison but it is currently one of the best preserved monastic complexes in Europe.

On entering the monastic city you go through two squares, one after the other. The second is dominated by the royal gateway of the Assumption. In the center of this square stands a Baroque statue of St. Bernard Calvo, the Cistercian abbot who founded the hospital of St. Peter of the Poor, just outside the monastic complex. On the south side you see the former abbot's palace, with its attractive patio, which now houses the town hall and a school. A few shops here and there bring the whole place to life. The atmosphere resembles a small old provincial town, but Santes Creus is happily less busy than Montserrat with its hordes of tourists. Cistercians preferred out-of-the-way places and thus they have remained (even the most visited abbeys attract three times fewer visitors

Facing page:
The terrace and well of the "royal palace". Built in the fourteenth century for Jacques II le Cérémonieux, who liked to stay at the abbey.

Above:
The lavatorium, seen from the east cloister walk.

Above:
The lavatorium. *Built before the cloister, it is similar to the* lavatorium *in Poblet. The openings have two arches surmounted by a tympanum, alternatively set with lozenges and oculi.*

Facing page:
Romanesque chapel in the north transept.

It is reinforced by wide transverse arches on engaged shafts which stop some ten feet (3m) short of the floor to rest on traditional Cistercian corbels, which here take the form of turned modillions. All you have to do is to take a good look at the elevation to see that the Gothic vault (about 1220) has replaced an earlier one (about 1180). Later a wide bay was added to the church front along with a beautiful rose window in the *chevet*. Later still came the octagonal tower over the crossing crowned by a lantern dome.

The cloister (1332–41) was the work of an English master builder who brought Flamboyant Gothic to Catalonia. As in so many other abbeys, the original cloister had just a simple, sloping wooden roof. The cloister we see today was the last thing to be built at Santes Creus, which explains why it is more refined and polished in style than the other buildings. They even took the liberty of carving the capitals.

By contrast, the sober chapter house, the beautiful lavabo opposite the refectory, the dormitory with its diaphragm arches under the roof, all these day-to-day rooms where abbey life carried on, were built at the same time as the church.

Outside the monastery quadrangle, an alley leads toward the Mediterranean garden in the "old cloister" (simple pointed arcades with no capitals) and on to the royal palace of Jaime II (the Ceremonious) with its refined patio and elaborate staircase. Kings and princes loved retreating to abbeys. At Santes Creus they could go and pray in the small chapel of the Holy Trinity, a jewel of Romanesque architecture with a beautiful barrel vault, tucked just inside the outer walls, well away from ceremony and intrigue. This chapel was built in 1158 just after the monks arrived on site.

Note

In 1977, the Catalan public and local authorities financed an incredible educational tour through Santes Creus that features an audiovisual show and systematic reconstruction of the abbey. The tour allows you to see and hear an accurate and beautifully presented summary of the Cistercian adventure.

than the Châteaux of the Loire), a fact for which true travelers are grateful…

The abbey church stands like a fortress at the center of the complex. Its massive front is topped by ramparts with six wide crenellations which prepare you for the austerity of the nave, the only place in the monastery with this characteristic. Enormous square piers support a rib-vaulted ceiling of quite primitive construction.

Right:
North aisle of the nave.

Facing page, above:
The chapter house vault comprises nine rib resting on four cylindrical columns with finely carved capitals.

Facing page, below:
The roll-molded corbels are characteristic of Santes Creus.

SEDLEC

Sedlecium

location: Kutna Hora (Central Bohemia), Czech Republic

founded: 1143, by Waldsassen (filiation of Morimond)

suppressed: From 1421 to 1700, and in 1783 (Joseph II)

present use: Parish church and cigarette factory

See also pp. 33, 110, 125.

Bibliography

Katerina CHARVATORA and Debroslav Libai, *Ràd Cisterci-ackv*, Prague, 1992.

Pierre CHARPENTRAT, *L'Art baroque*, Presses Universitaires de France, 1967.

J. M. RICHARDS, *Who's who de l'architecture de 1400 à nos jours*, Albin Michel, 1979.

Like many religious buildings in Bohemia, the Cistercian abbey of Sedlec saw two flourishing periods separated by the Hussite revolution. Its foundation in 1143 by Waldsassen was part of the policy of "colonization" of the lands in eastern Europe that the General Chapter of Cîteaux recommended should be pursued by Morimond through the intermediary of her daughter abbeys in Austria and Germany. Thus Waldsassen founded Osek (1199); Ebrach founded Plasy (1144), Zd'ar (1251), and Vyssi Brod (1259); and Heiligenkreuz founded Zlata Koruna (1263). In the thirteenth century, by the time these Bohe-

mian abbeys had in their turn set up daughter houses, there were eighteen Cistercian abbeys (thirteen for men and five for women).

The monastery met with many difficulties in the early years, for Bohemia was suffering from great poverty and famine. In 1282, however, the monk Heidenreich, elected abbot, set up a very sophisticated financial arrangement to enable the monastery to participate in the exploitation of the silver mines recently discovered at Kutna Hora, extending partly into territory belonging to the abbey. Legend has it that the discovery of the mines was made by a monk, hence the place name Kutna, meaning "monk's habit" in Czech. Abbot Heidenreich became friend to the princes of Bohemia: the monastery was able to lend them money and they entrusted the education of their heirs to the monks. Taking his inspiration from the great Cistercian churches of the Île-de-France, spectacular for their size and the lightness of their Gothic structures, but still bearing all the hallmarks of the austerity so beloved of Cistercians, Heidenreich embarked on the construction of a new abbey (1282–1320).

The townspeople of Kutna Hora saw this as a challenge, for they were concerned that their town, now the economic center of Bohemia and the site of the mint for the Prague gros, the unit of currency used throughout Bohemia, should demonstrate its importance. The beautiful church of St. Barbara was begun in 1384, in a spirit marked by the anti-Cistercian choice of ornamentation, stained glass, and statuary inspired by the cathedral of St. Vitus in Prague.

The Hussites put an end to this euphoria. The teachings of the former rector of the University of Prague had mobilized a crowd of disciples. His eloquence, and the rigor of his morality, had led him to denounce the vices and greed of the clergy, the scandals and simony, and the selling of indulgences that were all reappearing within the Church. He attacked the dogma of the Church in Rome, and agreed to go, protected by a safe-conduct from the emperor, to the Council of Constance to defend himself. He was thrown into prison, and kept in chains day and night for seven months. He was allowed no defense, was accused of heresy, and burned alive in 1415. His death was the signal for a popular uprising, of an extraordinary violence, against the prelates and abbeys. It continued for more than ten years. Sedlec was demolished in 1421, and the monks were forced to abandon the abbey. They returned in 1700, finding sufficient financial support to rebuild and decorate the abbey. The design for the church was produced by the architect Johann Blasius Santini-Aichel, better known as Santini. The famous "Gothicism" of the interlacing ribs of the vaults at Sedlec (1702–1707) takes the decorative possibilities of Gothic art to its extremes. This masterpiece influenced a whole school, and Santini repeated the procedure in many Bohemian churches, as well as for the Cistercians of Zd'ar around 1710.

The church was a parish church from 1783, the year of the decrees of the "enlightened" emperor, Joseph II. Since, according to Joseph, the contemplative Orders were useless to society, they were offered the choice of either leaving their monasteries or of performing pastoral duties in the parish. One such duty was to take charge of the pilgrimage to the ossuary-chapel known as All Saints. The story had it that a priest had returned from Jerusalem, in the thirteenth century, with a handful of earth from the Mount of Olives which he scattered in the town cemetery. In the years that followed, the place became sacred, and more than 40,000 people wanted to be buried there. In the sixteenth century, a blind monk began to decorate the interior of the chapel with human skulls and bones, and the work was finished off by the sculptor Frantisek Rint. It is an extraordinary example of a surreal "installation", similar to one in the Capuchin monastery in Palermo.

The Gothicism of the architect Santini gives the abbey church of Sedlec a lightness and exuberance rarely encountered in architecture. Still little known, this art is the embodiment of a religious lyriasm which should captivate those visitors who are now rediscovering the architectural richness of Bohemia.

SÉNANQUE

Sinanqua (Sana aqua)
location: Gordes (Vaucluse), Provence/Côte d'Azur region, France
founded: 1148, by Mazan (Bonnevaux-Cîteaux)
suppressed: 1780
present status: monastery of the Cistercian Order of Common Observance

See also pp. 44, 47, 60, 69, 88, 114.

Bibliography
Emmanuel MUHEIM, *L'Abbaye de Sénanque*, Ouest-France, 1982.
L'Abbaye de Sénanque, Éditions Gaud, Moisenay, 1993.

Approaching from the old village of Gordes, on a bend on the modern road that plunges abruptly into a rift in the Vaucluse plateau, the traveler suddenly sees from above, like an architect's model, exposed for all to contemplate, the abbey of Sénanque, standing alone in its grandiose surroundings.

It is a rugged site: the harmony of the brown stone of the roofs, the white stone of the walls, and the violet of the flowering lavender all around makes a striking contrast with the plateau, its rocky limestone outcrops, the poor vegetation of the garrigue, with, here and there, a *borie*, one of the dry-stone huts once used by shepherds or hermits.

In the time of the first monks, when the road now so busy with tourist traffic was not there, one approached Sénanque by the valley of the Sénancole. This approach reveals the site in a more gradual way. "It is in this way that we can most accurately grasp the full measure of the monument. There is a perfect matching of the proportions and the materials to the valley that surrounds it. The abbey had taken the material of which it is made from the mountain, distinguishable from it only by the rigor of its architecture."[1]

Like most Cistercian abbeys, Sénanque was the result of an agreement between an abbot of great spiritual vision and a good organizer. The first was Pierre de Mazan, a bishop sympathetic to the Cistercians. The second was Alfan de Cavaillon, a lord who provided the necessary protection. The family of Agoult-Simiane, who had suzerainty over Gordes, donated all the land in the valley of the Sénancole.

The abbey quickly became prosperous. Well irrigated, as the result of major works - dikes and channels that are still partly visible by the river - the lands of the abbey were able to support about thirty monks. The community was soon able to found a daughter house (Chambon), and establish some ten granges and town houses.

The revenues from these developments made possible the construction of the church between 1160 and 1180, the monastic buildings (1190–1200), and then the chapter house a few years later.

In the fourteenth century, a time of considerable difficulty for the Cistercian Order, Sénanque benefited from the political and economic influence of nearby Avignon, now the papal capital. Legend has it that Petrarch wrote his *De vita solitaria* (1356) after staying

Previous page:

The traditional "post-card" view of Sénanque: Well-kept lavender fields lap against the circular apse. Thus Cistercian architecture can be both Romanesque and Provençal!

Right:

The cloister walk and bell-tower. Each arm of the cloister comprises four arches resting on three piers enclosing three sub-arches. It is tempting to see a symbolism in the numbers.

in the abbey. Even under the system of benefices, the abbey was fortunate in having a saintly
abbot, François d'Estaing, the "Father of the
poor".

Monastic life came to an abrupt end in 1544,
when the Vaudois, or Waldensians, of Luberon
attacked the abbey, in revenge for the actions
of the Inquisition that had tried to convert them
by force, and had burnt down some thirty mountain villages. The Waldensians hanged several
monks, pillaged the storehouses, burned down
the library, and destroyed the lay brothers' range
and the refectory. They were not rebuilt until
the seventeenth century, when attempts were
made to revive the community. Vocations were
few, however, and in 1780 the last monk still
living at Sénanque was buried. At the Revolution, an old royalist officer bought the abbey
and turned it into a farm, thus saving the buildings from destruction.

In the nineteenth century, Sénanque was
one of the few abbeys to be returned to use as
a monastery. In 1854, Abbot Barnouin gathered
together a number of hermits following the
Common Observance. The number of novices
attracted to the abbey allowed it to expand to
Fontfroide, Hautecombe, La Garde Dieu, and
Segries, and to create a congregation with its
headquarters in Lerins. The laws passed on
congregations (1880 and 1901) forced the monks
to go into exile. Returning in 1928, their numbers
were too few to be viable. The abbey became
a study center, which, over a period of twenty
years (1968-88), restored the buildings and the
surrounding land and opened them to the public,
creating a collection of ethnological objects, a
center for medieval studies (the Georges Duby
Center), and a center for Gregorian studies.
Since 1988, the abbey has come back into use
as a priory, dependent on Lerins.

The first builders of Sénanque chose a Romanesque architecture of great formal perfection,
in the spirit of Cîteaux and following the standard Bernardine plan. By this time, throughout
the north of France, the Order was building in
the new Gothic style. The architects and masons
of Sénanque, by contrast, remained faithful to
the traditional ways. And so too have the restorers

of the succeeding centuries. Sénanque today is
the most visited Cistercian abbey, contributing
to the perpetuation of the widely held belief
that all Cistercian architecture should be
Romanesque. It can be, and at Sénanque it
stands as if in a state of grace.

*The nave aisle and its
quadrant vault.*

Above:
Capitals of the transept crossing.

Right:
Opposite the chapter house, a grotesque face reminds us that evils prowls around everywhere and that we have to fight against it.

Far right:
Capital with waterleaf ornament.

Facing page:
The chapter house has hree stone benches, on which the monks sit while listening to the abbot.

SILVACANE

Silva Cana

**location: La Roque-d'Antheron (Bouches-du-Rhône),
Provence, France**

founded: about 1111, by Morimond

church constructed: 1175–1230

dissolved: 1443

present status: owned by the state

See also pp. 53, 114.

Bibliography
Marcel AUBERT, *L'Architecture cistercienne en France*,
Vanouest, Paris, 1947.
Yves ESQUIEU, *Silvacane*, Ouest-France/CNMHS,
Rennes, 1995.

Silvacane Abbey looks as if it just ended up on the banks of the Durance by chance. Would there have been a Cistercian abbey on this very un-Cistercian site (apart from the rose gardens: *Silva Cana* means forest of roses) if the monks of Saint-Victor who held the ford or a ferry over the river had not appealed to the monks of Morimond to take over from them? They also promised gifts from Raymond de Baux and Raymond Béranger of Barcelona. The abbey, which rapidly grew rich, is a superb building. So fine that it aroused the jealousy of the Benedictine monks of Montmajour, near Arles, who did

not hesitate to seize the place and hold the monks hostage (1289). It took a mini-council of Provence to have the prisoners freed! Later on, the lord of Aubignan's men completely pillaged the monastery and its granges (1358). Poor harvests made the abbey's financial situation even worse (1364). The monks lost heart and gave up the place, which was incorporated into the chapter of Aix (1443).

What we have today is a monastic complex that was spared the transformations usually made by successive generations of builder-monks. Like its two other sisters in Provence (Le Thoronet and Sénanque), Silvacane is the work of an architect thoroughly versed in Romanesque techniques, since intersecting ribs were still only at the experimental stage in the south of France. The construction is completely coherent, since building work did not stretch out over decades. In the church, the nave, aisles, and transept have pointed tunnel vaults and there is an almost archaic intersecting rib vault at the crossing. The cloister walks are barrel vaulted with fully-rounded arcades. The chapter house, monks' common-room, and refectory were built later and have intersecting ribs whereas the dormitory is still barrel vaulted.

After photographing a hundred or so abbeys across Europe, Henri Gaud has a soft spot for the church at Silvacane: "It's the most beautiful!". Marcel Aubert, who refers to the abbey 75 times in his incomparable work, goes into great detail when describing the abbey church. He emphasizes "the power of its form and the grandeur of its presence, the wonderful balance of the buildings, the quality of the finish and the austerity of the decoration". This archeologist, who trained at the École des Chartes, has

The lavabo basin in the north-west corner of the cloister. Its shelter did not protect it from vandals.

The nave: a bay on the south side and (facing page) a crossing pier. The nave and the aisles are separated by stone benches which help to "absorb" *the unevenness of the ground. This restriction then became a functional element of the church.*

attentively studied every last wall and proudly describes it all in order to whip up his readers' enthusiasm: "The archivolt of the west front door has an extrados of stepped form!".

Perhaps the church at Silvacane is the most beautiful, but so are dozens of others. The truth is that no Cistercian abbey fails to move. You would need an encyclopedia to do them all justice, even when all that remains to discover is a fragment of wall, as is the case at Cherlieu. Those selected for this volume were chosen more by the chance of travel than by follow-

ing a program that listed in order of merit the sites born of the Cistercian adventure. You cannot help feeling moved when you encounter Vaucelles and its imposing monks' common-room; Valloires and the Baroque decoration in the choir; Longpont, Trois Fontaines, Chaalis, Preuilly, Notre-Dame du Lys, Aulps and their lofty ruins; Ourscamp and its elegant Gothic infirmary; Notre-Dame du Val and its dormitory filled with light; Maubuisson and the wonderful nuns' common-room; Les Vaux-de-Cernay and its sumptuous building complex; Mori-

mond and its romantic lake; Villers Bettnach and its chapel dedicated to St. Catherine; La Bussière, Vauluisant and their parks; Le Val des Choues that seems stranded at the end of the world; Bonport, Le Breuil Benoît, Fontaine Guérard, the Abbaye Blanche, Aiguebelle, Le Vignogoul, Villelongue, L'Escaladieu, Belloc, Cadouin, Bonnecombe, L'Étoile, Boquen, Clairmont, l'Épau and the sheer volume of Cistercian heritage that they contain; Mégemont, lost in solitude; La Bénisson Dieu with its beautiful roof of colored glazed tiles; Boschaud and its exceptional domes; Hautecombe alongside its lake and Tamié on its mountain…

In Spain, Sta. Maria de Huerta with the knights' cloister; Moreruela in Castille; Las Huel-

gas, the famous nunnery; Piedra among the waterfalls; Valdedios and the San Salvador chapel; La Oliva and its alabaster windows; Leyre on the mountainside; Oseta, the monastery-palace of Galicia; Valbonna, the third Catalan abbey…

In Germany, Eberbach with its ancient winepress; Ebrach with its Baroque church; Himmerod with its remains inspired by Clairvaux; Arnsburg and its chapter house; Bronnbach and its tall windows; Heina and its cloister of the mystic lamb; Heilsbronn and its retable of the auxiliary saints; Kaishem and its twelve-sided ambulatory; Altenberg and its church…

In England, Kirkstall and its beautiful ruins in the heart of Leeds… In Scotland, Culross and its ruins in the ancient royal town… In Wales,

Neth with its tower-porch. In Austria, Lilienfeld and its beautiful Gothic nave; the sumptuous Baroque of Schlierbach… In Belgium, Aulne and its wonderful chevet… In Ireland, Corcomroe, Grey, Inch, Kilbeggan and their ruins… In Italy, Valvisciolo, another Fossanova set amid olive groves; Fontevivo and its Virgin and Child in polychrome stone… In Switzerland, Bonmont, Hauterive and Montheron and the splendid remains they hold of the Cistercian spirit; Weltigen, discretely Baroque…

In Poland, Wachock, Kreszow, Henrykow and their Baroque churches, and the organ festival held at Oliwa every summer, not to mention the frescos at Mogila… In Greece, Daphne and its Byzantine architecture…

Left:
Aisle window.

Below:
The stone bench between the nave and the aisles of the church.

Facing page:
Romanesque simplicity: the cloister walks.

SILVANÈS

Silvanesium

location: Sylvanès (Aveyron), Midi-Pyrénées region, France

founded: 1136, by Mazan (affiliation of Cîteaux)

suppressed 1768

present status: Parish church and cultural center

See also pp. 54, 114.

Bibliography
Geneviève DURAND and Nicole Andrieu, "Sylvanès, ancienne abbaye Notre-Dame", in *Anciennes Abbayes en Midi-Pyrénées*, Addoc, Tarbes, 1991.
Robert AUSSIBAL and André Gouzes, O. P., *Sylvanès*, Éditions du Beffroi, Millau, 1989.

Underlying the origins of Sylvanès are the currents of violence and faith, that run through the early Middle Ages. Behaving more like a common brigand than the local lord of the petty nobility that he was, Pons de Léras had the unpleasant habit of holding to ransom any traveler crossing the Pas de l'Escalette, between the Auvergne and Languedoc. One Christmas night, moved by the sound of religious chant, he decided to return his victims' property, to go on a pilgrimage to seek pardon for his sins, and to become a monk with his companions in crime, who had also repented. A hermitage was established near Camarès in 1132 that was to become the abbey of Sylvanès in 1136. Work began on the church and monastic buildings

in 1151 and was to last for almost a century.

This violence and this faith can be seen transcended in the architecture of the abbey, placed uncompromisingly like a massive stone block straddling the valley. The work of constructing such a building must have aroused the enthusiasm of the monks, discovering their place of prayer, of the lay brothers involved in the building work, and of all those craftsmen who came to draw up the plans and cut the stones. To work here was to fight the elements, the rigors of the climate, and the difficulties of the site—a challenge to which feudal man would always rise. When building work was finished life became routine, saying the daily offices, endlessly working in the fields. From the end

Facing page:
General view of the abbey and its square east end.

Above:
The transept and the sanctuary. The large diaphragm arch and its three windows. The chevet with its three oculi and its Cistercian triplet of windows.

lancets, three rose windows, plus an oculus), evoking the Trinity. The monks' choir is lit by three windows in the diaphragm wall. The vault buttresses, integrated into the roof, are also reminiscent of Fontenay. During the construction of the church, the builders, recognized experts in the techniques of Romanesque architecture, tried to integrate the new Gothic techniques that were just then causing a revolution in the building sites of northern France. Marcel Aubert describes it thus: "The transepts have transverse barrel vaults that penetrate into the nave using very skilfully shaped stone blocks. The lower part of the vault is normal up to the intersecting curve, only becoming horizontal at the top of the vault. At the last bay of the nave, forming the crossing, a rib vault with wide carinate ribs is applied to the vault into which it penetrates, showing an attempt at a procedure whose rationale was not fully understood". The rib vaults are more successfully handled in the aisle and the cloister, the latter being the only monastic building still standing today and which unites, according to the Bernardine plan, the sacristy, chapter house, and monks' day-room, also used as the scriptorium.

Since 1969, when it was bought by the local council, Sylvanès has seen something of a renaissance. In 1975, André Gouzes O.P. and Michel Wolkowitsky launched the *Rencontres culturelles* program. In 1979, a start was made on the restoration of the historic buildings. Some 100,000 visitors and students come each year, contributing to the success of this important center for music in France. As well as concerts and musical activities, the center offers courses in instrumental music, choral singing, painting, dance, liturgy, theology, and philosophy, and hosts conferences, craft workshops, and exhibitions.

of the thirteenth century, the history of the abbey was relatively uneventful. A slow decline was punctuated by the usual vicissitudes experienced during the difficult years of monasticism: epidemics, wars, beneficed abbots holding the abbey *in commendam*, falling numbers of monks… In 1768, the Commission of Regulars, set up by Louis XV, recommended that the six monks left at Sylvanès should attach themselves to some other abbey. A few years later the abbey church became a parish church.

This monument is typically Cistercian. The west front is a plain and undecorated stone gable wall. The Gothic bay added on does nothing to detract from the austerity emphasized by the two little Romanesque doors that open laterally on to the nave. The fortress-like appearance of the building is reinforced by the shallow pitch of the roofs and their stone slab covering, as well as by the bonding of the closely-jointed sandstone blocks at the east end and in all the walls. The windows, and even the oculi, have the appearance of arrow slits.

And yet, on entering the church, one is struck by its lightness and spaciousness. The single nave is exceptionally wide, and as high as it is wide. A pointed tunnel vault leads up to the sanctuary with its square east end, under a low vault between square chapels, following the traditional plan of Clairvaux and Fontenay. The bright light of the rising sun falls on the altar through two sets of three windows (three

Above left:
The entrance of the chapter house

Facing page:
The lovely monks' door

STAFFARDA

Staffarda
location: near Revello (Piedmont), Italy
founded: 1135, by Tiglieto (filiation of La Ferté)
suppressed: c.1804
present status: parish church

See also pp. 60, 111.

Bibliography
Maria Carla PRETTE, *Guida all'Abbazia di S. Maria di Staffarda*, Mariogros, Turin.
Alessio MONCIATTI, *Staffarda* in *Architettura cistercense, Fontenay e le abbazie in Italia dal 1120 al 1160*, Edizione Casamari, Certosa di Firenze, 1995.

The Cistercians did not always found their monasteries in the "desert". Indeed at Staffarda the White Monks arriving from Tiglieto in Liguria were able to take advantage of work done by previous occupants. Reclamation work on the swampy site had been started by the Romans and now all the Cistercians had to do was to continue it. In the same fashion, all they had to do was set their own mark on a Benedictine monastery which had been there since 1122. But they did not come empty handed, since Manfredo I, the ruler of Saluzzo, gave them land. This must have been around 1135 although we do not have a charter to prove it. Other donations, this time documented, followed in 1138.

The abbey's Romanesque architecture capped by Gothic roofing is very consistent in character. In 1189, there was a fire so serious that the monks had to live in exile for a few years at S. Martino al Cimino. The abbey was then completely rebuilt at the start of the thirteenth century. It was from this time that a taste for decoration, of which the original Cistercians would not have approved, began to creep in—as can be seen from the combined use of brick and stone. At Staffarda the true Cistercian spirit survives in the *fonasteria*, the large infirmary room in which two Gothic aisles were supported by sturdy stone columns crowned by very discreet, plain capitals.

But Staffarda was not spared its share of troubles. From 1463 onwards, it was run by absentee abbots, or commendatories. It was (partially) destroyed during the War of the Spanish Succession (it was at Staffarda that on 18 August 1690 Maréchal Catinat won fame when he defeated King Victor Amadeus II of Savoy who, in turn, had to pay damages). The abbey was then pillaged by French troops in 1799. The Cistercians could no longer keep their monastery going and Pope Benedict XIV turned it into a "perpetual sinecure" of the Military Order of S. Maurizio. But they abandoned it in 1804 and the church was taken over by the local parish.

Since 1826 there have been attempts at work to save the abbey from slowly falling into ruin. This was put on a systematic footing from 1923 onwards. Thanks to this, one of Piedmont's finest abbeys has been saved.

Far left:
The cloister south gallery and the awkward buttress which had to be built to prevent the church from collapsing into the cloister. The master builders are not as perfect as monks!

Left:
Elaborate brick decoration.

Above:
The monks of Staffarda as immortalized in one of the abbey wall paintings.

SWEETHEART

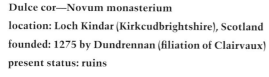

Dulce cor—Novum monasterium
location: Loch Kindar (Kirkcudbrightshire), Scotland
founded: 1275 by Dundrennan (filiation of Clairvaux)
present status: ruins

Bibliography
Henry THOROLD, *The Ruined Abbeys of England, Wales and Scotland*, Harper Collins, London, 1993.
Richard FAWCETT, *Scottish Medieval Churches*, Historic Buildings and Monuments Department, Edinburgh, 1985.
J. S. RICHARDSON, *Dundrennan Abbey*, Historic Scotland, 1994.

The ancient abbey of Sweetheart exudes solemnity through its the walls, all of which are still standing even after centuries of neglect, unlike the vaulted roofs which have long since fallen in. It is an important site, since it contains the remains of the last Cistercian abbey to be founded in Scotland. And the effect of the red sandstone walls against the verdant green of grass produced by Scottish rain is flamboyant.

Although built in the fourteenth century, the church's Gothic architecture is fairly rudimentary. There are no wide bays in the nave, and the façade is devoid of the kind of beautiful rose window beloved of English architects. With an enormous square tower rising above the crossing of the transept, the complex gives rather the impression of a fortress awaiting invaders from the nearby Irish Sea. The gigantic dimensions of the outer abbey wall reinforce this notion.

What was there to protect in this abbey at the end of the world? Perhaps the embalmed heart (sweetheart) of John, Lord Balliol, founder of Balliol College Oxford, who died in 1269, and of his wife, the Lady Devorgilla, who entrusted it to the monks of the abbey. When she lay dying in 1289, she asked to be buried alongside the casket containing his cherished remains. It was she who gave the funds needed to establish the abbey.

Above:
The church's square east end.

Facing page:
Church nave, almost intact.

LE THORONET

Thoronetum

location: Le Thoronet (Var), Provence, France

founded: 1136/1176, by Mazan (filiation of Cîteaux)

dissolved: 1791 (French Revolution)

present status: owned by the CNMHS (Ministry of Culture)

See also pp. 38, 47, 60, 114, 116, 117, 137.

Bibliography

François CALI and Lucien HERVÉ, *La plus grande aventure du monde, Cîteaux*, Arthaud, Paris, 1956 (with preface written by Le Corbusier).

Fernand POUILLON, *Les Pierres sauvages*, Seuil, Paris, 1964.

Yves ESQUIEU, *L'Abbaye du Thoronet*, Ouest-France and CNMHS, Paris, 1985/1995.

Raoul BERENGUIER, *L'Abbaye du Thoronet*, CNMHS, Paris, 1973.

Le Thoronet exerts a special fascination for modern architects, who strive to come up with cost-effective solutions to complex projects. They have discovered at least one connection between the master builders responsible for devising Cistercian functionality and today's construction industry: both must work within similar constraints.

Le Corbusier was fascinated by Le Thoronet. He visited it with his friend Lucien Hervé, who was at the time working on his wonderful volume of black and white photographs of the abbey, now sadly impossible to find. There was no peace until Le Corbusier wrote the introduction to the book:

"Here every element of the building adds a creative value to the architecture.

The architecture is the tireless addition of positive gestures. The overall work and the detail are as one.

Stone is man's friend: the sharpness of its ribs encloses areas like rough skin. [...].

Light and shade are the heralds of this architecture of truth, calm, and strength. There can be nothing else to add.

In an age of "raw concrete", such a wonderful encounter along one's path is welcome indeed."

Facing page, right:
General view on the church and the apse. Some contemporary architects described Thoronet's special volume stucture as "geometrism".

Left:
Lavatorium *and* lavabo. *The latter was reconstituted in the nineteenth century by the architect Revoil, who used a fragment that had been found by archeologists.*

The cloister. Along the wall of the collatio *walk is a stone bench where the monks used to sit reading sacred books from the* armarium, *which was located on the upper level of the cloister gallery. This gallery leads to the* lavatorium. *When everything is silent one hears only the sound of water falling into the basin. The Rule allowed every brother to ask the Cantor for books from the* armarium *for the* lectio divina. *As the saying goes:* Claustrum sine armario, castrum sine armamento *("A cloister without an* armarium *is like a fortress without weapons").*

Fernand Pouillon was equally fascinated by Le Thoronet. He copied its plans, deciphered its charters, excavated its foundations until he was able to identify so completely with the abbey's architect that he could write a masterly book recreating the imaginary diary of the building works. Apart from the unquestioned literary value of this work, *Les Pierres sauvages* [Wild Stones] provides us with a vivid account of life on a medieval building site as well as being a precious document as far as the architectural creative process is concerned.

Like Le Corbusier, Fernand Pouillon emphasizes the perfect way in which the stone was hewn and the balance given to the complete work by the actual bonding of the stone.

"Inside, the facing shall be as smooth and regular as possible. The blocks shall be laid in horizontal courses [...] and then soaked in lime-wash [...]. We cannot risk anything coming apart and the blocks shall only be laid this way on the inside, where they are sheltered both from frost and the scorching sun. The jointing will hold fast for centuries, for once the lime has set it becomes as hard as stone.

[The external facings shall be] dry walled, that is to say laid without mortar. This method is not often used today but was common in Antiquity. Nowadays it is unusual even when dealing with small stones. It needs so much care! The faces of the stone must be perfectly dressed for the horizontal courses. If the thickness of the jointing is just slightly out, it is difficult to lay and any rough edges must be corrected in situ [...]. It takes at least twice as long to dress and lay the stone [...]. This method of laying the stone will bring a touch of luxury to the poverty [...].

If packed jointing and smooth surfaces bring an element of solace to the shadows inside the monastic buildings and the church, in full sunlight this type of packing or mortared jointing would clash with the precision of the perfectly-fitting stones. The outer walls of our monasteries, rising thick and straight, cry out for the most beautiful finish possible."

Everything about Le Thoronet is summed up in this text. What does it matter that the idea for the abbey came from Raymond Béranger, that the monks first lived at Tourtour in Val de Florège, that they were poor, then rich, then exploited by an absentee abbot, then went soft in the eighteenth century before they were turned out by the Revolution...? What does it matter is that Prosper Mérimée and Viollet-le-Duc went there and that they too were fascinated by the place—as ever the first to be so. Indeed we owe to them everything that is fascinating in France today. It was they who started restoration work on this masterpiece of ashlar, with or without jointing, that was built almost to the letter of St. Bernard's plan.

Far left:
Cloister staircase.

Left:
A cloister capital.

Above:
Chapter house.

Facing page:
Cloister arcade.

North aisle of the church.

Chapter house capitals.

TINTERN

Tinterna major

location: **Chapel Hill (Gwent), Wales**

founded: **1131, by Aumône (filiation of Cîteaux)**

dissolved: **1538 (Act of Dissolution)**

present status: **ruins**

See also pp. 38, 72.

Bibliography
Anselme DIMIER, *L'Art cistercien*, vol. 2, Zodiaque, La Pierre-qui-Vire, 1971.
David M. ROBINSON, *Tintern Abbey*, CADW, Cardiff, 1995.
Henry THOROLD, *The Ruined Abbeys of England, Wales and Scotland*, Harper Collins, London, 1993.
E. C. NORTON and D. PARK (eds.), *Cistercian Art and Architecture in the British Isles*, Cambridge 1986.

Romantic countryside with Romantic ruins celebrated in verse—that is what Tintern is!

It is true that the Wye Valley winding its way between wooded hills is particularly picturesque. As for the abbey, surely it is more beautiful as a ruin than it ever was at the height of its splendor? These sketches should already be sufficient to give you a taste of the picture, without it all being colored in… At Tintern, the missing architectural elements have become a virtue. You can view the abbey church as it is today and imagine that this is how it really should be. William Wordsworth, father of English Romantic poetry, was the first to sing of Tintern's splendor. One of his poems bears the annotation: *Lines composed a few miles above Tintern Abbey, 13 July 1798.*

> *[…] and again I hear*
> *These waters, rolling from their mountain springs*
> *With a soft inland murmur—once again*
> *Do I behold these steep and lofty cliffs,*
> *That on a wild secluded scene impress*
> *Thoughts of more deep seclusion; and connect*
> *The landscape with the quiet of the sky.*

The Duke of Beaufort owned the abbey in Wordsworth's day and was undoubtedly the man responsible for our infatuation with the ruins of Tintern. He was passionate about the heritage left to him and, rather than restoring it, set about preserving its condition as the perfect ruin. No easy task, as it calls for a combination of both the architect's and the gardener's arts. Ivy binds the walls together and adds to the charm of the ancient stones. But too many climbing plants can loosen the mortar and bring whole sections of wall tumbling down. The English are past-masters at the art of beautifully managed ruins.

As soon as they arrived at Tintern in 1131, the monks built a small, single-nave church, like the monks of Étoile, their French mother house, had already done. Then, more than a century later, in 1269 they set about endowing the abbey with the most beautiful Gothic church they could build. At the time, the close of the thirteenth century, Cistercian architects were absolute masters of the rib vault and huge traceried bays.

While the conventual buildings were razed to the ground and can now only be distinguished from their foundations, the church itself is almost intact with its four elevations, huge choir, and aisles still standing. We can leave the specialists to describe this in the right words. "The main elevation presents a twin-arched, tierce-point portal with twin doorways separated by a pier and framed by two twin-light, false windows and surmounted by a great seven-light lancet window, with intricate radiating tracery carrying the eye upward toward the surmounting oculus. Under the gable at the top is a large arched window. A small doorway surmounted by a triple-light window and a small lozenge-shaped oculus open on to the south aisle." (Anselme Dimier).

On the other hand, you can forget about the words, stop trying to analyze everything and take a stroll around the vast ruins as if you were exploring a huge open-air sculpture accessible both inside and out.

The church in its pure perfection. As if the interrupted construction was about to restart.

TINTERN MINOR

Cinn Eich, Tinterna Minor
location: Duncannon Castle (Co. Wexford), Ireland
founded: 1200, by Tintern Major (affiliation of Cîteaux through Aumône
dissolved: 1536 (Dissolution)
present status: privately owned (house)

Bibliography
Roger STALLEY, *The Cistercian Monasteries of Ireland*, Yale University Press, London, 1987.

The abbey of Tintern Minor, that owes its name to that of its mother house, Tintern Major in Monmouthshire (Wales), is reached by a pretty medieval bridge, as romantic as one could wish for. But everything about the history of this monastery has an air of romance.

First, there is the story of its foundation, the result of a vow made by the count of Pembroke, William Marshal, who had just escaped with his life from a shipwreck after a terrible storm on the Irish Sea, when he was returning home from England. Then there were the decorations, carried out in 1447 during the abbacy of a monk who had brought with him into the monastery a sufficiently large fortune to allow him to bear the entire cost of the work. Lastly,

the fate of the abbey after the Dissolution in 1536: the property was given to Sir Anthony Colclough, whose descendants lived in the abbey until 1963, converting the choir and nave of the church into a neo-Gothic house.

Important excavations carried out in 1982 attempted to reconstruct the ruins in their original state.

Above:
The Gothic bridge of the abbey.

Facing page:
The church and its "perpendicular" tower (fourteenth century).

TISNOV (PORTA COELI)

Porta Coeli

location: Tisnov (Southern Moravia), Czech Republic

founded: 1234 (nuns)

suppressed: 1782 (by Joseph II)

See also p. 100.

Bibliography
Josef ZACPAL, *Porta Coeli* Nakladatelstvi, Brno, 1997.

Cistercian nunneries were most often founded by queens. Like Blanche of Castille at Maubuisson or Queen Berengaria at L'Épau, it was Queen Konstancie, daughter of the Hungarian king, Bela III, and widow of the king of Bohemia, Premysl Otakar I, who founded Porta Coeli in 1234.

The triple-aisled Gothic church, consecrated in 1239, has a very beautiful western portal that has survived the centuries, despite the vicissitudes experienced by the abbey, which was pillaged in 1241 by the Tartars and in 1425 by the Hussites. The majority of the buildings were restored in the fifteenth century, but without altering the original cloister and chapter house.

After the suppression of the monastery by Joseph II in 1782, the monastic buildings were turned into a textile factory, while the church was used as a parish church. Since 1899, the monastery has been occupied once again by Cistercians, without interruptions, despite the difficulties encountered whilst trying to live according to the Rule under the Communist regime, when the monks were obliged to work outside the monastic enclosure and were forbidden to share their liturgical life with the local people.

Work on the restoration of the abbey has made it possible for tourists to visit this "living" abbey without disturbing the monastic life. The little pots of flowers, one in each window of the cloister (that still has a fine apple tree in the middle), are evidence that, despite their cloistered lives, the nuns are happy to welcome these visitors.

Facing the famous portal of the abbey is a long building known as the "former provost's house". Here, since the 1950s, is to be found the museum of regional history of Podhoracko ("the valley beneath the mountain").

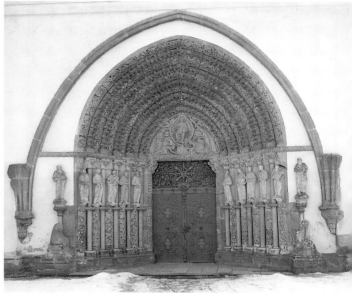

Facing page, right:
The abbey barn, hops stores which used to serve for brewing beer.

Left:
The cloister (closed) gallery. The enclosed nuns who have lived in the abbey since the "velvet revolution" use it as a greenhouse for their pot plants.

Above:
Porta Coeli. Some say this beautiful portal was inspired by Chartres.

The church, south aisle and nave.
The baroque period did not affect the thirteenth century Gothic architecture.

VALCROISSANT

Valais Cresceus

location: Die (Drôme), Rhône-Alpes region, France

founded: 1188 (possibly 1140, date disputed) by Bonnevaux (filiation of Cîteaux)

dissolved: 1568 (abandoned) and 1791 (French Revolution)

present use: farm

Bibliography
Marcel AUBERT (and the Marquise de Maillé), *L'Architecture cistercienne en France*, Vanoest, Paris, 1947.
Bernard PEUGNIEZ, *Routier des abbayes cisterciennes de France*, Signe, Strasbourg, 1994.
Serge DURAND, *L'Abbay cistercienne Notre-Dame de Valcroissant*, (2 vols.), Die, 1997.

Some of the abbeys which were buried in almost inaccessible places and that had already been abandoned by their monks before the Revolution have simply been forgotten. This indeed is the case for most Cistercian granges as well, which were just turned into ordinary farms save that the cows were in the chapter house and hay was stored in the abbey church. Today we are rediscovering these sites. Some of them get restored once locally elected councillors realize, usually after prompting by a cultural association, that they are of interest to a wider public and could give the local area a special identity and develop green, non-polluting tourism. Mégemont (Puy-de-Dôme) has just been through this process and Valcroissant is currently undergoing it.

The Marquise de Maillé was with Marcel Aubert while he re-drew the plans of Valcroissant. Fifty years ago, however, they found it so difficult to get there that Aubert produced the only "literary" description in the whole of his unsurpassable Cistercian encyclopedia. "The abbey stands in the bottom of an imposing ring of towering mountains, scarcely connected to the outside world except by a narrow path running along the bed of a mountain stream [...]; the buildings, which are now used as a farm, huddle in a slightly sheltered hollow at the foot of Glandasse in a bare and wild setting which is alternately scorched by the sun and chilled by frost. They farm just manages to grow a few walnut trees, some scanty crops of rye, barley, carrots, and cabbages close to the mouth of the stream where they are sheltered from the violent winds and avalanches of snow by a few scraggy pines and firs."

Ten years ago Bernard Peugniez, another tireless traveler round the Cistercian abbeys, also conjured up the difficulties of the road to Valcroissant. However, he added that there is a moving reward awaiting anyone who reaches this mountain monastery.

Indeed, the location did not permit communal life to achieve a balance between the hard toil needed to survive and spiritual life. The abbey buildings conform to St. Bernard's plans for a Cistercian monastery but are on a smaller scale: the nave of the church is of only two bays, the cloister garth measures 40ft square (12m x 12m) while the chapter house is only 20ft square (6m x 6m). In 1496 there were only four monks. After being attacked in 1568 by Protestants, who pillaged the place, the last monks left the abbey. The church, sacristy, and book cupboard, the chapter house, slype, novices' dormitory, refectory, and part of the kitchen are all still standing.

The beautiful vaulted
room, located between
the church and the
chapter house was
probably used as a
sacristy and armarium.

VALLE CRUCIS

Madog ap Gruffydd Maelor, ruler of Powys, to start a new abbey in Wales, the country had still not been colonized by the English. Nevertheless, there were continuous skirmishes in the Marches and it would not be long before King Edward secured his conquest (1282–83). A number of Welsh monks were then deported to England. There is no question that it was at this time the monks of Valle Crucis added the capital, that can still be seen today, showing an upside-down fleur-de-lys symbolizing their denial of the sway of the English throne.

Strolling through the ruins you will come across a small sacristy used as a cellar, remains of the spiral day stairs, a lovely *armarium* or book cupboard, a square well in the middle of the cloister, the restored chapter house whose windows overlook lovely countryside… and the reflection of the east end of the church in the waters of the fishpond.

Vallis Crucis—Llanegurist

location: Valle Crucis (Clwyd), Wales

founded: 1201, by Shata Marcella (filiation of Clairvaux)

dissolved: 1536 (Act of Dissolution)

present status: ruins

See also p. 54.

Bibliography

Henry THOROLD, *The Ruined Abbeys of England, Wales and Scotland*, Harper Collins, London, 1993.

E. C. NORTON and D. PARK (eds.), *Cistercian Art and Architecture in the British Isles*, Cambridge 1986.

The Cistercian Order was a multi-national united by its Rule. Having said this, the monks also knew how to defend the local conditions prevailing at their own sites as they were the key to protection and donations. Thus, there is little doubt that the monks of Valle Crucis were Welsh when they were dealing with the Welsh. On the other hand, the very name of their abbey is an explicit reference not the Cross of Christ but to the Pillar of Eliseg, a ninth-century cross near the monastery. This was erected in homage to the ancient Celtic kings of Powys whose armed intervention also contributed to maintaining Welsh independence after the Norman Conquest in 1066. When in 1201 the monks of Shata Marcella (Yshad Margel) were invited by

Facing page, below:
The monks' passageway, between the cloister and the garden.

Left:
The chapter house, which was restored in the fourteenth century (vaulting with drying moldings, rather than capitals).

VALMAGNE

Valais Magne

location: Die (Hérault), Languedoc, France

founded: 1155, by Bonnevaux (filiation of Cîteaux)

dissolved: 1790 (French Revolution)

present use: vineyard

See also pp. 73, 91, 118.

Bibliography
Marcel AUBERT, *L'Architecture cistercienne en France*, Paris, 1947.
Diane GAUDART d'ALLAINES, *Abbaye de Valmagne*, SAEP, Colmar, 1989.

As at Poblet, a sea of vines laps against the walls of Valmagne, another Languedoc citadel belonging to the Order of Cîteaux. But apart from its imposing church, which still trumpets the power of the monastery, the place is now imbued with a kind of Tuscan charm, doubtless emanating from the exceptional atmosphere created by the flowers and water in the cloister garth, bathed in the typically soft light by the banks of the Étang de Thau.

It all began in 1138 when Raymond Tuncavel and a number of lords within the diocese of Agde invited the monks from Ardorel in the diocese of Albi to come and live in lower Languedoc, not far from the still much-used ancient Roman road, the Via Domitia, that connected Narbonne to Montpellier. Ardorel was a daughter of Cadouin, one of the abbeys founded by Gérard de Sales, a disciple of Robert d'Abrissel (Order of Fontevrault), and which rapidly adopted the Cistercian Rule. Ardorel and Cadouin attached themselves to Pontigny. The new abbey at Valmagne also wanted to join the Cistercians and in 1145 the pope affiliated them to Bonnevaux, a direct daughter of Cîteaux, something which did not go down too well with its previous mother houses. It is clear for all to see that the "branches" of the Order of Cîteaux were competing with each other...

Valmagne grew fast and wide. Gifts flowed in and the abbey archive, which covers only the period 1185–1225, contains more than 900 charters. Granges were given to the abbey as far afield as almost the very gates of Béziers (Ortes). Later, the abbey benefited once more when it was given toll rights over the Lunel bridge on a salt-trading route. Furthermore, the white monks were in territory which provi-

sionally belonged to Aragon—a kingdom which tolerated the Cathares—but they gave stalwart support to the pope in his fight against this heresy. They were well rewarded. In 1257, the abbot demolished the original Romanesque church that had been built 100 years earlier. In its place he put a church of cathedral dimensions, whose size equaled anything else within the Order. The abbot called in master builders from the north of France who were to introduce the new Rayonnant style of Gothic architecture to Languedoc, twenty years before the naves of Saint-Just in Narbonne, Saint-Étienne in Toulouse, or the cathedral at Rodez. 272ft (83m) long, 75ft (23m) high, in the form of a

Facing page, right:
Lavatorium *and*
fountain.

Left:
View of the cloister from
the chapter house.

Latin cross, with seven chapels opening on to the ambulatory, this church also spells out a desire for aesthetic achievement that runs counter to the Cistercian spirit. So the choir piers crowd closer and closer together as they approach the chevet, generating ever more pointed arches, which in turn increases the effect of perspective. Just as happened when other cathedrals were constructed, the building work was financed by selling the famous indulgences that were to spark the Lutheran Reformation.

The Black Death, the Hundred Years War, and absentee abbots all contributed to ruin the abbey, which at the same time needed to fortify itself (hence the towers on the façade). The Wars of Religion "destabilized" it. One abbot who had supported the Reformation pillaged Valmagne to feed his Protestant troops. Abandoned, the monastery narrowly escaped demolition. It had to wait a century before the monks returned, repaired the church, put a new vault on the fourteenth-century cloister (1610) and asked Jacques and Pierre Hugolz, the master fountain builders from Saint-Jean-de-Fos, to re-install a fountain fed by water from a stream which had been diverted into a canal running underneath the abbey-church. In 1768 they built "the pretty pavilion that frames the fountain, a simple corona of radiating ribs around a central keystone, incorporating fragments from an earlier building" (Marcel Aubert). This is the abbey's jewel. One of the absentee abbots, Cardinal Pierre de Bouzi, loved both the Languedoc region and Valmagne monastery. He was very good for the place and endowed the abbey with all the trappings of a palace (1680–97). This meant that the few remaining monks were able to survive there until the Revolution.

After it had been pillaged by the local peasants, Valmagne was sold off as a national asset. The new owner installed huge vats in the lower part of the nave and the chapels of the abbey-church. For over two hundred years they were used to age the estate wines and thus saved the abbey from being demolished. In 1838 the Count

Above:
Cloister walk.

Facing page:
The "vineyard's cathedral" with its wine casks nestling in the sides of the aisles. The rich smell of the wine cellar pervades the huge luminous nave which was built by the Cistercians, who were also wealthy wine growers.

of Turenne acquired the property which has remained in his family for over 150 years. Now restored, the abbey has been open to the public since 1975 and in 1985 it was awarded a prize given to those who have saved "endangered masterpieces".

VERUELA

Veruela

location: Vera de Moncayo (Aragon) Spain

founded: 1146, by Escaladieu (filiation of Morimond)

dissolved: 1835 (repayment of national debt)

present use: cultural center

See also pp. 44, 91, 118.

Bibliography
Monasterio de Veruela, guia historica, anthology, General Counsel of Saragossa, 1993.
Eladio ROMERO GARCIA *Monasterio de Veruela*, Quinel, Huesca, 1996.

Not far from Tarazona, a sleepy little town in deepest Aragon, Cistercians from Fitero inherited in 1146 some land donated by the king of Navarre. In 1171 his place was taken by Raymond Béranger, the ruler of Aragon, under whose protection, therefore, Veruela was born. The white monks rapidly cultivated plantations of wheat and barley, olive groves and vineyards, flax and hemp. This venture was so successful that they were soon able to finance building an abbey, whose church was completed in 1190. But Veruela lies close to Castille and in 1357 it was subjected to the type of destruction that all frontier zones know when wars are waged. The monks were forced to flee before the advancing Castillian invasion and to rebuild their abbey upon their return. They continued to enlarge and embellish it right up to the eighteenth century. Then came a troubled period during which Spanish monasteries were disbanded (1835), pillaged for years on end and only saved when they were listed as national monuments. Veruela became a hotel then a Jesuit college. Today it is used for a number of activities, including a wine museum, training center, conference center and so on.

The abbey is completely walled in by tall ramparts reinforced by towers. The entrance is through the porch to the keep, brightened by Plateresque decoration. The effect of the fortifications is reminiscent of an opera set and scarcely seems to relate to the monastic purpose of the place. The main courtyard boasts a wonderful avenue of trees which runs along the sixteenth-century abbot's palace right up to the front of the church. Here you are struck by the Romanesque portal with five archivolts resting on foliated capitals. The abbey church

has three aisles in six bays covered by intersecting rib vaults in the strictest Cistercian spirit. The sanctuary has a simple diagonal vault and is surrounded by an ambulatory with five apsidal niches.

The cloister at Veruela is interesting as it is on three levels and uses different styles. The lower cloister is Gothic and serves the chapter house, refectory, kitchen and parlor. An enormous lavabo, which unfortunately has lost its basin, unusually opens on to the cloister garth not through a light arcade generally associated with this type of building, but rather through portals with five large archivolts of the kind that you would expect to find on the church front. The upper cloister is an elegant Renaissance piece of work with fully-rounded arcades decorated with Plateresque motifs. This leads to the dormitory and to the sixteenth-century abbot's house.

The two-storey cloister.

Left:
The multifoil oculi are
closed with stained-glass
windows made with
white alabaster.

Facing page, right:
The cloister gargoyles.

VILLERS-LA-VILLE

Villarium

location: Villers la Ville (Brabant), Belgium

founded: 1146, by Clairvaux

dissolved: 1796

present use: cultural center

See also pp. 37, 41, 47, 51, 56, 71, 80, 136.

Bibliography
Henri GILLES *Abbaye Notre-Dame de Villers en Brabant*,
S. I. de Villers, Villers-Brussels, 1989.
Victor HUGO, *Pierres*.
Roger MASSON, *Abbaye de Villers*, Masson, Villers, 1993.
Thomas COOMANS, *Analyse critique des gravures anciennes
de l'abbaye de Villers*, Villers-Brussels, 1988.

A huge and truly beautiful abbey could do nothing but leave behind huge and really lovely ruins. This is what it feels like when you discover Villers and its extensive ruins as you approach along a winding forest road. Time and space are banished from this enclosed setting where history seems frozen. Victor Hugo came here to meditate during his long exile in Belgium. He also spoke of the melancholy feeling that surrounds the abbey:

["… Thus I used to meditate

At Villers, the ruined and wild abbey

Where every evening at sunset I saw,

Heading back to nests concealed among the tombs,

Flocks of rooks arriving with noisy caws."]

Legend has it that it was Bernard of Clairvaux who sent out some of his monks to found Villers in 1146 and that he himself came to help them choose the final site for the abbey and to sort out the hydraulic work required on the valley's watercourse. Historical fact attributes the initiative to found Villers to the lord of Marbais who chose a site that was already partly occupied and provided with running water. But it is not impossible that the famous abbot may well have visited and given some instructions to his "new daughter" in January 1147, before traveling on to Vaucelles. He was indeed fond of giving instructions about everything and he had already visited sufficient abbeys to have informed opinions.

At the end of the twelfth century, the eighth abbot of Villers, Charles de Seyne (1197-1209), reaped the rewards of his predecessors' wise management, and decided that the abbey was now sufficiently rich to build an abbey church and to update the monastery's temporary buildings. This adventure was to last seventy years. A century later, Villers reached the height of its power in both the spiritual and temporal domains. It had produced an abbot for Clairvaux (Guillaume de Dongelbert), founded two daughters (Grandpré and Saint-Bernard-sur-Escaut), overseen the establishment of a nunnery at Cambre, and managed to get a declaration that several of its abbots "died in the odor of sanctity". In addition to this the abbey owned 45,000 acres (18,000ha) of cultivated land, meadows and woods and had set up numerous granges. By then, 100 monks and 300 lay brothers lived at Villers.

Like all houses in the Order of Cîteaux, from the sixteenth century onwards Villers would never regain the power and the glory of its first

East windows of the monks' refectory. The art of growing a vegetal scenery on ruins was perfected in Villers. Such an architectural recomposition is a poetic enterprise which bears the burden of constraints (unstable ruins and plants) but also of seductive charm.

two centuries of existence. The abbey lay at the heart of that stretch of Europe which was regularly sacked by warring armies or decimated by epidemics. At times, the monks even left the abbey for long periods to take refuge in their town house. They lived there for sixteen years during the sixteenth century and fled there on at least four occasions during the Franco-Spanish wars.

But the abbey always held on to its estates which allowed the eighteenth-century abbots sufficient funds to set about transforming and embellishing Villers. An abbot's palace was constructed, the church was given a majestic portal and henceforth the monks slept in indi-

vidual cells. The abbey's new-found splendor did not last long and the revolutionary movements at the end of the century were to deal it the death blow. First, the abbot was exiled because he opposed Emperor Joseph II of Austria who he believed to be anti-religious. Then after Fleurus, the abbey was disbanded.

Its destruction started once the abbey had been sold as a "national asset". The purchasers used the buildings as a stone quarry and the locals regularly pillaged it. In 1855 a railroad was built through the estate. The roofs fell in and the walls cracked. The abbey had to wait until 1892 for the Belgium government to expropriate the property and save what remained.

The architect Charles Licot's name is associated with the restoration work undertaken by the Highways Department. A keen student of Viollet-le-Duc, he set about piecing together a complex which, despite the destruction that had occurred, can still be considered one of the most important sites of the great Cistercian abbeys of the Middle Ages.

His aim was to stabilize the buildings that were still standing and to enhance their value, as British "architects of ruins" had already been doing for several decades. Both ethics and aesthetics underlie this line of action which combines a number of disciplines: archeology, that is generally concerned about maintaining things

as they are; history, which is very willing to reconstruct things in an identical fashion; and architecture, which claims the right to build "town upon town" by adding contemporary work to the foundations of the past. The debate could go on for ever...

Villers is surrounded by a wall over a mile (1,700m) long. In order to understand the site, you are best advised to enter by the Brussels gate and imagine that the road crossing the lower courtyard has already been moved. Then, before approaching the imposingly large front end of the church, you should take a look at the extent of the buildings in the service range, which was used by the lay brothers. The mill

has been turned into a restaurant and brasserie (a use which some have questioned), which should be much appreciated by all drinkers of "Trappist" beer. When you get to the monastic quadrangle, the forest of truncated pillars, gaping vaults and open walls is impressive. Nonetheless, you can still make out St Bernard's plan and the architecture is plainly in the Cistercian spirit. Black schist, green grass and ivy, sky through the windows all offer a "spectacle" which reaches its climax at the heart of the abbey church. This majestic building speaks more of mystery today than it ever could have done before being almost demolished.

VYSSI BROD

Altovadum

location: Vyssi-Brod (Southern Bohemia), Czech Republic

founded: 1259, by Wilhering (Ebrach and Rein—affiliation of Morimond)

suppressed from 1946 to 1992

present status: monastery of Cistercian Order of Common Observance

See also pp. 18, 22, 56, 125, 131.

Bibliography
Milan HLINOMAZ, *Vyssi Brod, Cistercian Abbey*, VEGA.

Close to the beautiful little town of Cesky-Krumlov, on the edge of the legendary valley of the Vltava, the abbey of Vyssi-Brod has managed—like Osek—to revive its monastic vocation. A number of elderly monks, who were forced out in 1950 and since then found refuge in Rein, returned to their cells, and look after the venerable buildings first developed there under the patronage of the illustrious Vok of Rozmberk.

For ten generations, from the thirteenth to the seventeenth centuries, the Rozmberk family endowed the abbey. It was able to extend its area into still uninhabited territory, owning 500 villages, and two small towns with their markets (Vyssi-Brod and Horice). Occupied, but not damaged, by the Hussites in 1422, the abbey continued to expand through the centuries. Joseph II's reforms did not affect it, because it had already begun to look after the parish churches in 1629. It still had sixteen in 1939. Today, walking through the fortified tower of the abbey gatehouse, we discover the numerous monastic buildings standing abandoned in the long grass.

The Gothic church, a lofty hall of 1259, enlarged in 1370, retains the simplicity required by the Rule, though the furnishings add a Baroque appearance. The stalls in a reddish wood are surmounted by statues of SS. Peter and Paul standing in declamatory attitudes. The great retable of the sanctuary covers the glass of the windows in the apse, so that the gilded wood-carving catches all the better the light from the candle flames. One of the statues represents Robert of Molesme carrying two abbeys, the one which made his name famous in history, and Cîteaux.

Amidst all these eighteenth-century masterpieces are two colored ceramic statues, typical of the Society of Saint-Suplice, one of St. Joseph with the infant Jesus, and the other of the Sacred Heart. They remind the art historian of the considerable expansion that took place in 1900 of the factory at Vendeuvre in Champagne, whose Christian art flooded the world at that time with more than 10,000 statues a year!

There are real masterpieces in the abbey library, which is worthy of comparison with more famous libraries, like those of Saint-Gall or Melk. It houses 70,000 volumes and some 1,000 manuscripts, parchments, and incunabula in two specialized rooms—the philosophy room which also houses scientific works, and the theology room. In the neighboring picture gallery can be seen the famous retable by the Hohenfurth Master, showing scenes from the life of Christ.

*The baroque library
(philosophy section).*

*The tripartite vault of
the chapter house.*

The choir and the Baroque sanctuary.

ZDÁR

Fons Sancta Maria in Saar

location: **Zdár (Southern Moravia), Czech Republic**

founded: **1251, by Nepomuk (affiliation of Morimond)**

dissolved: **1784 (Joseph II)**

present status: **parish church and cultural center**

See also p. 34.

Bibliography
Katerina CHARVATORA and Dobroslav Libal, *Ràd Cisterciackv*, Prague, 1992.
Pierre CHARPENTRAT, *L'Art baroque*, Presses Universitaires de France, 1967.
J. M. RICHARDS, *Who's who de l'architecture de 1400 à nos jours*, Albin Michel, 1979.

Little is known about the circumstances in which Zdár was founded. Poor planning led to the failure of the first attempt, by five monks from Osek, to establish a monastery in 1240. A second attempt, on the initiative of a local lord, to found a monastery, known as Bernhardi Cella, only survived for five years. The third attempt was more successful, allowing monks from Nepomuk to build a church between 1253 and 1264, to make further enlargements until 1330, to repair it after damage by the Hussites (in 1422) between 1458 and 1471, and then to have major alterations carried out by Johann Blasins Santini Aichel, known as Santini (around 1710).

Santini's work at Zdár followed on from his Gothicizing experiments at Sedlec, and was clearly a significant moment in the history of the abbey. The masterpiece of Zdár—and of Santini—is, in fact, a few hundred yards away, on the grassy hill on which is found a cemetery enclosed within a ten-sided cloister articulated by ten chapels. In the middle is a beautiful and unexpected little centrally-planned church, dedicated to St. John of Nepomuk. Since the Council of Trent the Church had placed increased stress on the cult of the saints as privileged intercessors of the faith. Pilgrimages were made to those places where relics were housed and, if miracles were witnessed, such holy places became desirable places to be buried. The abbot of Zdár possessed the hyoid bone of St John of Nepomuk, and had organized a very popular pilgrimage. The pentagonal church designed by Santini consists of an ambulatory entirely enclosing a nave made up of five ellipses, linked together by five curvilinear triangles. Perhaps this is a reference to the five stars that floated on the waters of the Vltava when the martyr of the secret of the confessional was thrown in to drown. The interior is Baroque, of a delicacy similar to the beautiful Bavarian church of Weis. The roof and tower give an air of the Orthodox Church, further increased by the appearance of the roofs of the ten side chapels.

Santini's work deserves to be better known.

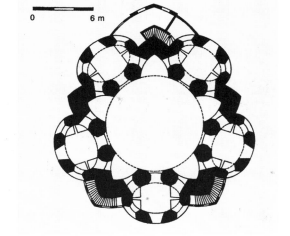

The pentagonal church of St. John of Nepomuk in the middle of the Zdar cemetery.

This masterpiece from Santini is a major work of Baroque art.

ZLATA KORUNA

Aurea Corona

location: Zlata Koruna (Southern Bohemia), Czech Republic

founded: 1263, by Heiligenkreuz (filiation of Morimond)

dissolved: 1785 (by Joseph II)

present status: parish church

See also pp. 34, 37.

Bibliography
Jindřich SPINAR, *Zlata Koruna*, Zlata Koruna District, 1995.

The abbey was originally to be called Santa Corona, because the king Premysl Otakar II had managed to buy one of the spines from the Crown of Thorns from St. Louis, and presented it to the monastery. But before long the name had changed to Aurea Corona (Crown of Gold, or Zlata Koruna), for reasons that are not entirely clear. Possibly it was an allusion to the wealth of the abbey.

At that time, Premysl Otakar II was king both of Bohemia and Austria. The abbey was intended to have a unifying effect on the two populations. For this reason, it was established near the frontier, on the road between Prague and Vienna, not far from Cesky-Krumlov. The fact that the father abbot of Heiligenkreuz had been asked to be the "immediate father" of the new abbey was considered a politic move with regard to the Austrians. It did not, however, prevent the loss of Austria in 1276.

Zlata Koruna found it was endowed not only with the Holy Thorn, which would bring in a significant income from pilgrims, but also with large areas of unexploited and uninhabited forest, thought to be about 340 square miles (880 km^2). It was the abbey's mission to develop them. Colonization led to the creation of a hundred new villages. "Zlata Koruna was then like salt in the eyes of the local nobility." During the war against the Hapsburgs, so damaging to Premysl Otakar II (1276), the monastery was attacked and burned down by a group of vassals who had risen up against their king. Everything returned to normal, however, and new royal donations enabled the abbey to enjoy the largest territories in all Bohemia

The power of Zlata Koruna could not withstand the Hussite revolutionaries who burned

down the abbey in 1420. They wished to do away both with kings and landowning monasteries, in the name of equality for all. The rich Rozmberk de Cesky-Krumlov family took over the monastery estates. The monks did not return until 1599, henceforth only receiving tithes from their former properties. Nothing was as it had been before and Joseph II closed the abbey in 1785.

The beautiful Gothic church is very high, and has a Cistercian simplicity. The white plaster of the inner walls contrasts with the engaged piers of brown stone. The light floods in. Only the sanctuary was altered, in order to install a large Baroque retable dedicated to the glory of the Fathers of the Church. The best preserved original Gothic structure at Zlata Koruna is a two-storey chapel (today reduced to a single storey), built at the beginning of the thirteenth century to serve as a royal chapel.

Major restoration work has been undertaken. The cloister, the former abbot's palace, and the library remind us that the monks of the eighteenth century still had considerable financial resources, which enabled them to update their abbey in line with prevailing fashions.

Facing page, right:
Detail of the cloister vault.

Left:
The cloister. Chapter house gallery.

ZWETTL

Claravallis

location: Zwettl (Waldviertel), Lower Austria

founded: 1137, by Heiligenkreuz (affiliation of Morimond)

suppressed: never suppressed

present status: monastery of the Cistercian Order of Common Observance, with school

See also pp. 47, 129, 131.

Bibliography
Johann TOMASCHEK, *Zisterzienserstift Zwettl*, C. Brandstatter Verlag, Vienna, 1989.

The sumptuous abbey of Zwettl has benefited from repeated architectural enrichment over the centuries. In flagrant transgression of the General Chapter's requirement that low belfries of wood be built rather than stone towers, it has the highest tower of any Cistercian abbey, at the top of which, 325 feet (99m) up, is a gilded statue of Christ blessing the world. On the other hand, the Cistercians adhered scrupulously to the ideas of the Counter-Reformation and the religious Baroque style, the magnificence of which was designed to dazzle both princes and commoners, diverting them from the growing influence of reform, enlightened ideas and those people who would bring revolution to the whole of Europe.

The Baroque remodeling of Zwettl did not destroy older parts of the abbey, such as the bridge that crosses the river Kamp, once used by the carts bringing granite for the early building work. The chapter house, monks' dormitory, and the cloister still have a very characteristic Romanesque core (1159–80) beneath ribbed vaults (1180–1240) of perfect Burgundian form. Because of the difficulties involved in quarrying for stone, the period of building work stretched out over many decades. This explains the development in styles through the four walks of the cloister. The Austrian builders' skill in the Gothic style can be seen in the choir of the church with its corona of fourteen chapels (1343–48) and its high nave (1360–90), symbolic of a renewed vitality after the Black Death.

The abbey survived the Hussite revolution and the Thirty Years' War without too much damage. In the seventeenth and eighteenth centuries, it was fortunate in having a number of outstanding abbots. The first of these was Abbot Link (1646–71), the scholarly author of the *Annales Austrioclaravallenses*. He was followed by Caspar Bernhardt (1672–95) who had extensions to the monastery built in the form of a series of closed courtyards characteristic of urban Baroque architecture. The Abteihof, ornamented with a fountain in the middle, has white façades with pale yellow plaster. The windows and Tuscan-style door are the only elements to suggest the sumptuous decoration of the ceremonial rooms on the upper floor.

But it was Abbot Melchior Zaunagg (1706–47) who transformed the church of Zwettl, adding two bays to the nave in order to raise the famous tower above the west end, creating an immense retable above the altar, summoning the best

The chapter house. Presumably built as early as 1160.

painters, sculptors, stucco craftsmen, cabinet makers, stained glass makers, and fresco painters of the day to decorate the walls and furnish the empty spaces of the abbey. Like Bernard of Clairvaux or Suger in their time, the abbot discussed every detail of the plans with his architect (Joseph Mungenast), visited the building site, and worked out the programs of the painting with the artists. The great master of Baroque art, Mathias Steinl, assisted by advising the abbot.

The wonderful unity of the whole is due in great part to this collaboration between the abbot as master builder, and his architect. Together they managed to avoid the sometimes overloaded extravagance of the Baroque that can swamp a building with its gilding and its exuberance. Despite the extent of excellent Baroque work, the great purity of the Gothic architecture, the Cistercian rigor, emerge in all their strength and majesty.

Above:
The ambulatory vault.

Facing page:
Free opening of the
chapter house on to the
cloister.

NOTES DE LA PREMIÈRE PARTIE

Avertisement
To ease reading, the quotations of historic texts have been printed in italics, while quotes by contemporary historians have been inserted in roman letters.

Chapter 1
For additional reading on this chapter, see:
– Jean Daniélou, *L'Église des premiers temps*, Le Seuil-Points, Paris, 1963.
– Jacques Le Goff, René Rémond, et al., *Histoire de la France religieuse* (volume 1), Le Seuil, Paris, 1988.
– *Encyclopédie catholique Théo*, Droguet-Ardant et Fayard, Paris, 1989.

Chapter 2
1. Adalbero of Laon quoted by Jacques Le Goff, *La Civilisation de l'Occident médiéval*, Arthaud, Champs Flammarion, Paris, 1964/1982, p. 234. Adalbero was bishop of Laon from 977 and one of the accomplices of Hugh Capet in 987. He wrote a lengthy poem on the mores of his time.
2. Paul Zumthor, *Guillaume le Conquérant*, Tallandier, Paris, 1978.
3. Ordéric Vital, *Historica ecclesiastica* quoted by Eliane Vergnolle, *L'Art roman en France*, Flammarion, Paris, 1994, p. 26.
4. Commission d'histoire de l'Ordre de Cîteaux, *Bernard de Clairvaux*, Alsatia, Paris, 1953, p. 48.
5. Jean Berthold Mahn, *L'Ordre cistercien et son gouvernement, des origines au milieu du XIIIe siècle (1098-1265)*, Éditions E. de Broccard, Paris, 1982, p. 23.
6. Marcel Durliat, *L'Art roman*, Éditions d'art Lucien Mazenod, Paris, 1982.
7. The architectural context. This frame refers to the chronology suggested by Alain Erlande-Brandenburg and Anne Merel-Brandenburg, *Histoire de l'Architecture françoise, du Moyen ge à la Renaissancee*, CNMHS and Mengès, Paris, 1995.

Chapter 3
1. Jean Berthold Mahn, op. cit. p. 41.
2. Marcel Pacaut, *Les Moines blancs*, Fayard, 1993.
3. The Commission d'Historie de l'Ordre de Cîteaux in 1953 proposed to keep the name of Aubri, only derivative of the Latin Albertticus; the traditional Albéric is an "obvious barbarism". However, few works published after the proposal take up this suggestion.
4. Frère Marcel Lebeau, *Abrégé chronologique de l'histoire de Cîteaux*; Cîteaux, 1980, p. 9.
5. As expressed by Robert Folz quoted by Marcel Pacaut, op. cit. p. 41.
6. J. A. Lefevre, *Saint Robert de Molesme dans l'opinion monastique*, Analecta Bollandiana LXXIV, 1956, p. 68 and 80/83.
7. *Cîteaux, documents primitifs*. Commentarii cistercienses, Cîteaux, 1988.
8. Commission d'Histoire de l'Ordre de Cîteaux, op. cit. p. 31.
9. Frère Marcel Lebeau, 1980, op. cit. p. 10.
10. Commission d'Histoire de l'Ordre de Cîteaux, op. cit. p. 32.
11. Guillaume de Saint Thierry, *Vie de saint Bernard*, III.15, F. X. de Guibertet OEIL, Paris, 1997.
12. Frère Jean-Baptiste Auberger, OFM, *L'Unanimité cistercienne primitive : mythe ou réalité ?* Cîteaux Commentarii cistercienses, Achel 1986, p. 1.

Chapter 4
1. Jean Leclercq, *Nouveau visage de Bernard de Clairvaux, approches psycho-historiques*, Cerf, Paris, 1976, p. 155.
2. Guillaume de Saint Thierry, *Vita prima*, VII. 33.
3. *Dictatus papae* by Gregory VII, paragraph 2.
4. Commission d'Histoire de l'Ordre de Cîteaux, op. cit. p. 379.

Chapter 5
1. The number twelve is obviously symbolic, referring to the Twelve Apostles, but it was not always respected.
2. *Voyage de deux bénédictins de la Congrégation de Saint Maur* (1717-1724).
3. P. Dalloz, *L'Architecture selon saint Bernard*, appendix of the translation of St. Bernard, *De la Considération*, Cerf, p. 177.
4. *Apologie à Guillaume*, translation by François Cali, *La plus grande aventure du monde, Cîteaux*, Arthaud, Paris, 1956.
5. Quoted by Marcel Aubert (and Marquise de Maillé), *L'architecture cistercienne en France*, Vanoest, éditions d'art et d'histoire, Paris, 1947, volume I, p. 97.
6. Viollet-le-Duc, op. cit., volume 1, article Architecte, p. 107/116.
7. Marcel Aubert, op. cit. p. 97.
8. Alain Erlande-Brandenburg, op. cit.
9. Anselme Dimier, *Recueil de plans d'églises cisterciennes*, Paris, 1949.
10. Jacques Le Goff, *L'Imaginaire médiéval*, Gallimard, Bibliothèque des Histoires, 1985, p. 59 (in reference to Ch. Higounet, M. Bloch and G. Roupnel).
11. Bernadette Barrière, *Les Cisterciens d'Obazine en Bas Limousin*, in *L'hydraulique monastique*, Rencontres de Royaumont/Creaphis, Giane, 1996, p. 13/33.
12. Paul Benoit, *Vers une chronologie de l'hydraulique monastique, in L'hydraulique monastique*, op. cit., p. 475/485.
13. Jacques Laurent, *Les Noms des monastères cisterciens dans la toponymie européenne* in *Saint Bernard et son temps*, volume 1, 1928, p. 168/204.
14. *Dialogues inter Cluniac. et Cisterc.* in Marcel Aubert, volume I, op. cit. p. 53.
15. On the symbolism of the orientation of the church, see M. M. Davy, *Initiation à la Symbolique romane*, Champs Flammarion, Paris, 1977, p. 196.
16. On Villard de Honnecourt see M. M. Davy, op. cit. p. 182.
17. Benoît Chauvin, *Le Plan bernardin*, in *Bernard de Clairvaux, histoire, mentalités, spiritualité*, colloquium of Lyon-Cîteaux-Dijon 1990, Cerf, Paris, 1992, p. 339.
18. Marcel Aubert, op. cit. volume I, p.320.
19. Dante, *Divine Comedy*, tenth song of fourth heaven, 1321, in Jean Gimpel, *La Révolution industrielle au Moyen Âge*, Seuil (Points-Histoire) Paris, 1975, p. 145.
20. André Stirling has reconstructed the clepsydra of Villers from texts found on slate during the 1894 excavations. He presented it at the colloquium of *Villers, una abbaye revisitée*, APTCV, 1996, p. 135.
21. Marcel Aubert, op. cit.
22. Gérard de Champeaux and Dom Sebastien Sterckx, *Le Monde des symboles*, Zodiaque, 1980.
23. Thérèse Glorieux de Gand, *Le Langage des signes chez les cisterciens* in colloquium *Villers, une abbaye revisitée*, op. cit. p. 157.
24. Bernard Garnerin, *La Musique française du Moyen Âge*, PUF, 1961, p. 5 à 22.
25. This note owes a lot to Sam Baruch, acoustic engineer, and his documentation, notably J. M. Fontaine, *Un système historique de correction sonore: les vases acoustiques*. Camille de Montalivet has likewise patiently highlighted, for this note, the placement of the 55 vases of Vitruvius set in the vaults at the abbey of Loc Dieu.
26. Léo Moulin, *La Vie quotidienne des religieux au Moyen Âge X^e^-XVe siècle*, Hachette, Paris 1978, p. 166.
27. Léo Moulin, op. cit.
28. Régine Pernoud and Georges Herscher, *Jardins de monastères*, Actes Sud, 1996.
29. Sylvie Fournier, *Brève histoire du parchemin et de l'enluminure*, Fragile, Tiralet, 1995, p. 5.
30. Yolanta Zaluska, *L'Enluminure et le scriptorium de Cîteaux au XIIe siècle*, Cîteaux, 1989, p. 113. See also André Vernet avec la collaboration de J. F. Genest. *La Bibliothèque de Clairvaux au XIIe et XIIIe siècle*, Paris, 1979; Françoise Bibolet, *La Bibliothèque de Clairvaux* in *Vie en Champagne*, special edition *Abbaye de Clairvaux*, 1986, p. 22.
31. Marcel Aubert, op. cit. p. 122.
32. Viollet-le-Duc, op. cit. volume VI, p. 172.
33. Georges Duby, *Saint Bernard, l'art cistercien*, Flammarion, Paris, 1976.
34. Quoted by Michel Miguet, *Les Convers cisterciens, l'institution, les hommes, les bâtiments*, unpublished manuscript.
35. Robert Fossier, *La Vie économique de l'abbaye de Clairvaux, des origines à la fin de la guerre de Cent Ans 1115–1471*, archives de l'Aube, série J.
36. *L'Espace cistercien*, sous la direction de Léon Pressouyre, Comité des travaux historiques et scientifiques, Paris, 1994.
37. Viollet-le-Duc, op. cit, volume III, p. 482.
38. Bertrand Gille, *Origines de la grande industrie métallurgique en France*; Paul Benoît and Denis Caillaux, *Moines et Métallurgie dans la France médiévale*, Paris, 1991.
39. Catherine Verna, *Les Mines et les forges des cisterciens en Champagne du Nord et en Bourgogne du Nord*, AEDEH, Paris, 1995, p. 34/35.
40. Louis J. Lekai, op. cit. p. 261/263.
41. Viollet-le-Duc, op. cit. tome I, p. 275.
42. Marcel Pacaut, op. cit., p. 261, according to the map drawn by J. F. Leroux in *L'Abbaye de Clairvaux*, Vie en Champagne, 1986, p. 11.

Chapter 6
1. La lumière cistercienne. Serge Clavé, *Entretiens avec Pierre Soulages* in *Architecture cistercienne*, Architecture moderne, document dactyl. 1996. *Cahiers du musée d'Art moderne*, March 1980.
2. La lumière cistercienne. Georges Duby, preface of *Conques, les vitraux de Soulages*, Seuil, 1994, p. 8.
3. La lumière cistercienne. Document établi par Dom Olivier Briand, abbé d'Acey.
4. La lumière cistercienne. Georges Duby, Préface de *Noirlac, Abbaye cistercienne, Vitraux de J.P. Raynaud*, EMA Paris, p. 11.
5. Alain Erlande-Brandenburg, op. cit., p. 247
6. Heinfried Wischermann, *L'Architecture romane en Grande-Bretagne* in *L'art Roman*, Könemann, Cologne, 1996, p. 235/236.
7. Erwin Panofsky, *Architecture gothique et pensée scolastique*, Éditions de Minuit, Paris, 1967, p. 69
8. The beautiful restoration of the lay brothers' building at Clairvaux was done by the late Jean-Michel Musso, deceased in an accident in 1998.

Chapter 7
1. Louis J. Lekai, op. cit.
2. René Locatelli, *L'Expansion cistercienne en Europe*, in *Dossiers de l'archéologie*, December 1997, p. 20; and Marcel Pacaut, op. cit., p. 129.
3. Stephen Tobin, *The Cistercians: Monks and Monasteries of Europe*, Woodstock, N.Y., Overlook Press, 1996, p. 188. The number of 754 abbeys mentioned by Tobin corresponds to the number presented by Frédéric Van der Meer in his important *Atlas de l'Ordre Cistercien*, Editions Sequoia, Paris, Brussels, 1965.
4. The expansion zones of the first four daughters in Europe are depicted in the sketches taken from *Cysterci W kulturze Sredniowiecznej europy*, Pozen 1992.
5. Lucelle, granddaughter of Morimond, via Bellevaux, today lies in France, in the Haut-Rhin (Upper Rhine) department.

Chapter 8
1. Louis J. Lekai, op. cit. p. 74.
2. Jacques Berlioz « *Tuez les tous, Dieu reconnaîtra les siens* », *la croisade contre les albigeois vue par Cesaire de Heisterbach*, Loubatières, Portet, 1994, p. 9.

Chapter 9
1. Louis J. Lekai, op. cit. p. 265.
2. H. d'Arbois de Jubainville, Etudes sur l'état intérieur des abbayes cisterciennes et principalement de Clairvaux aux XIIe et XIIIe siècles, Durand, Paris, 1858, p. 277.
3. H. d'Arbois de Jubainville, op. cit. p. 279.
4. H. d'Arbois de Jubainville, op. cit. p. 281.
5. See the map of the Granges de Clairvaux
6. H. d'Arbois de Jubainville, op. cit. p. 295.
7. Charles Higounet, *La Grange de Vaulerent*, Paris, 1965 and François Blary, *Le Domaine de Chaalis, XIIe-XIVe siècles*, ECTHS, Paris, 1989 p. 382.
8. Marcel Pacaut, op. cit. p. 260.
9. Marcel Aubert, op. cit. volume II, p. 161.
10. Michel Miguet, op. cit., 1997.
11. Jean Gimpel, *La Révolution industrielle au Moyen Âge*, Seuil Points Histoire, Paris, 1975, p. 69 with reference to J.S. Donnelly, *The Decline of the Medieval Cistercian Laybrotherhood*, Fordham U.P., New York, 1949, p. 32.
12. Marcel Pacaut, op. cit. p. 276.
13. Benoît Chauvin, *Notes et documents pour servir à l'histoire du sel au Moyen Âge : Les archives de l'abbaye de Clairvaux (1173-1234)*, in *Actes du Colloque sur l'histoire de Clairvaux*, op. cit. p. 303.
14. Gilles Villain, *Trois granges de l'ancienne abbaye de Clairvaux* in *L'Espace cistercien*, op. cit. p. 581.
15. François Blary, op. cit. p. 106.
16. Claude Royer, *Les Vignerons, usages et mentalités des pays de vignobles*, Berger-Levrault, Paris, 1980, p. 34.
17. Was the wine of the Côte des Bars, made by the lay brothers of Clairvaux naturally sparkling? Should one attribute to them the first champagne-type wine, many years before the benedictine dom Pérignon?
18. Louis J. Lekai, op. cit. p. 270.
19. Richard Hoffmann, *Medieval Cistercian Fisheries Natural and Artificial*, in *L'Espace cistercien*, op. cit. p. 401.
20. Jean Gimpel, op. cit. p. 19.
21. Louis J. Lekai, op. cit. p. 273.
22. Paul Benoît, *Moines et métallurgie dans la France médiévale*, AEDEH Paris, 1991, p. 355.
23. Louis J. Lekai, op. cit.
24. Louis J. Lekai, op. cit.

Chapter 10
1. Marcel Aubert, op. cit. p. 127 et 133.
2. Marcel Aubert, op. cit. p. 128.
3. Fernand Pouillon : *Les Pierres sauvages*, Seuil, Paris, 1964, p. 175.
4. Jean-François Dhuys, in *L'Architecture selon Emile Aillaud*, Dunod, Paris, 1983, p. 18.
5. François Cali, op. cit.
6. Raymond Oursel, *L'esprit de Cîteaux*, Zodiaque, St. Léger-Vauban, 1978, p. 15.
7. Marcel Aubert, op. cit. p. 218.

Chapter 11
1. Frédéric Van der Meer, *Atlas de l'Ordre cistercien*, Sequoia, Paris-Bruxelles, 1, p. 32.

Chapter 12
1. P. Colomban Bock, *Les Codifications du droit cistercien*, Westmalle, p. 51.
2. Louis J. Lekai, op. cit.
3. Louis J. Lekai, op. cit. p. 100.

Chapter 13
1. Louis J. Lekai, op. cit. p. 140.
2. Louis J. Lekai, op. cit.
3. Jean-Marie Pérouse de Montclos, *Histoire de l'architecture française, de la Renaissance à la Révolution*, Mengès and CNMHS, Paris, 1989, p. 190.
4. Dominique Fernandez, *Le Banquet des anges*, Plon, Paris, 1984, p. 50.
5. Dominique Fernandez, op. cit.
6. Jacques Foucart-Borville, *Simon Pfaff, un sculpteur autrichien en Picardie*, Paillart, Abbeville, 1996.

Chapter 14
1. Marie Gérard Dubois, *Le Bonheur de Dieu, souvenirs et réflexions du père abbé de la Trappe*, Robert Laffont, Paris, 1995, p. 372.
2. François Cali, op. cit.

Jean-François Leroux-Dhuys would like to recognize the experts on the history of the Cistercians who during the past several years have contributed significant new studies that visibly enrich the information contained within this volume.

Henri Gaud would like to express his profound thanks to the guides at Cistercian sites who received and assisted him during his research. Thanks to them and the love they hold toward their abbeys – which they are eager to disclose – an ever-increasing public is discovering on-site the history and architecture of these abbeys as well as the spiritual message they have continued to spread from centuries ago till today.

Photo credits

© Bibliothèque municipale de Dijon - Cl. François Perrodin
pp. 29, 42b, 46, 70g, 70m, 98
© Bibliothèque municipale de Troyes
pp. 38, 70d
©Prim'dias "La Goélette," Saint-Ouen
p. 32
© SDAVO, 1997, V. Lemoine
p. 47d